UNCOMFORTABLY OFF

UNCOMFORTABLY OFF

Why the Top 10% of Earners
Should Care about Inequality

Marcos González Hernando and Gerry Mitchell

Foreword by
James Perry

Afterword by
Danny Dorling

First published in Great Britain in 2024 by

Policy Press, an imprint of
Bristol University Press
University of Bristol
1-9 Old Park Hill
Bristol
BS2 8BB
UK
t: +44 (0)117 374 6645
e: bup-info@bristol.ac.uk

Details of international sales and distribution partners are available at
policy.bristoluniversitypress.co.uk

British Library Cataloguing in Publication Data
A catalogue record for this book is available from the British Library

ISBN 978-1-4473-6752-9 paperback
ISBN 978-1-4473-6751-2 hardcover
ISBN 978-1-4473-6753-6 ePub
ISBN 978-1-4473-6754-3 ePdf

Cover design: Mecob
Front cover image: Shutterstock/wk1003mike

Contents

List of figures   vi
About the authors   vii
Acknowledgements   viii
Foreword by James Perry   x

Introduction: Why bother with the well-off?   1

1   Not billionaires, but well-off?   21
2   On the ubiquity and invisibility of the upper-middle class   38
3   'Work is life, that's it'   55
4   Don't rock the boat: politics and the well-off   76
5   Business class tickets for a sinking ship   100
6   Jumping ship, but where to?   124
7   Barriers to being comfortably off   146
8   'When the facts change, I change my mind'   161

Conclusion: Accepted truths, social distance and discomfort   183

Afterword by Danny Dorling   189
Notes   193
References   207
Index   241

List of figures

0.1	Income thresholds before tax by percentile point, UK, 2019/20	7
1.1	Occupation by income decile, UK, 2016	25
2.1	Agreement with statement 'Government should reduce differences in income levels' by income decile, UK, 2008–18	43
4.1	Agreement with the statement 'Social benefits and services place too great a strain on the economy' in the UK, 2008–16	93
4.2	*The New Yorker* cartoon, by Barbara Smaller	99
6.1	'Daddy!' by Peter Schrank	131

About the authors

Marcos González Hernando is Honorary Research Fellow at UCL Social Research Institute, Postdoctoral Researcher at Universidad Diego Portales and Adjunct Researcher at the Centre for the Study of Conflict and Social Cohesion. He is also a Fellow of the Royal Society of Arts and has a PhD in sociology from the University of Cambridge. Marcos has experience working in universities and think tanks, both in Latin America and Europe. His research interests include think tanks and policy experts, intellectual change, attitudes towards inequality, and economic and political elites. He is also the author of *British Think Tanks after the 2008 Global Financial Crisis* (Palgrave, 2019). He recently moved to Santiago, Chile, where he lives with his wife, Irina, and his cat, Lily.

Gerry Mitchell is a freelance policy researcher and writer. Experienced in research, political campaigning, community engagement and teaching, she has degrees from Cambridge and the London School of Economics and Political Science where, based in the Centre for Social Exclusion, she completed a PhD in social policy. She has recently worked with Compass (London), the Edinburgh Voluntary Organisations' Council, the Foundation for European Progressive Studies (Brussels), Friedrich-Ebert-Stiftung (Stockholm and London) and the Think-tank for Action on Social Change (Dublin). She lives in Woking, Surrey, with her partner, Gareth, and their two children, Lilya and Noah, where she chaired Woking Labour Party and stood as its parliamentary candidate in the 2019 general election. She currently chairs local Compass and Make Votes Matter groups, is a secondary school governor and in 2022 opened Canalside Community Fridge.

Acknowledgements

We would like to begin by thanking our interviewees for sharing their time, personal experiences and thoughts with us. They were all extremely generous, interesting and thoughtful.

We also wish to thank our colleagues in the top 10% research report on which this book is based at Arena Idé, Compass, Foundation for European Progressive Studies, Fundación Alternativas and the Think-tank for Action on Social Change. They are Amy Barker, Belén Barreiro, Sylvia Byrne, Susana Cristo, Frances Foley, Jack Jeffrey, Johanna Lindell, Sidney Moss, Michelle O'Sullivan, Kishan Patel, Lisa Pelling, David Rinaldi, Jesús Ruiz-Huerta, Jorge San Vicente, Paul Sweeney, Rob Sweeney, Remco Van der Stoep, Gonzalo Velasco and Diana Volpe. Special thanks to Neal Lawson and Shana Cohen who have advised and supported us throughout the process.

We are also grateful to the team at Policy Press, particularly Kathryn King, Jessica Miles and Victoria Pittman.

We cannot forget our immediate families, for putting up with us (it can't have been easy). This book would not have been written without their love, support, generosity and patience: Irina, Marco, Marcela, Daniela, María Francisca, Gareth, Lilya, Noah, Margaret and Mary.

This book is also informed by the insightful comments of our readers: Valentina Ausserladscheider, Shana Cohen, Daniel Edmiston, Roxana Chiappa, Rodrigo Cordero, Nurjk Agloni, Danny Dorling, Naim Bro Khomasi, Ruth Lister, Victoria Redclift and Macarena Orchard. It also draws from the writings and conversations with Katharina Hecht, Martina Yopo, Katie Gaddini, Alfredo Joignant, Patrick Baert, Michaela Franceschelli, Jorge Atria, Michèle Lamont, Jordan Tchilingirian, Luis Garrido, Aris Komporozos-Athanasiou and Simon Susen.

James Perry, as readers will notice, wrote an extremely sharp and readable foreword. He was also gracious, patient and perceptive throughout the process and we cannot thank him enough.

We also cannot imagine having written this book without the influence and support of colleagues and friends: Rebecca Gibbs, Andy Berriman, Ognjen Bubalo, Carmen Campeanu, Franko Cancino, Fabien Cante, Manuela Cisternas, Zara Coombes, Eduardo Lobos, Nat O'Grady, Mark Perryman, Marcela Santana, Steve Sawh, Marita Unepiece, Thiago Vilas-Boas, Israel Yamaguchi, Compass colleagues, Woking Labour CLP and Make Votes Matter.

Finally, we wish to dedicate this book to the memory of Sir John Hills, Barbara Ehrenreich, Nigel Dodd and David Graeber.

Foreword

Something isn't working. Everyone can feel it. Why, when we live in an age of unparalleled prosperity does it seem so hard to make ends meet?

But surely the top 10% are okay, right? Everything is relative, and of course, their problems are largely 'first world problems'. But they're still problems.

A deep dive into the data shows that the distribution of income and wealth in the UK has experienced a hollowing out of the middle class over recent decades. And surprisingly, it shows that this hollowing out has also affected the top 10%. Where has all the wealth creation gone? Mostly to the top 1%. As the generation of new wealth has increasingly drifted into the hands of a very few, it has left behind most of us, even a largely professional 'top 10%'.

This top 10% aspire to a lifestyle that is increasingly beyond them. While from the outside they look like they are living the dream, in reality, they are beset by anxiety. Life to them is a hamster wheel, a constant struggle to keep the high-paying jobs that allow them to service their mortgages and keep up with expectations. They worry about their and their family's future, and so education becomes an arms race to ensure their children are fast enough to be able to get onto, and stay on, that same hamster wheel.

They believe in public services and, in theory, see that the burden for their cost should fall more on those doing well for themselves. But they don't count themselves among those people. Theirs is an uncomfortable existence, squeezed by the accelerating hamster wheel of expectations, both at home and at work. In short, a majority of this group has become uncomfortably off.

Meanwhile, in the higher reaches of the top 1%, there has been almost a total decoupling from everyone else. A super-class of extreme wealth has emerged – those at the top of the pyramid who have made great riches from finance, business, sport, showbiz.

This small group holds an astonishing amount of wealth and lives in a through-the-looking-glass world of privilege. The top 10% has become a microcosm of the entire wealth distribution in that those at the bottom of it are struggling to meet their expectations with an income of £55,000 to £60,000 while those at the top enjoy the compound annual growth of their wealth, accruing at a rate far faster than they could ever spend.

The implications for this modern phenomenon reach into everything. The state is no longer able to make enough tax revenue from the squeezed 99% to cover the social contract. Structural deficits lead the public debt markets to baulk, or at least to increase the interest cost on the national debt to a level greater than the budget of many government departments. Wealth continues to go untaxed, and discussion of any meaningful reform to the 13,000-page UK tax code has been made taboo by certain sections of the media – even in the face of high levels of political consensus on the necessity of some obvious simplifications and changes. Meanwhile, public services, on which the top 10% still rely, become ever more decrepit, unable to metabolise the needs of a population which gets more complex – whether in social care, health, education, social services or justice. And with all the local fires to put out, the government increasingly lacks the bandwidth or political will to meaningfully address the global fire that is about to engulf us all – climate breakdown. The intractability of these structural problems plays out in a political permacrisis. While the top 10% may have the most potential influence over our politicians, are they sufficiently aware of the underlying issues and long-term trends causing their own anxiety?

The discomfort of the top 10% is a logical conclusion to the system we have created. It is a symptom of prioritising individual advancement at all costs, as opposed to the wellbeing of the whole, so the only purpose (and duty) of business and finance is the maximisation of profits. People are reduced to individualised units of labour and consumption – whether consuming the products and services of business or of the state.

The core design idea that underpins our system is individualism. Yet, the truth is that if we are to move beyond our discomfort we have no choice but to look beyond ourselves. To replace the organising idea of individualism with the deeper truth of our interdependence. In recognising that we do not exist in a vacuum, we have no choice but to give prominence to the wellbeing of the whole if we are to create wellbeing for individuals.

The top 10%, the uncomfortably off, are the best-placed cohort in society to address this imperative for deeper change – to transition from individualism to interdependence. It is they who design, regulate and operate the current system. They are the people with both the knowledge and the access to design a better arrangement, based on the truth of our interdependence.

This important and timely book should be seen as a call to arms and a manual for this uniquely placed group, the uncomfortably off. If you are reading this, you may be one of them or perhaps closer than you thought. And if you want to feel comfortable, then the opportunity lies before you to mobilise and rethink the systems that you operate – for everyone in society, and so for yourself. And now, before it is too late.

James Perry
November 2022

James is co-Chair of COOK (www.cookfood.net), a certified B Corp since 2013. He co-founded the B Corp movement in the UK (www.bcorporation.uk), and serves on the global board of B Lab and the board of B Lab Europe. He is also a member of Patriotic Millionaires UK, a founding partner of Snowball (www.snowball.im) and a multi-asset impact investment manager.

Introduction:
Why bother with the well-off?

Three weeks before the UK's 2019 general election, a middle-aged man spoke up among the audience on BBC *Question Time* and briefly became a minor celebrity. Clearly angry, Rob Barber, an IT consultant from Lancashire, said that the Labour Party was lying to the public by claiming that people like him wouldn't be taxed more by a Labour government: "You are not going after the billionaires, you're going after the employees because it's easy money and I have no choice because it's PAYE [pay as you earn]. I have no choice."

The Labour Member of Parliament (MP) Richard Burgon, on the programme's panel, assured him that the proposal only targeted the top 5% of income earners, so most of the public wouldn't qualify and Labour would not be touching their taxes. Unconvinced, Barber retorted: "But you are! Because I've read your policy. It's above £80,000. And I am nowhere near the top 5%, let me tell you. I am not even in the top 50%."

At this point, a few other members of the audience muttered back "But you are!" and Burgon repeated that £80,000 would indeed make you part of the top 5%, but Barber remained undeterred: "Every doctor, every accountant, every solicitor in this country earns more than that. [...] The top 5%, they don't even work! They're not employees!"

For a few days, the exchange became the subject of much media attention. Most pieces on the topic mocked Barber for not realising he was a high earner. As inequality researchers, in the months before that programme we had been interviewing high-income earners just like him, and few if any of our respondents had guessed correctly where they sat in the income distribution.

But is there something to be learnt from this incident beyond Barber's lack of knowledge of income statistics? After all, that assurances had to be made repeatedly about the actual number is evidence itself of a much more generalised ignorance about the economic lives of others. This ignorance, we argue, is not politically anodyne. The fact that Barber and many of our respondents thought they are not even in the top 50% – that is, below the median income, a figure that rarely goes over £30,000 regardless of the statistical source – may paint a much rosier picture in their minds of the circumstances of their fellow citizens than is the case. This assured belief in where they sit is, we will argue, at least partly a result of a tendency to think of ourselves intuitively as 'normal', situated somewhere around the middle. They may have thought if most people are broadly like themselves, they probably earn roughly the same, and therefore their finances are also similar – that is, more likely to be negatively affected by a marginal income tax hike for earnings above £80,000 than benefited by the potential strengthening of welfare provision those funds may allow for.

These misunderstandings about incomes at the top, nevertheless, hide a kernel of truth. For many, the figure of the top 5% evokes images of Jeff Bezos, Elon Musk, yachts and private jets. These are the 'masters of the universe', the truly wealthy, whose economic reality is completely foreign to most. Although Barber may have underestimated the threshold for that kind of wealth, his insistence that he isn't part of it was not unjustified.

Torsten Bell, Head of the Resolution Foundation, wrote one of the best op-eds about the *Question Time* episode. He explained that the real hikes in the income distribution begin around the top 1% and even above.[1] It's no wonder, then, that a relatively well-earning employee or small business owner might resent being put in the same bracket as people whose incomes are exponentially larger. In absolute terms, those at the 5% mark sit much closer to the median income earner than to the super-rich and are arguably much more likely to fall below the former than to ever join the ranks of the latter.

It is also worth remembering that, when we refer to the top 5%, we are talking about 1.635 million people in employment (the total employed population in Britain, as of 2022, being 32.7 million).[2] This is not an insignificant number and one which can even decide elections on its own considering that, as studies have repeatedly shown, the higher your income, the more likely you are to vote.[3]

The fact we are generally unaware of the economic circumstances of those socially distant from us is only compounded by the taboos that exist around money. When we chat with friends and colleagues, we might talk about families, houses, our children, the intricacies of our health issues, our sex lives even, but it is beyond rude to ask about the details of someone else's finances. Money, even if it's everywhere and touches everything, is a subject too private to talk about. It is culturally both 'dirty' (linked to selfishness and philistinism) and 'valued' (associated with social esteem, effort and success). In other words, talking frankly about money makes the social and economic distance between us noticeable and leaves us feeling naked and objectified. If our incomes are higher than those around us, we fear being seen with resentment, or if they are lower, being considered inferior. However reasonable that taboo may be for interpersonal relationships, one important consequence of not broaching it is difficulty in understanding and connecting with the economic realities of others. The ignorance that derives from this may easily inform our politics.

Burgon later told the audience, trying to win them over, "the enemy of someone who is on 70 or 80 thousand pounds a year isn't someone on 20 or 25 thousand pounds a year [...] the people getting away with murder, in reality, are the billionaires, and it's the billionaires who are backing the Conservative Party". Regardless, three weeks later, a majority of the British electorate, Barber presumably included, gave the Tories their largest majority in decades.

At the time of writing (October 2022), the same misperceptions of the income distribution remain by those earning higher incomes. Kwasi Kwarteng, the Chancellor between 6 September and 14 October 2022, announced in a September mini-budget that the 45p tax rate for earnings above £150,000 was going to be abolished.[4] After much public backlash, he reversed the policy. Tony Parsons, a 68-year-old successful author, journalist and broadcaster living in London, tweeted in response to public outcry at the initial policy announcement: "If you think the men and women earning £150,000 a year are 'the super-rich,' you need to get out a bit more."[5]

This book is addressed to those who, like Rob Barber, are affluent in relative terms but do not necessarily feel so. For our purposes, this will include anyone who is part of the top 10% of income earners but is not near the very top – that is, what we believe to be an arbitrary but reasonable cut-off point for the upper-middle, professional-managerial class.[6] We aim to answer the following questions: what do members of the top 10% think about inequality, politics and their position in society? How will they react to the economic crisis, the cost of living, cuts to public services and the climate emergency? And how can a case be made for tackling inequality that appeals to this segment of the population?

But before we do any of that, we ought to have a clearer idea of who belongs to this group. After all, the boundaries of what constitutes being 'well-off' are fuzzy and depend on where we stand. Barber did not think he was, even though he is better off than 95% of the British public. Readers may wonder where they themselves sit. We asked ourselves the same thing.

Who exactly are we talking about? And who is doing the talking?

In current debates on economic inequality, most attention has been given either to the top 1% and their capacity to influence politics and shape society, or to those with the lowest incomes, and for good reason. However, the remainder of the top 10% of the income distribution, the top decile in statistical terminology, is just as significant for understanding how inequality works and is maintained. This group includes, for instance, engineers, head teachers, IT specialists, HR managers, senior academics and accountants, who are affluent but not excessively so.

Unless otherwise stated, the subject of this book is those in the top decile but below the top 1% or, if in the top 1%, only just – we were not recruiting for CEOs or tycoons. At this point, it is important to say that these are arbitrary cut-off points. It could be argued that the truly global elite only begins at the 0.1% mark,[7] or that the top quintile (20%) shares similar sociological characteristics with the top decile. We would agree; the economic distribution is not static, after all. Most of our examples will come from the UK, but given our previous research experience and the degree of international mobility and global outlook of this group, we also refer to other countries in Europe and the Americas.

Even though the overwhelming majority in the top 10% do not own yachts or have direct access to senior politicians, they still have disproportionate political influence. Indeed, almost by definition, this group includes all British MPs and most of the top echelons of government, as well as a sizeable proportion of decision makers in the media, the third sector, political parties, business and academia; not to mention senior doctors, lawyers, most judges, consultants and the like. In other words, they make up much of the higher ranks of the professions and institutions dominating the economy, politics and public conversation – with the possible exception of finance, which is firmly the remit of the 1%.

We, Gerry and Marcos, met in 2018, working on a research project focused on the top 10% of income earners in four European countries (Ireland, Spain, Sweden and the UK) led by TASC and FEPS, Irish and European Union (EU) think tanks, respectively. The evidence collected – which includes 110 interviews in those four countries – is the basis for this book.[8]

The report asked to what extent this group was sociologically distinct from the rest of society and whether its attitudes to welfare and redistribution were any different. We focused mostly on income (what people earn) rather than wealth (what they own). Some suggested it would perhaps be better to concentrate on the latter: it is even more unequally distributed than income and, as Thomas Piketty has shown, returns from owning (for instance, property or stocks) are increasing in importance relative to returns from working.[9] Nevertheless, also following Piketty, we thought looking at those at the top of the income distribution would be particularly interesting as they may see their work pay less and less and increasingly rely on what they own instead.

While we were carrying out those interviews, three well-established facts struck us about the literature on the top 10%. First, according to estimations from the HMRC survey of personal incomes, in the 2019–20 tax year, you only needed to earn over £58,300 to be part of it.[10] Many of those earning this amount are not necessarily part of the top 10% of households, especially if they have young children, but a couple where both partners earn around that are significantly above the top 10% mark.[11] Most people, be they interviewees, colleagues and friends, thought this figure was way too low. Perhaps for some readers, this doesn't sound like much either, especially if they are based in a large city such as London where well-paying jobs tend to concentrate and the cost of living is highest. But, and this is key if you are earning £58,300, it means that 90% of the population earns less. See Figure 0.1 for a dramatic representation of how incomes shoot up after the 90th percentile, and how far away the top 1% is from everybody else.

Second, if you are just about into the top 10%, or even the top 5% (£81,000, according to the same HMRC source quoted above for 2019/20), you are still further away from those in the top 1% (£180,000 and over) than from the UK's median income (around £26,000). The higher you go up the distribution, the steeper the climb. As many have noted, including Richard Burgon and Torsten Bell, the earnings of the truly rich are almost unimaginable for most. And as we climb closer to the very top of the distribution, those earnings are increasingly backed up by what people own (in other words, their capital) rather than only their wages. Furthermore, reporting actual income at both the top and the bottom of the distribution is difficult to ascertain, so the distances may be even bigger than we imagine.[12]

Third, while members of that top 10% tend to have relatively socially progressive attitudes to immigration, abortion, minority rights, same-sex marriage and foreign policy, their attitudes on all things economic are not so left of centre. Both surveys and interviews show they are more likely than the rest to oppose redistribution and to accept meritocratic explanations of social mobility.[13]

As bringing up the subject of income is often awkward, finding interviewees wasn't always easy.[14] We used our extended networks and LinkedIn, recruiting to reflect the composition of the top 10% in a few key respects. The most important of these was occupation, which we took as a proxy for income as we did not want to begin the interview with our respondents being immediately aware that they were in the top decile. In most cases that variable was enough to identify who should be

Figure 0.1: Income thresholds before tax by percentile point, UK, 2019/20

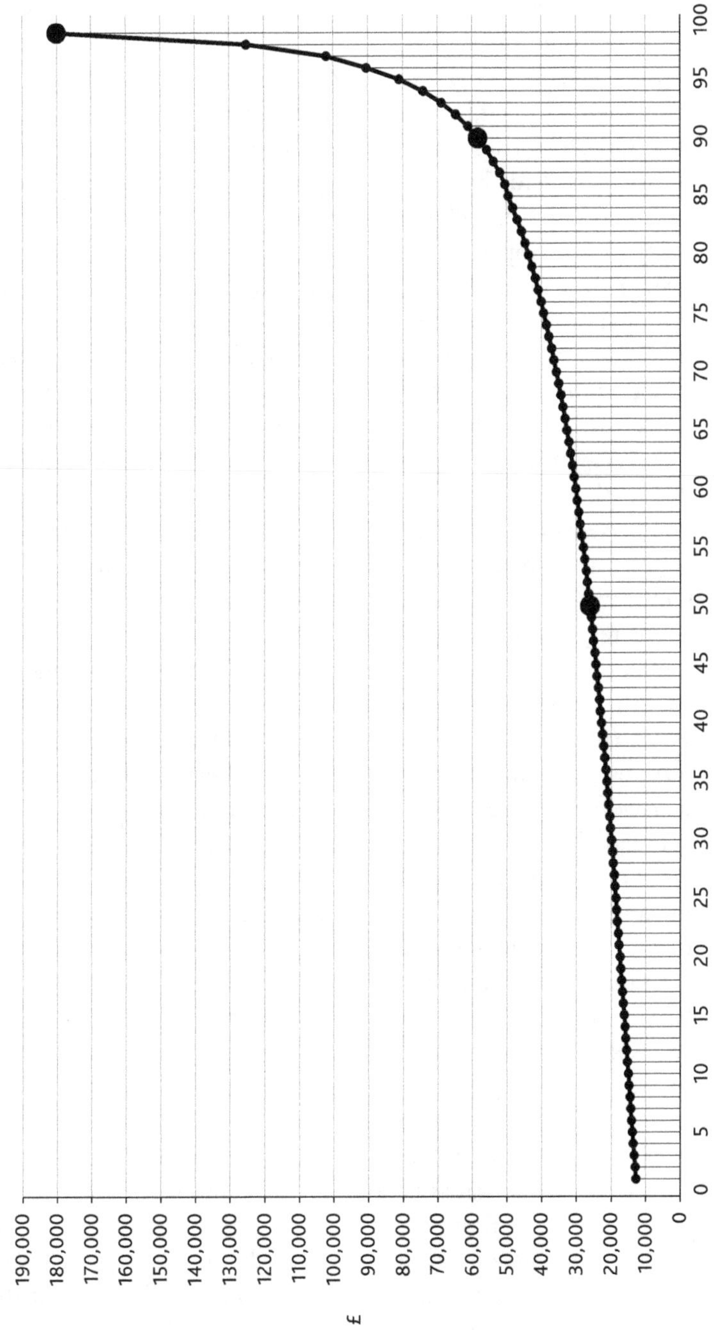

Source: HMRC, 2022

interviewed, with the exception of a young IT professional who earned significantly less.

To further reflect the top 10% in statistical terms, two thirds were men, ranging between 26 and 66 years of age, most being in their late forties and early fifties. A majority were White, married and had children.[15] Most lived in or close to the capitals or largest cities in each of the four countries; 16% of Londoners belong to the top 10%.[16] In the UK, that meant our respondents lived mainly in south-east England, perhaps a consequence of us both living there and the concentration of higher-paying jobs in this most affluent region of the country.[17] We acknowledge that this is a limitation and that the perceptions and attitudes of high earners living in other parts of the UK warrant further study.

Interviews were conducted between August 2018 and August 2019, plus a series of follow-ups between January and May 2022. A majority of these were carried out online, but some were in person. Most took just over an hour and all used the same semi-structured interview guide. We began with questions about respondents' biographies, followed by asking them about their work, careers and professional trajectory.[18] Later, we moved on to their attitudes on inequality, the rich and the poor; their views on taxation, the public and private sectors, and public services (including which ones they use); their social and political behaviour: whether they vote, participate in politics or volunteer. We ended with questions about their self-perception. Do they feel privileged? To what extent has hard work, good decision making and luck determined their status? Where do they think they fit in the income distribution?

At this stage, it's important to explain why we found this group worthy of attention and how it may affect how we see it. When we were carrying out this research, we were an early-career sociologist looking for a footing in a precarious, internationalised academic labour market and a freelance social policy researcher who had moved out of London to Woking, a solidly Conservative constituency, and ran as Labour's parliamentary candidate in the 2019 general election.

Marcos is the son of upwardly mobile doctors from Chile – themselves of middle-class background in the US sense of the term. He grew up during the decades that followed Pinochet's dictatorship, which saw his country become one of the wealthiest and most unequal in Latin America. In 2009, he came to the UK to study at some of the most prestigious universities in the world. For his Cambridge PhD and first book on think tanks after the 2008 financial crisis, he interviewed some elite figures of British policy making. After graduating, he spent a few years doing freelance research and taking occasional teaching and lecturing jobs across UK universities, because it was difficult to find permanent work. As anyone who knows academia will tell you, teaching means being paid only for the time spent in the classroom at a rate, when preparation and marking time are added, that often amounts to less than the minimum wage. The unspoken assumption is that this will only be temporary as junior academics work their way up the hierarchy. However, for many, this is not what happens, as evidenced by the increasing reliance of universities on underpaid fixed-term labour, without which they could not deliver their courses.[19] Marcos only found a more secure foothold when he was contracted by University College London to cover a permanent member of staff on maternity leave, after almost four years of applying for jobs. This is not uncommon.

Gerry is an only child and the first in her mother's family to go to university and private school. Though she moved around quite a bit during her childhood, she spent many years behind the scenes in luxury hotels in London, where her mother and stepfather worked as managers. Her classmates were children of some of the wealthiest families in the city. Living in such environments during the Thatcher years made her keenly aware of inequality. Following her undergraduate degree, Gerry spent ten years working in publishing, public sector and non-profit organisations, at which point she returned to university in the 2000s, completing a PhD at the London School of Economics and Political Science (LSE) on the impact of Tony Blair's New Labour welfare to work programmes on young people. At the same time, she also took contract teaching, lecturing and research positions at LSE and was a freelance Hansard reporter in parliament. She then took a career break to raise her own family, moving to Woking, just outside London. Before returning to research, Gerry worked in local schools and voluntary organisations and became heavily involved with the Labour Party. In those years, she saw the impact of austerity on her community, ostensibly one of the most affluent in the UK.

From that brief introduction to two people with fairly different backgrounds, it is apparent that there is much we share. We are both from families who became socially and geographically mobile, who provided privilege on the tacit expectation that our trajectories would be equally successful. Both of us have experienced the anxiety such expectations can often bring and owe our positions not only to scholarships but also to the early privilege provided by our parents being professionals or managers and finding the cash for private schools. Very few, even in the top 10%, ever get to write a book. Less than 2% of their children go to Oxbridge or the LSE. We share these privileges with many working in the social sciences, a relatively 'posh' academic subject. While as individuals we are not in the top 10%, we have been supported by our partners and wider network of relatives, friends and colleagues, many of whom are in this group themselves or have been for much of their working lives.

Having entered the privileged world of academia, we have both been broadly invested in the institution of the university, from which we expected to get the legitimacy to have something to say about society and the prerogative to belong to the middle class, however vaguely defined.[20] We have spent decades studying alongside, being taught by and working with individuals in academia and the policy research world who were – or could be expected to become – high-earning professionals and managers. However, neither of us expects to join the top 10% anytime soon, however close we are to some of its members in professional, educational or personal settings. The ground rules have changed and a PhD isn't able to guarantee the income it may have just a few decades ago.

Our own position, as authors of this book, is therefore instrumentally and ethically loaded. On the one hand, our professional biographies give us a keen understanding of how inequalities function and our relative proximity to our research subjects gives us a unique opportunity to identify their ways of thinking. On the other hand, there are ethical and methodological risks in that we find our own perspectives becoming entangled with worldviews that reflect and reinforce the status quo, and which are then given further legitimacy through our work. Our own relationship with the top 10% is, therefore, both potentially transformative (we have unique access) but also dangerous (it may reproduce current frames of thinking).

Conducting interviews with high-income earners, we were struck by the seeming familiarity of many of their views. Most were to the right of Jeremy Corbyn and to the left of Boris Johnson (or at least of his post-Brexit version). Those closer to the right (a majority, but not an overwhelming one), tended to have the kind of 'pro-austerity' views that are prevalent in the media and gave meritocratic explanations and values to justify their opposition to greater redistribution. Those closer to the political left often held similar ideas to those found in *The Guardian* and the kinds of institutions we are both familiar with (universities, NGOs, left-of-centre think tanks and political parties). Therefore, a crucial hurdle in deciphering this group was that – discounting their distorted sense of their own economic position – what they told us often simply sounded like the prevailing 'common sense' in media and politics.

We also soon discovered that the dominance and ubiquity of the top 10% in the public conversation perversely renders it almost invisible. We have become accustomed to its ways of thinking – including meritocratic explanations of its success – and its cultural trappings. It's the unspoken background of the dominant political culture in Britain, as represented, for example, by the BBC. Members of the top 10%, while not always identifying with that description of themselves, see the economic and social structures that support them simply as 'commonsensical' and 'reasonable'. Therefore, they are perplexed when confronted with anger against them. In their minds, a more irrational 'populism' seems to have taken over, especially in the fallout of the Brexit vote and after Trump became US president. We started wondering whether these ways of thinking, though seemingly unremarkable, are part of the explanation for our growing social divides.

The difficulty of making sense of the fact that their views are both apparently omnipresent and perceived to be under siege made us think. Academics frequently tend to 'other' their research subjects, ostensibly to give a voice to people we don't usually hear from or understand. In our case, the difficulty was exactly the opposite – we needed to interrogate the 'us' of the 'us and them'.

The research world is not immune to the naturalisation of such views, which makes writing this book particularly uncomfortable – reflecting on the growing distance between ourselves (the researchers), the people we study (most often those who are 'othered'), and those we report to (quite frequently, members of the top 10%). While nobody we know in the top decile would refer to themselves as 'us' or to the rest of the population as 'them', the structure of our work assumes a 'professional' distance between the researcher and a researched 'subject'. We study others through 'fieldwork' and return to elite environments to present 'findings' to our peers and employers to, in the best-case scenario, inform policy and the public conversation.

This privileged viewpoint comes with the tacit acceptance of a commonly held but rarely voiced view: if you are a high-income earner, you have proven yourself worthy of being in charge of your own life and politics and the state should leave you be. From that viewpoint, even researching the relatively well-off may seem indulgent. This book argues the opposite, that social structures affect the lives of 'us' as well as 'them'. For that reason, we look at high-income earners as a group to be studied sociologically and anthropologically, reflecting on how the failure to do so obscures so much of the dynamics of inequality. In that sense, thinking about the 'subjects' of our work requires what anthropologists call 'estranged intimacy': becoming intimately involved, while at the same time standing back.

That being said, we do not want to simply reproduce the kind of 'anti-metropolitan elites' arguments that have poisoned the well in Britain and elsewhere. As the last decade has made all of us painfully aware, denunciations of highly educated professionals and experts quite frequently mask reactionary politics under the guise of anti-elitism – and lead to trust being deposited into even more moneyed elites. We do not want to refuel nativist, anti-intellectual denunciations of the 'citizens of nowhere', which often end up benefiting the truly wealthy, the owners of capital. As we explore later in the book, taking that route – as countries like Hungary, Russia and increasingly the UK seem to have done – results in less free, less solidaristic and less sustainable societies.

Another issue we face with our chosen subject group is that while we don't want to antagonise the top 10%, we also don't want to seem excessively sympathetic to those who are, by definition, a privileged segment of society. They tend to be more mobile, healthy, educated, professionally fulfilled, economically secure and optimistic about the future than the 90%. Even though their incomes decrease at a larger rate after economic downturns, they recover faster and capture most subsequent growth.[21] More likely to hold a university degree, to access cheap credit and to feel financially secure, they have also been insulated from the worst effects of austerity and the post-COVID-19 economic crisis.

What we want instead is to prompt this group to question whether they are simply 'normal' and whether their own experiences and achievements can and should be the basis to judge the lives of everyone else. After all, soon after being granted a privilege, you get used to it, at which point it becomes normal, part of the background. However, this tendency becomes harmful when it forces on the majority standards that are increasingly beyond their reach. In other words, we want to elicit more 'sociological imagination' in a group in which those who have a voice in how society is run tend to concentrate.

Is all well with them?

As privileged as members of this subset of the population might be, we argue that cracks are beginning to show in their sense of security and self-worth. This has opened up a space to offer alternatives. In Ireland, for instance, a country that depends to a great degree on international capital flows, with some of the highest nominal earnings and fastest growth rates in the EU, we found that 28% of the Irish top 10% declared that they had difficulties 'making ends meet' in 2016, a year in which its economy grew by 5.2%.[22] Surely, part of the answer to that was that 'making ends meet' means something very different to the well-off, right? Or is something else going on?

To be sure, the top decile has thrived since the advent of globalisation, but not nearly as much as the top 1%. According to the World Inequality Database, while the top 10% captured 36.1% of all income in Britain in 2018 (up from 28.5% in 1980), it was the top 1% who received most of it (from 6.8% to 13.1%).[23] This leaves a 1.3% share growth for the remainder of the top 10%, and raises the question of how much of it was seen by those at the bottom of the top decile. Furthermore, as Piketty has famously shown, wealth is much more unequally distributed than income, and the more income you have, the more likely it is that a greater proportion of it derives from your wealth rather than only from your work.[24]

Given the above, we argue that growing inequality and the spectacular concentration of wealth at the top in recent decades – once touted as necessary for a thriving economy – now risk hurting even many within the top 10%. This is not only because of their perceived indirect effects (for example, crime and insecurity), but also because keeping up with the top 1% may prove increasingly hard for most. It is precisely because of this ambiguity surrounding the top 10%, the fact they are both privileged and mostly dependent on their work to make a living, that we decided to focus on them rather than on owners of wealth more directly, who are much more likely to align themselves with the interests of capital. By the same token, we acknowledge the increasing number of high earners in Britain who are also owners of the most wealth. Inequality expert Branko Milanovic tweeted: "your neighbourly CEO […] is in the top 1% by labor income and also in the top 1% by [the] shares he owns."[25]

Anti-elitism, precarity, automation and higher costs of living also risk undermining the social and economic status of the top income decile. Our interviews revealed some veiled anxieties. Despite their relative advantages, comfort and insulation, those in the top decile do not feel politically empowered and fear downward mobility. Like all of us, they live in a world affected by climate change, higher costs of living, an eroding social safety net, and what they see as rising populism and political polarisation. Aware of intergenerational inequalities, they worry that the world their children will inherit will be worse off.[26] Like most of us, they know there's something wrong and unsustainable about how we live our lives, but don't know exactly what it is or what to do about it.

Recently, we found ourselves reflecting on how the top 10% may interpret the momentous changes the UK and the world are undergoing, and whether their lives and views have changed since the start of the pandemic. We know that their political and social attitudes develop from everyday concerns about good schools for their children, affordable housing and access to healthcare if they need it: a desire to be secure. How will this group respond when faced with societal shocks and the wider realisation that the gap between those in the top 1% and the remainder of the top 10% is significant and only likely to grow?

Before the pandemic, they were already facing a choice between an ever more unsustainable status quo and the far right. In 2020, they experienced significant changes to their lives and, if not becoming the direct recipients of state transfers through furlough and business-support schemes, witnessed their widespread use among people not too different from themselves. Meanwhile, as Gary Stevenson, a former trader in the City of London, has shown, the COVID-19 response represented an unprecedented transfer of wealth towards the rich, boosting the savings and assets of the already wealthy while the rest are left to struggle with rising inflation.[27] Since late 2021, high earners have seen a cost of living crisis and market instability that have increasingly threatened them too. The choice they have to make in the coming years is one between isolating and protecting themselves even further or reaching out and connecting with others, in the understanding that their concerns aren't ultimately that different from those of the median earner: being able to afford a good quality of life in an ever more expensive and uncertain world.

Chapter outline

The remainder of the book is structured as follows. Chapter 1 sketches a broad picture of the top 10%, examining what they look like and how they are different from the rest in sociodemographic terms. Perhaps unsurprisingly, they are doing rather well. We show how members of this income group are more likely than people lower down the distribution to hold a university degree and to have seen their incomes grow. However, the top 10% is also internally diverse, and there is a noticeable distance between those at the top and the bottom of the bracket.

In Chapter 2, we look at high-earning individuals in qualitative terms: what they tell us in interviews about their backgrounds and life stories. By most reasonable definitions of the term, they are the 'upper-middle class' but they would flinch if called that. They believe that they are merely average. This tells us that there is a distortion in how those who earn more than 90% of their fellow citizens think about themselves and others. What impact is this having on how they think about the society they live in?

Chapter 3 examines their views on work: its importance for their self-definition and how they derive moral and social worth from paid employment and educational attainment, measured by income and professional status. This logic explains why even high-income earners who hold progressive views on the economy often come across as hierarchical rather than egalitarian. Those with the most career achievements and educational credentials are, according to an unspoken meritocratic truism, better positioned to lead the state, steer the public conversation and decide over the public purse.

Chapter 4 zeroes in on the politics of the top 10%, in both formal and informal terms. It does so by acknowledging that public opinion can be complex and conflicting and that it is an oversimplification to align principles, behaviours, morals and values to either the right or left of the political spectrum.[28] Notwithstanding, previous research has positioned the top 10% broadly on the right on economics and on the left on issues such as same-sex marriage, abortion and immigration. Recently, these views have been under strain, especially after the populist waves of the 2010s and, in the UK, the emergence of Brexit and Jeremy Corbyn. We also explore some of the reasons why voters in the most affluent constituencies of the UK continue to support the Conservatives at the same time as being quite critical of their lurch to the right.

According to surveys, this group has higher levels of trust in political institutions than the rest, as well as being more likely to vote and to believe they have a say in how their countries are run. However, and seemingly in contradiction with that, our respondents also show a certain mistrust of politics, fearing political instability, populism, corruption and the erosion of democratic norms. This might be explained by the fact that, although they have a detached familiarity with national political debates, they rarely engage with small 'p' politics. Given their tendency to prioritise work and competition and to surround themselves with those of similar socioeconomic status, they frequently feel detached from the communities in which they live, which are often quite segregated. Moreover, their lives have been relatively insulated from the effects of austerity and their knowledge of how hard it is at the bottom is mostly theoretical.

In Chapter 5, we underline the challenges that mounting inequality presents for high-income earners. As is well established, inequality threatens not only those in poverty but the whole of society on a wide range of social indicators: insecurity, crime, climate change, public health and even political polarisation.[29] Although most of our interviewees agreed inequality was something we should be concerned about, they were much more pessimistic about society's future than their own. This speaks of an imagined distance from the rest and an ontological sense of security. There will continue to be opportunities for them and they will be able to get out of whatever circumstances they find themselves in, despite their anxieties and concerns, through the hard work that got them where they are in the first place.

Even so, holes are beginning to appear in their narrative of constant social advancement. Access to housing, jobs, opportunities for career progression and places in elite universities is becoming scarcer and competition fiercer. Many are also aware that catastrophic events such as illness or accident could derail their career trajectories. In tandem, intergenerational inequalities are becoming more accentuated, as Millennials and Generation Z find the transition to adulthood increasingly difficult. Education does not seem to guarantee income the way it once did, as income and status are becoming closely linked to inheritance and wealth. Our respondents' optimism was less pronounced about the world their children will inherit.

Chapter 6 asks what the top 10% will do when faced with such pressures, considering their mobility and their ability to isolate themselves. As globalisation was emerging, sociologists highlighted the increasing mobility and flexibility of a globalised workforce. This especially applies to the well-off, driving the process of 'brain-drain' and the interconnectedness of fields such as science, finance, business and education. Commuting and moving for work and education also means that many high-income earners lack a strong connection to any one place. Interviewees who were originally from less-privileged backgrounds described their upward mobility as individual exercises of 'getting out' of environments offering few prospects.

However, in an increasingly nationalistic post-COVID-19 world, our respondents' ability to cross borders is endangered while competition for services (increasingly offered online) threatens to become global. If they cannot escape these societal shocks, what are the alternatives? They could hunker down, insulating themselves from the worst effects of inequality, or seek to acquire as many advantages as possible for their children. While these are all attractive in the short term, they are also becoming more difficult and less effective, both because of the magnitude of the crises we are facing and because of the distance the very top has already secured from everyone else.

Chapter 7 identifies some of the barriers to a wider sense of belonging created by their perspectives, including a dominant belief in meritocracy. As we establish in Chapter 3, high earners' identities are mostly centred on homogeneous workplaces. High earners also tend to live either in high-income areas or at a 'social distance' from less-affluent communities near them. Although confident about their occupational status, many didn't feel they made a wider contribution to society and felt disempowered by corporate structures.

We believe there is a need for this group to tear down some of these barriers and strengthen their connection with their communities. While relatively protected, the pandemic has shown all of us – including the top 10% – that we depend on each other, especially on many of those we pay the least. COVID-19 will have also altered their work-life balance and led to more time spent locally. It might be time for high-income earners to rethink their assumptions about which parts of society are valuable, the meaning of citizenship and what work is 'essential' and worthy of respect.

Chapter 8 may make uncomfortable reading because rather than mapping out a positive vision of the future, it instead suggests some of the ways the top 10% could reset their attitudes towards the lives of others and re-examine their relationship with the private sector, public services and the state. It starts by reminding us what we know: that while they told us they largely defined themselves through work, they rarely thought about the contribution of their work to society beyond the bottom line. They also worried their older selves may not remain 'ahead of the curve' in a global market and that their children might be unable to climb the meritocratic ladder as they did. They acknowledge the value of public services, but, prior to the pandemic, tended to focus on education and equality of opportunity. They were generally supportive of public spending on healthcare and education, partly because they touch the lives of individuals in spheres mostly outside their influence. By the same token, many viewed those receiving welfare as somehow deficient.

The book's conclusion reflects on how high-income earners may react to societal shocks as it becomes increasingly apparent that their previous strategies are becoming ineffective. It questions whether the economic structures that have, until now, served them well will continue to. The first obstacle is that the very definition of elite implies a distance from non-members. For meritocratic high-income earners, the rationale for this distance cannot be ascribed status: it has to be the reward for effort, whether in the form of work or educational credentials. Therefore, one of the first tasks is to question the concept of 'reward' and its linkage to social goods and status. Our respondents were beginning to see that this link is getting weaker, that hierarchical employment structures and hiring demands are changing – with a hollowing out of middle-class jobs – and that social mobility is coming to a standstill. They are aware that their children, notwithstanding their education, will not have the same opportunities or standard of living, and their choices for work and consumption will therefore have to change.

High-income earners, particularly those working in the private sector, appear compliant with a meritocratic, pro-austerity common sense. However, they were likely to consider the limits of this logic when encouraged to reflect on the tensions between their own needs (and those of their children) and the requirements of global capital. We have seen that they have mostly sought to meet the former by serving the latter. They may prefer paying for advantages for their children while at the same time erecting fences to keep other people's children out, in the understanding that the benefits of doing that are much more direct and tangible than building a less unequal country. But as the fence grows taller and the club's fees become more expensive, this may not continue to work. And this means that we will need to promote the need for, and value of, new models of ownership (both at work or locally) and the legitimacy of other work, life and consumption roles and choices. If not, high earners may continue to see the distance between the idea and the reality of meritocracy only grow, to the point where only capital is truly valued.

The well-off are uncomfortably off, intuitively coming to terms with the awkward truth that they cannot be, as Markovits puts it, 'both rich and free'.[30] Living at the current level of competition has negative effects on their wellbeing while directly relying on other people's exclusion. Their imagined sense of self cannot be dissociated from the economic structures they live within. This book's aim is to invite the top 10% to consider a future in which, for the price of giving up the barriers through which they seek to distinguish themselves from the rest, they could become less anxious, more secure and less isolated. Their children, who will increasingly struggle to retain the position they were born in, are likely to push them in that direction.

1

Not billionaires, but well-off?

This chapter describes the top 10% in statistical terms, based mostly on survey data. It explores what, if anything, makes them a recognisable group that can be distinguished from the rest of the population.[1] However, an important caveat is that incomes at the very top are sometimes difficult to fully detect, and increasingly so the higher up you go. Top incomes are under-reported in surveys when compared with tax data[2] – and tax data also underestimate the riches of the truly affluent.[3] This may be because the higher you climb, the more likely you are to have incentives and the capacity to hide your true income, for tax reasons or otherwise. Many within the top 10% (as well as among our interviewees) are business owners and can decide what to take from their businesses as a salary rather than rely on a fixed monthly amount. Nevertheless, using the lower bound of the top 10% as a benchmark, what we show in this chapter holds as a rough sociological sketch of those who are doing *relatively* well. There will be many exceptions, but at an aggregate level, there is much that distinguishes this group from the other 90% of the population (though, of course, the boundary between 'well-off' and those 'not quite there' is always fuzzy).

How to define the top 10%

Posh, well-off, privileged, upper class, elite. In societies where the lives of their citizens are ruled by the possession of money such as ours, these words are loaded and contradictory. On the one hand, being well-off has positive connotations: being able to provide for oneself and one's family, but also being articulate, well travelled, confident, educated and successful – it implies being a member of society whose contribution is valued enough to deserve a decent living. On the other hand, calling someone well-off also insinuates they might be spoiled, cloistered, arrogant or unrelatable: always at risk of engendering distance and envy. For that reason, being (or being perceived as) well-off is a sensitive affair that has both societal and interpersonal dimensions, that touches on both history and the everyday. Hence our attitudes towards what is apparently a strictly economic category are also political, cultural and moral.

Not only are our attitudes to affluence contradictory, but also relative. In the UK, you might not think of the working class of post-industrial northern England as privileged, but arguably they are compared to most in Eritrea. Similarly, a family of doctors from South America might be by many definitions well-off, but their income is minuscule compared with the fortunes of the tech barons of Palo Alto. Given both how laden and relative this issue is, it is easy to see why delimiting who is and who is not well-off is problematic. The lower boundary is always fuzzy, dependent on our vantage point, and riddled with danger. A 2016 Gallup poll in the US found that those earning under $20,000 a year and those earning between $150,000 and $250,000 both identified as middle class at similar rates (roughly 30%).[4]

All of this poses difficulties for anyone studying the relatively privileged. Those familiar with income statistics will know there are many ways to break down the population that implicitly address the question of who should be considered well-off, middle class and poor. Quintiles and deciles are probably the most common – dividing a population into five or ten groups ordered by an unequally distributed variable such as wealth or income.

To be sure, there is some arbitrariness involved. The cut-off point could conceivably be the 50%, 13.9%, 4.8% or 0.2% mark, or not based on income or wealth numbers at all. Nevertheless, for the sake of simplicity and comparability, they tend to be used not only as reference points to detect relative wealth or deprivation but also as the basis for indexes to measure inequality. For instance, the Palma ratio aims to reflect the extent of inequality by comparing the share of the total income of the top 10% of the population with that of the bottom 40%. Only in particularly equal countries such as Sweden does the Palma ratio approach one, meaning that both groups capture about the same percentage of the country's income. In the UK, according to the Organisation for Economic Co-operation and Development (OECD), it was 1.57 in 2019.[5] In other words, for every pound earned by the bottom 40%, £1.57 is captured by the top 10% – and the bottom 40%, it may be obvious but needs restating, is four times larger.

In that sense, though focusing on the top 10% is arbitrary, it has its advantages. The first is quite prosaic: several measures use that benchmark. Besides the Palma ratio, there are the 90/50 and the 90/10 ratios, measuring the distance between the threshold for the top 10% and the earner right in the middle of the distribution (90/50) or the one at the top of the lowest decile (90/10). According to the OECD, these numbers in 2019 were 1.9 and 4, respectively, meaning the poorest member of the top 10% earns almost twice as much as the median earner and four times more than those in the poorest 10%.[6] Another advantage of using the top decile as a cut-off point is that, although few would argue that the top 10% are affluent relative to the rest of society, this population is broad and diverse enough to encompass many who may not necessarily feel so. As we will show, within that group you can find both billionaires and people who would struggle to get a mortgage.

Research by the Trust for London in 2020 identified five levels of progressively higher living standards, which were not equally spaced: minimum income standard, surviving comfortably, the (securely) comfortable, the wealthy and the super-rich. Focus group discussions found 'there is no agreement on what it means to be rich'. Attitudes are nuanced and narratives of the deserving and undeserving rich emerge – such as consideration of how the rich get their money, how they spend it, and whether it is used for the good of others.[7] The researchers concluded that:

> The concept of a 'riches' line, if defined as a line above which people are considered to have 'too much' [...] (rather than a *descriptive* line above which someone can simply be defined as rich) is by nature a normative evaluation. If public consensus on this *normative* view

(that it is wrong to have too much) could be found it would be a valuable addition to debates about the scope for the redistribution of wealth or for the curbing of high income, including the compressing of pay differentials. But the idea of surplus, excessive or unnecessary income, consumption or wealth is open to many different interpretations.[8]

In what follows, we argue that drawing the line at the 10% mark makes sense sociologically, not because the top 10% is cohesive or homogeneous, but because at an aggregate level they have some distinct characteristics compared with everyone else. Doubtless, they are a diverse group, but what they share says a lot about them too. Among those variables, probably the two most immediate are occupation and education.

What is peculiar about the top 10%?

Unsurprisingly, the top 10% is massively overrepresented among managers (28% of them are part of the top 10%, according to data from European Union Statistics on Income and Living Conditions [EU-SILC]), professionals (21%), and, to a lesser extent, associate professionals (8%), with the notable but not numerous exceptions of the armed forces and some elite technical occupations such as pilots and railway operators.[9] There are very few clerical staff, skilled agricultural, fisheries and forestry workers, trades and crafts workers and machine operators in the top 10% and almost none among those employed in elementary occupations such as cleaners and carers. None of the other categories have more than 5% of their members in the top 10%, and clerks, sales and service workers and those in elementary occupations barely have anyone among their ranks (see Figure 1.1).

At this stage we should remind readers that, according to the Office for National Statistics (ONS), in 2018, professionals and managers account for, respectively, 11% and 20% of all workers in Britain, and professionals and managers in the top 10% are a smaller group still.[10] Even so, a 2016 NatCen Social Research study found that 47% of professionals and managers in Britain declare themselves to be working class.[11] Comparing

Not billionaires, but well-off?

Figure 1.1: Occupation by income decile, UK, 2016

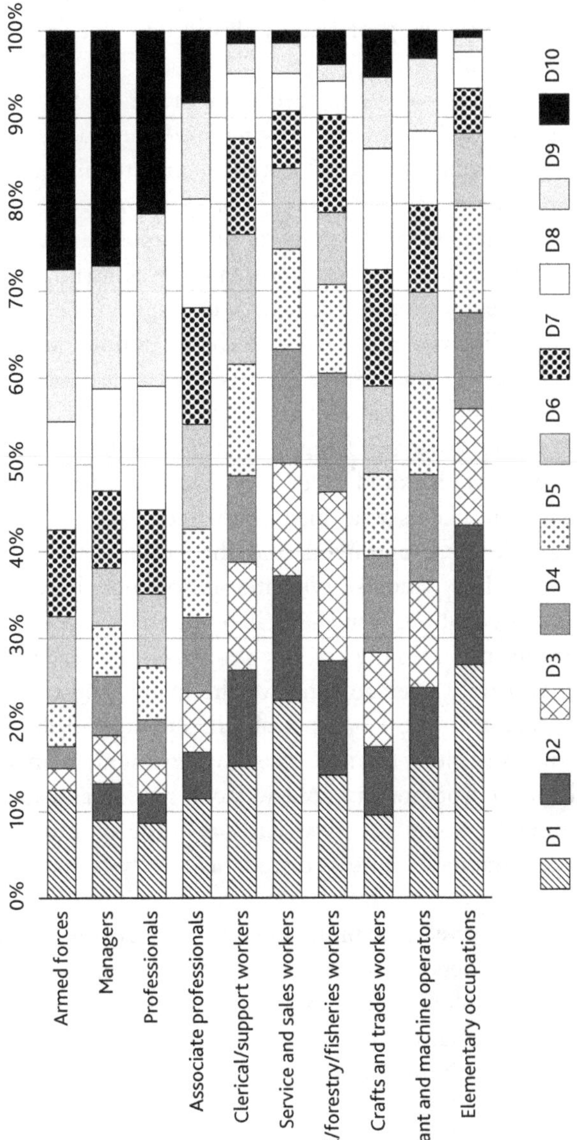

Source: Eurostat, 2018

these results with the US Gallup poll mentioned earlier, British people's understanding of class is clearly different from that of the Americans.

Occupation has, to be sure, several important effects on people's lives. As we grow older, and leaving aside our social networks associated with family and education – and arguably to a lesser or diminishing degree, churches, hobbies and neighbourhood – work is the place we make many of our friendships. It shouldn't be surprising because we spend most of our waking hours there. If that is the case, most of our immediate colleagues (or at least those we are most likely to relate to), will share a similar occupational status with us: in the case of professionals and managers, that usually means other professionals and managers.

Work shapes to a large extent the kinds of people we have daily contact with. This could include, in the case of the top 10%, colleagues and clients who may be sociologically very different (for example, civil engineers and the builders they oversee; doctors and their patients), but often it does not. Indeed, many well-paid occupations, especially in a country as welcoming to international capital as the UK, seek to attract the very wealthiest clients. You only need to think of the many industries geared towards selling to the 1%, especially in and around the City of London: investment finance, asset management, management consultancy, corporate and tax law, stock trading and so on, but also, closer to home for us as authors – the elite universities selling postgraduate courses to students largely from families in the top 10%.

Even where a well-paid profession is not mostly oriented towards the top 1%, access to its ranks may still be defensively policed, making it difficult for outsiders or those without the connections, money or 'cultural fit' to join. This immediately recalls the top echelons of media and politics: in 2019 it was reported that two thirds of Boris Johnson's cabinet attended Eton College (for those not from the UK, an elite boys' school that charges up to £48,500 a year).[12] The truth, however, is that this phenomenon is much more widespread than at the apex of the political elite. According to the Institute for Fiscal Studies, the average annual net private school fees in Britain are £13,700, while total state school spending per pupil is about half of that, £6,900.[13]

According to Sam Friedman and Daniel Laurison in their celebrated book on social mobility, *The Class Ceiling*, over 50% of those working in elite fields such as medicine, journalism, law, life sciences, management consultancy, academia and advertising have parents who were professionals and managers themselves.[14] More specifically, Friedman and Laurison also show that the children of doctors are 24 times more likely than the rest of their cohort to become doctors; the children of lawyers, 17 times more likely than the rest to become lawyers; and the children of people working in film and television, 12 times more likely to have the same occupation as their parents.

Friedman and Laurison found that people whose parents were from lower socioeconomic backgrounds tend to be paid less for the same job than high-income earners with parents who had elite occupations. How does this square with 47% of professionals and managers who describe themselves as 'working class'? Interviewing people in elite jobs, they conclude that part of the explanation is the 'way in which working class ways of being have been ruthlessly appropriated by the upper-middle class as a way to make money and cachet from authenticity'.[15] With increasing levels of inequality and the dominance of elites in many occupations, class certainly seems to remain relevant in the UK in explaining people's life trajectories.

Income is correlated with who is most likely to work from home. Studies following the COVID-19 pandemic have found that the industries where high-income earners tend to be concentrated (finance and insurance, IT, professional services) are also among the most adaptable to be carried out remotely, while elementary and manufacturing occupations are much less so.[16] Coincidentally enough, these are also the kinds of jobs which often require being more mobile and at ease with globalised, innovation-driven labour markets and also those where much of the top 10% are concentrated.

While all of this is happening, the structure of the labour market is changing. More professional-level jobs are appearing, while at the lower end the structure of the labour market is shifting away from skilled work and manufacturing towards clerical and blue-collar service occupations. A 2020 Eurofound report (in which the UK was still considered), found that between 2011 and 2018, white-collar, highly skilled jobs were by far the fastest to expand in Europe (2.4%), especially in services. Most other occupational categories, meanwhile, dwindled, especially highly skilled blue-collar and construction jobs. The only exception was blue-collar, low-skilled jobs in private-sector services (for example, retail and catering).[17] Meanwhile, growth in full-time, permanent employment was almost completely concentrated in the first income quintile (top 20%), while the proportion of part-time, temporary jobs is increasing across the economies of Europe. Conceivably, the only way for this process of deindustrialisation not to generate insurmountable societal pressures is if the numbers of professional, well-paid service jobs continue to increase and are captured by the children of blue-collar workers. But how likely is that, considering what we know about social mobility trends? And if the children of blue-collar workers do seek to become professionals and managers, won't that generate further incentives to police access to elite occupations for those already 'in' them?

Unsurprisingly, having a high income is also strongly correlated with years spent in formal education. EU-SILC data show that 36.8% of the UK population have at least a tertiary education (meaning at least a university degree). For the top 10%, that number is 75.8%, (in Ireland these figures are 39.8 and 81.7%, and in Spain 29.6 and 71.6%).[18] Considering the concentration of professionals and managers in the top 10%, this is perhaps unremarkable. However, even though the great majority of high-income earners attended university, over two thirds of people with degrees in the population at large are not part of the top 10%.[19]

Not only are the years in education important, but also the perceived quality of that education and how much it is valued in the labour market. For instance, the diminishing returns of getting a PhD versus an MBA, or a degree from post-1992 universities versus one from Oxbridge. According to data from The Sutton Trust, 41% of senior public servants, 31% of politicians, 39% of media elites, and 17% of business leaders attended either Oxford or Cambridge, compared to 1% of the population.[20] In recent years, much has been written about Oxford and Cambridge's outreach efforts to increase their uptake of state school students (93% of all pupils). Yet, in 2020, these universities reported as a success story that 69.1% of admitted applicants to Oxford and

70.6% of those at Cambridge were from state schools.[21] One reason that these percentages were reported as success stories is that they are higher than many other elite universities. In 2021, Oxford Brookes University, formerly Oxford Polytechnic, appeared to take more children from private schools than Oxford University. However, more importantly, 51% of Oxford's students and 46% of Cambridge students are postgraduates – and most are paying very high fees.[22] Put this way, the undergraduate stats provide a 'shop window' that hides the extent to which Oxbridge students come from privileged backgrounds.

Another characteristic shared by the top 10% is location. A majority live in large cities where the best-paid jobs tend to be concentrated and the cost of living is highest. The ONS has reported that the highest incomes in Britain are found mostly in and around London, with important pockets in Buckinghamshire, Surrey and West Kent, plus a few others further afield in places like Edinburgh, Cheshire, North Yorkshire and East Cumbria.[23] Truly high incomes at an aggregate level, however, are mostly found in Central and West London. In particular, the boroughs of Kensington & Chelsea and Hammersmith & Fulham have an average yearly income of £63,286, which would position the average earner living there firmly in the top 10%.[24]

One of Friedman and Laurison's most interesting arguments in *The Class Ceiling* is that among the most important mechanisms by which privilege is reproduced at the top is the fact children from privileged backgrounds can rely on what they call 'the bank of mum and dad'.[25] In other words, the children of affluent parents have the possibility of delaying their entry into the workforce even while living and studying in places like London, where housing costs and salaries are highest. This allows privileged children to work in unpaid internships, spend more time in education, grow their networks and hone their skills so that they can compete in ever more specialised and credentialled labour markets.

In terms of gender, the figures are no more encouraging. Women comprise the majority of earners at each and every of the six poorest deciles, and their share diminishes the higher you go. Notwithstanding big differences among European countries, EU-SILC data show that although women were slightly over 50% of the European workforce in 2016, they were around 70%

of the poorest 10% of workers and around 33% of the top 10%. This tendency doesn't stop even within the top decile, as they are only 17% of the top 1%.[26] According to the ONS, the gender pay gap increases substantially in high-paying jobs in the UK, driving up the overall gender pay gap numbers, a gap that is also much more pronounced for workers below the age of 40.[27] Coincidentally, the highest average incomes in terms of age and gender are concentrated in men aged 45–49 and 50–54 (£55,300 and £54,100, respectively), while women of the same age can expect to earn much less (on average £36,300 and £35,200).[28]

Regarding race and ethnic origin, ONS data show that White, Chinese and Indian are the only ethnicities well represented in the top quintile, meaning at least 20% are part of the 20% of highest earners. The numbers for other ethnicities are dire: only 3% of Bangladeshis, 5% of Pakistanis and 11% of Black African/British/Caribbean workers are part of that top quintile, and 47%, 42%, and 31% respectively are part of the poorest.[29] Of the total economically active population in March 2022, estimated to be 33,792,000, 29 million are classified as White, 1 million as Indian and 194,000 as Chinese. However, even though high-income earners may look overwhelmingly White (90% of the top 20% of income earners are), they make up a lower percentage than the comparable 50+ age group in the rest of the income distribution.[30]

What can we conclude about high earners from these data? That they are mostly southern, middle-aged, White and male, even if most southern, middle-aged, White males are not high-income earners. Similarly, they are mostly professionals and managers, but a majority of professionals and managers are not part of the top 10% either.

From the data, it can be surmised that many factors are at play – both in terms of innate characteristics and upbringing – that make it likely that an individual will or will not be part of the top 10%. However, perhaps the single most noticeable variable identifying this group is the years spent in education. This does not mean that everyone with a university degree is a high earner, but that high earners are especially likely to have been to university. Education is crucial, not only to secure access to highly paid professional and managerial occupations but also as a cultural marker. It is through education that the economic and cultural signifiers of wealth come together, as well as the social prestige and lack of stigma that diminishes the possibility of finding fault with someone's CV to justify overlooking it. We also wager that this group is the kind whose children are all but guaranteed to go to university; for many, it isn't even a question. The top 10% are, on paper, those who have dotted all the I's and crossed all the T's.

Are they all that secure?

Previous research by Piketty and Saez, as well as by the OECD, on the impact of the 2008 financial crisis showed that the immediate effect of the crash was to suppress incomes at the top, briefly lowering inequality – at least for a couple of years.[31] However, soon after, the top deciles rebounded while incomes in the rest of the distribution remained stagnant. Based on these data, it is possible to argue that high incomes are more sensitive to economic shocks, at least initially, but that the proceeds of subsequent growth are also more likely to end up benefiting them.

Even so, nothing guaranteed that those in the top 10% before the financial crisis would still be there after it. Be it because of economic downturns, a health crisis, a bad financial or professional decision, or because of sheer bad luck, many who were once in the top 10% will have fallen out of it. Furthermore, the fact that high incomes tend to be concentrated in the middle of an individual's working life (roughly between the ages of 40 and 65) means that most people who belong in the top 10% will not be there for the majority of their lives.

This also applies across generations. Friedman and Laurison showed that although more than half of those in elite occupations had parents who also had elite occupations, many of the children of the professional-managerial class do not end up at the same level or above in the socioeconomic hierarchy.[32] Jessi Streib wrote a fascinating book, *Privilege Lost*, on the downward mobility of the children of the US upper-middle class.[33] Streib explores how values, interests and resources affect the decisions of young people on their transition to adulthood. She shows that many of the paths that granted a relatively comfortable experience to parents – and therefore influenced how their children were raised – cannot currently ensure the same level of economic security.

In addition, there is the internal diversity of high-income earners. The top 10%, by definition, has no upper limit. The poorest 10% has a lower bound of 0 (or negative numbers if one considers debt), while the rest are bound by the distribution itself. Among the top 10% are doctors, barristers, engineers, accountants, head teachers, senior academics and small business owners, but also billionaires. That is why median incomes are a better indication than averages: the latter are too sensitive to outliers. Nicanor Parra, the Chilean 'anti-poet', used to say: 'You eat two pieces of bread. I eat none. Average bread consumption: one per capita.'

Mindful of that phenomenon, we devised what we call the 99/90 ratio: a measure of the distance between the income of the lowest member of the top 10% and the lowest member of the top 1%. We found that, based on the same EU-SILC 2016 figures, that ratio was, for many countries, comparable to the distance between the bottom of the top 10% and the median income earner. In the UK, in terms of gross earnings, while the bottom of the top 10% earns 2.42 times more than the median earner, the bottom of the top 1% earns 2.78 times more than they (the bottom of the top 10%) do. Or, to make the comparison even more extreme, the 1% threshold equals 6.74 times the median income.[34] This does not even consider that within the 1%, inequalities are even sharper and that incomes at the very top are famously tricky to ascertain.

These inequalities, if anything, are getting more pronounced. According to the World Inequality Database,[35] the share of total income taken by the top 10% in the UK has gone from 28.5% in 1980 to 36.1% in 2018, while that of the bottom 50% has dwindled from 22.6% to 20.2%. However, most of the growth in the share of the top 10% has gone to the top 1%, which rose 6.3 points from 6.8% to 13.1%, leaving only 1.3% of the increase in the share of total income to the other 9%. And although one could argue this increase in inequality is irrelevant if the overall size of the economy continues to grow healthily, the truth is that real wages have mostly flatlined since the year 2000 – even without considering the cost of living crisis that is raging as we write. The tide rose, but not all boats were lifted.

One thing that puzzled us was that 12% of those in the top 10% in the UK declare facing difficulties in making ends meet –

and this figure was almost 30% in Ireland, the country with the highest nominal earnings in Europe![36] Surely, what 'making ends meet' means for different groups in the distribution is subjective and varies. For some, spending on private education, for instance, might seem like a bare minimum. However, even if that is the case, this phenomenon means something. We are not asking for commiseration for high-income earners – far from it – but merely saying that if this is the state of affairs, something is amiss.

Unsurprisingly, perhaps, high-income earners are the most likely to have access to a mortgage. However, it is important to point out that for the top half of the 1%, mortgages are for 'the little people' – in other words, they can buy their property without incurring debt. Still, according to EU-SILC data, the proportion of people who own their houses outright is much more representative of the whole distribution than that of those who hold a mortgage: 58% of the top 10% of households have one, while 5% of the bottom 10% do.[37] According to the ONS, the average house price in the UK was £278,000 in March 2022, up £24,000 from the year before, and it was £524,000 in London.[38] With those figures, it is not particularly shocking that mortgages are concentrated at the top of the distribution – a tendency that is only set to grow, considering interest rate hikes and a reduction in the range and generosity of mortgage products after Liz Truss's premiership. Still, considering that mortgages tend to be in the region of four to five times a person's annual salary, it is conceivable that a sole-income earner at the tail end of the 10%, earning roughly £60,000, may struggle to get a foothold on the housing ladder without family help.

Another interesting aspect about the top 10% concerns income from capital. Although we have said that we will focus to a lesser extent on capital, it is important to briefly mention some findings from the TASC report we previously worked on.[39] Based on EU-SILC data, we were able to identify income from wealth (renting, stocks, investments and so on) at the household level and how it has evolved. The poorest eight deciles did capture some of the share of total income from capital in 2008, but much less than the top 10%, let alone the top 1%. By 2016, however, almost all income from capital was captured in the top 20%. This is interesting because, as we are talking about proportions of the total share, the wealthiest deciles may conceivably have retained a similar level of income from capital, at the same time as the wealth from everyone else collapsed. These results chime with the findings of Berman and Milanovic, who argue that those at the very top of the income and wealth distribution are increasingly becoming the same people. They explain: 'In 1985, about 17% of adults in the top decile of capital income earners were also in the top decile of labor-income earners. In 2018 this indicator was about 30%.'[40]

In other words, lower deciles may have had some participation in income from capital in 2008, but this had mostly flatlined by 2016, the year of Brexit. Meanwhile, the participation at the top 10% level has either remained the same or grown – perhaps even without substantive increases, the share would automatically rise given the losses in the lower deciles. The Resolution Foundation also found similar results for the UK.[41] Comparing 2006–08 with 2016–18, they found that the lowest three wealth deciles (which include those with negative wealth: more debt than assets) saw no change, while deciles 4 to 7 saw their wealth decline by almost one percentage point. Only decile number 8 saw no change, while the top two (and especially the first) increased their wealth. Much may have changed in the overall wealth distribution, increasing wealth inequality significantly, and the top decile may not have even noticed.

Where is the top 10% going?

Back in 2018, we found ourselves at the entrance lobby of a large multinational in Canary Wharf, London, for the first interview in this project. William, our interviewee, approached us: middle aged, White, well mannered, wearing a nice suit, handkerchief in his jacket pocket, with earnings that would situate him just into the top 1%.[42] As we were at the beginning of our research into high-income earners, he ticked many of the boxes of what we thought we could expect. We asked him: do you see yourself as privileged? He told us:

> 'I feel fairly middle of the road and average, but objectively I know this is completely untrue. I know I

am at the top of the income percentile, but I also know I'm miles away from the very rich. Everything I earn goes at the end of the month. Whether it is school, holidays, et cetera. I never feel cash-rich.'

The top 10% are, by definition, a privileged group. William knows this at a theoretical level but does not feel particularly wealthy. He is not alone. Inequality expert Danny Dorling showed in his 2014 book *Inequality and the 1%* that those at the bottom of the 1% often declare that they are struggling to keep up with expenses, particularly school fees.[43] There are at least two explanations for this tendency. One is that they are simply out of touch and do not know what struggling or want means. This is certainly a possibility, but we did not want to start on the basis that our interviewees are simply wrong. If nothing else, it is bad form for a social researcher: our respondents have access to a world we do not necessarily know and the whole point of asking them is to try to understand it.

In a fascinating book on the lives of the very wealthy in New York, sociologist Rachel Sherman[44] argued that many among her interviewees were what she called 'upward-oriented', meaning that they thought they were situated somewhere in the middle of the income distribution: first, because most of the people they socialised with had similar or even higher incomes; and second, because there will always be the Bill Gates and Elon Musks of the world, whose fortunes dwarf everyone else's.

Considering this, a more feasible second explanation for William's unease is that those at the cusp of the top 1% have been prospering, but not necessarily so compared with some of their colleagues in Canary Wharf. They are well-paid, high-achieving professionals, often with advanced degrees and with all the respect associated with this. They have been doing well for themselves and, in their view, have done everything right: most of our interviewees (as well as Sherman's) justified their position by saying that they had arrived there through hard work.

However, raising children who have a fair chance of continuing an upward trajectory – and let's remember, their success will to a great extent be measured against how well their parents did – is becoming more expensive. Private schools cost on average over

£13,000 a year, but the type of private school that churns out prime ministers costs close to £50,000. Based on rough estimates, the top 10% have more children than average so their children make up 6% of the 7% who go to private schools; but half the children of the top 10% attend – often quite exclusive – state schools. Roughly one in seven children in private schools comes from the bottom 90%.[45] Despite this, the more the top 10% feel that they absolutely must commit to this expense, the more they will say they struggle to make ends meet. It is ultimately an arms race.

Society tends to view social mobility positively because of its upward direction; but the fear of a downward trajectory is part of the equation too, and throwing money at the problem seems to be the most immediate response to it. These are the concerns likely to be found among those in the top 10%. Those earning, say, £60,000 a year, especially if they are the only earner in their household and do not have wealthy relatives, though not poor, may not have access to the same quality of housing, private schools, or the same level of savings that would allow them to feel economically secure and competitive against the top 1%. And we have not even mentioned possible unexpected expenses, poor pensions or the impact of economic downturns. Amparo, a small business owner we interviewed in Spain, told us:

> 'I'm not doing badly. I'm happy; I've recovered my old customers who, after the [2007–08 financial] crisis, are finally doing better. It's not as good as it was before [...] but I'm doing fine. But I do worry that if at any given moment I will start doing worse, my children depend on me. I am 52 years old. I know that if I do badly as a businesswoman and I have to close down [my business], I won't be hired by another company.'

Could we really say she is wrong to worry?

In a 2017 Eurofound report, statistician Veli-Matti Törmälehto argues that measures of the well-off should be considered at an absolute rather than relative level.[46] That is, instead of defining who earns well by their position along the spectrum, we should focus on the income itself. In other words, someone right in the top 10% may be close to the top 1% in the graph, but in terms of income and lifestyle, they may be worlds apart. The top 10% of income earners, although doubtlessly privileged in relative terms, may not necessarily be affluent in absolute terms.

Our research confirms that there is much anxiety at the top. High earners, for example, may be so afraid of not being able to afford private school fees that they overwork and go without holidays. This is in the context of private schools offering much less advantage than they did in the past when they guaranteed a university degree, which in turn was a golden ticket. At the same time, student debt is growing; only 10% of UK students can attend university without incurring debt.[47] This level of pressure creates tensions throughout society. If, as these tendencies suggest, economic and social insecurity near the top is not an exaggeration, then we should all worry.

2

On the ubiquity and invisibility of the upper-middle class

In this chapter, we explore where the top 10% tend to think they sit in the income distribution, why they are often inaccurate in this estimation, and the connection between that inaccuracy and how they understand richness, privilege and worth. We argue that high-income earners could roughly be divided into two groups which, following Thomas Piketty's formulation, we call Brahmins and Merchants. We also claim that high-income earners' lack of knowledge of their own place in society is both cause and consequence of their disconnect from the rest.

We asked interviewees about their views on the rich, on those less well-off than themselves, and where they position themselves along the spectrum. Towards the end of each interview, we also asked each respondent about their income and then showed where it would situate them in the income distribution. We did not reveal that information beforehand because we wanted to avoid framing them as 'high-income earners' from the get-go and because we were curious about how they would react to the information. We simply told them in advance they were 'high-achieving professionals and managers' and that the interview would be about their views on inequality and politics. As we go on to show, they rarely, if ever, recognised themselves as high-income earners, let alone rich.

When speaking of class self-identification, discussing terminology is almost unavoidable. After all, it is through vague yet loaded terms that we tend to position ourselves and others socioeconomically and culturally. In the UK, the term 'upper class' is rarely used in casual conversation, though probably most would agree it's fair to describe the top 10% of income earners as such, socioeconomically speaking. Similarly, the 2013 Great British Class Survey defined 'elite' as the top 6%, and though that label is emotive and politically sensitive, it is also justifiable. Nevertheless, we met many who would qualify for that bracket who railed against elites, the establishment or the rich. Few high-income earners declare themselves to be upper-middle class either, and, if they did, it would seem vaguely like a confession. We also feel uneasy about using 'elite' or 'upper-middle class' to refer to our interviewees; not because these terms wouldn't be defensible, but because they sound like a veiled accusation.

In the UK, the labels 'middle class' and 'working class' are much more common (interestingly, rendering the upper class near-invisible).[1] However, 'middle class' does not completely shake off the negative connotations of upper-middle class. That distinction, instead of being mainly about money, generally refers to cultural signifiers: accent, vocabulary, demeanour, level of education, dress sense, taste and so on. As we mentioned in Chapter 1, according to a 2016 NatCen Social Research survey, 47% of professionals and managers – who, let's remember, account for around 80% of the top 10% – declare themselves to be working class.[2] A corollary of this way of thinking is that someone with many years in education and the 'right' accent but struggling to pay rent can be considered of a higher social class than a well-earning businessman with no degree and a northern accent. Although belonging to the upper-middle class undoubtedly has many advantages, overt bragging rights doesn't seem to be one, especially where meritocratic discourse holds sway. At the same time, declaring yourself to be middle class is seen as a great achievement and declared with pride by many – 'look where I have got to' – but it can also feel like a confession. The lengths that the 2022 Conservative Party leadership election candidates went to, to underplay their advantaged backgrounds, is an example of that.

Pinning any of this down is tricky, even more so following the advent of globalisation and the 'end of history', when many declared class to be 'dead' – society was deemed too complex and fluid for class to retain any explanatory power.[3] As Oly Durose wrote in *Suburban Socialism (or Barbarism)*, social classes have become more complex and internally diverse and 'to leave a polarised class untouched, in the hope that "the middle" disappears, is conceptually dishonest'.[4] However, ambiguously defining the middle class isn't an option for Durose, a left-of-centre campaigner seeking to appeal to the suburbs, because it has significant political consequences. Parties and leaders don't simply 'win over' the middle classes but construct them to pave their way to power. Drawing from his experience campaigning in Brentwood and Ongar – an affluent commuter hub in Essex and a safe Conservative seat since its creation – he describes suburbia as 'a space in which to *construct* a particular notion of the middle class for political gain. More specifically, parties have found suburban success by equating "middle class" identity with individual aspiration.'[5]

All of this means that how class is understood is not a given. It depends on which resources are valued; it is a construction, but one that uses the ideas and materials at hand. Pierre Bourdieu – the French sociologist who, while writing mainly about French society, has been most influential in the UK – provided one of the most popular ways of conceptualising class.[6] He argued that education and cultural signifiers are resources in themselves that, not unlike money, help distinguish those who have them from those who don't. He coined the term 'cultural capital': having the right knowledge, degree, demeanour and references – and even the right sense of humour – to do well in elite spaces. Easy to identify but hard to measure precisely – though proxies do exist (countries visited, framed degrees on walls, having books on your shelves – and making sure they're the right ones) – cultural capital can open or shut doors. For instance, according to Friedman and Laurison, in the context of interview panels for elite employers, cultural capital determines who *fits in*, which candidate is considered *polished*, and therefore who is hired.[7]

Put this way, though money is certainly crucial, it's not the only measure by which class manifests itself. Having spent many years in formal education (and being exposed to the associated behaviours) can be in itself a mark of privilege; it signals both investment by others (be it the state, parents or charities) in that person's education and, at a minimum, increased prospects for future earnings. The British focus on culture and education in matters of class is defensible, but it is disingenuous in that it allows for a certain confusion and partially dissociates class from money, or, at the very least, money in the here and now.

More than one way of being at the 'top'

The partial dissociation of class from money, therefore, allows a distinction between at least two kinds of privilege and, by extension, two kinds of high-income earners who are often lumped together: Piketty's 'ideal types' – Merchants and Brahmins.[8] Merchants derive their status mainly from their income and their position in the market. They are particularly common in the top 1% and among those in direct service to it in industries such as finance, in functions such as accounting and sales, and as landlords, investors or owners of their own businesses. They study for MBA degrees, invest and have a hard-boiled attitude to economic matters. Meanwhile, Brahmins base their status mainly on their employment, which often depends on their possession of cultural capital, meaning particularly high levels of education. They tend to be concentrated in bureaucracies and in the liberal and cultural professions: academics, lawyers, doctors, scientists, civil servants, artists and so on. One way to think about the difference between these groups is to consider who is more likely to be mentioned in casual conversation: Michel Foucault or Warren Buffett. Piketty's assertion is that, over the past decades in the Western world, Merchants have remained the bastion of the right while Brahmins have increasingly turned towards the left, which was not necessarily always the case. In other words, education is increasingly becoming a source of political divisions.

We are aware that these classifications are analytical tools that can be implicitly used by the Brahmin elite – of which we, the writers, are arguably a part (if not by income, by education) – to chastise another elite (the Merchants), and it's therefore important to apply them with a dose of scepticism. A Brahmin could be someone earning an income anywhere between 15% and 2% on the income distribution – at the bottom, it includes bishops on about £50,000 and, at the top, university vice chancellors and high court judges. The categorisation is therefore a coarse overgeneralisation (where would most engineers fit, for example?)

and exceptions abound (despite the stereotype, not all academics are on the left and all bankers on the right). Nevertheless, we find it a useful device with which to look at inequality in British society more closely. And although other variables intervene (age, gender, the urban/rural divide), there is ample evidence that years in education is one of the strongest predictors of liberal or conservative political views, especially in the last few decades.[9] However, we would like to add another dimension to the relationship that Piketty draws between politics and education: the distinction between political matters that are economic or, for lack of a better word, cultural in nature.

In 2012, US political scientist Martin Gilens showed that the top 10% of income earners are more likely than the rest to lean left on issues such as immigration, foreign policy and same-sex marriage.[10] However, that is not the case when it comes to the economy, as they are the most likely income group to oppose tax hikes and expansions of the welfare state. We found the same in our interviews: most people we spoke with were liberal on cultural issues, but a slight majority were against redistributive policies or raising taxes. As Figure 2.1 shows (based on European Social Survey figures), in the UK, the anti-welfare inclination of the top 10% compared with the rest is noticeable, but not static. It was particularly sharp before 2012 but, for whatever reason, it has begun to recede as most of the population has become increasingly supportive of government welfare provision.

Our interviews broadly aligned with what Gilens found. Most respondents were fairly liberal when it came to immigration, for instance, though these results may be subject to social desirability bias, especially considering that one of us is an immigrant. Most, whenever those issues arose, were also quite supportive of initiatives to ameliorate the exclusion of women, minority ethnic groups and LGBTQ+ people. However, there was an important difference between those supportive of more taxation and redistribution and those less so.

If we had to summarise what both Merchants and Brahmins have in common, it is a small 'l' liberal attitude to most issues: everyone is an individual responsible for his or her own actions and, as long as they don't hurt anyone else, they should be let be. The main difference between both views is one of emphasis:

Figure 2.1: Agreement with statement 'Government should reduce differences in income levels' by income decile, UK, 2008–18

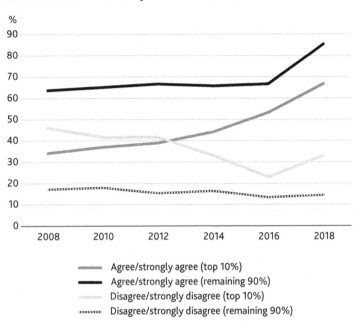

Agree/strongly agree (top 10%)
Agree/strongly agree (remaining 90%)
Disagree/strongly disagree (top 10%)
Disagree/strongly disagree (remaining 90%)

Source: ESS data, 2010–20

Merchants tend to prioritise the rights of individuals and economic freedom, whatever its results may be, while Brahmins are most concerned about freedom from discrimination and want. That is why both groups, in the main, share an animosity against biases based on gender, race and sexuality, but less so in relation to class.

Crucially, in our interviews, the Merchants were in a slight majority and mainly worked in the corporate and finance sector, while most Brahmins were highly educated professionals, often with postgraduate degrees. Roy, chief financial officer (CFO) of a small firm in the City of London, told us "I don't think much about inequality in the UK, because even the very poor have a bit with welfare. I don't think they are poor enough for me to feel sorry for them." Sean, owner of an HR consultancy, similarly said "If I'm funding people who are sitting at home and don't want to work, then I'm not happy about it. If I'm contributing to people who are below the poverty line, fine. But do I want taxes to go up for higher earners? No. I pay more than enough."

Stephen, a law professor, meanwhile, said that the current level of inequality "is the most obvious source of shame for civilised Western democracy. I find it unacceptable," and Paul, an architect, said, "Thatcher's effect on Britain was to make people insecure and greedy."

Put this way, there is a divide among high-income earners between those who have the view that the state should be small and the market robust and those who see the need for the state to actively shape and support our economies. After all, the discourse on whether the state or the market should prevail structures most political debates in the West and, we would claim, signals the split between the two types of elites who derive their status from their position in either the public or the private sector. Arguably these are the groups the Labour and the Conservative parties traditionally represent: workers and professionals versus owners and bosses, the highly educated versus the wealthy.

However, this view exaggerates the tendency of professionals to prioritise the public sector wholesale. Many Brahmins support a combination of both state and market solutions, especially after the end of the Cold War, as since then statist and pro-union policies have fallen out of fashion. It suffices to recall that top Labour politicians these days are much less likely to come from trade unionist or working-class backgrounds than they were in the past. According to the House of Commons library, in 1975, 98 MPs came from manual labour backgrounds. In 2015, the equivalent figure was 19.[11]

Moreover, even if our own professions were ever to put us in the top 10% and qualify us as Labour-voting Brahmins, we do not want to simply state that Brahmins have it right and Merchants do not. If nothing else, the electoral results and political climate of the last few years should warn us about such an easy conclusion. Here the role of life trajectories is crucial. Sean also told us he had a difficult childhood, growing up in deep poverty and with an alcoholic parent. In his account, he 'pulled himself by the bootstraps' and, understandably, resents the idea that those on a low income are simply victims and cannot do anything about their situation. He thinks everyone can succeed in Britain if they work hard and values what he sees as the market's fairness and appreciation of graft. Gemma, a consultant based in London, similarly, told us about how her 'escape' from Hull allowed her to move upwards. Simon, a manager in a City of London IT firm, said something similar about his experience of living in a housing estate in Sheffield when he was younger.

In her 1992 book, *Money, Morals, and Manners*, sociologist Michèle Lamont argued that in both France and the US at least three forms of justification for the position of elites in society could be identified.[12] She exemplified the *money elite* with the owner of a car-leasing business, a CEO, and a real estate developer; the *manners elite* with an architect, an economist and an academic administrator; and the *morals elite* with a labour arbitrator, the inheritor of a furniture plant and a finance executive for the US Department of Defense. Roughly, Brahmins would be comparable to the manners elite and Merchants to the money elite. The question of who would represent the moral elite (or who could be convinced to join its ranks) is an interesting one, but one corollary of Lamont's argument we would like to explore here is that different forms of elite produce powerful boundaries around themselves.

According to Lamont, each of these elite groups engages in constant 'boundary work': seeking to determine who is in or out based on shared norms over what is valued and what is not. Crucially, the norms these elites use differ in how they justify their own position and disparage others, and these justifications make sense from within each worldview. In such a way, members of the money elite can chastise manners elites for their perceived elitism and pretentiousness, while the manners elites see the former as philistine and short-sighted. In other words, the values espoused by the two elites (graft or sophistication) determine both what they admonish (laziness or bigotry), their cardinal sin (materialism or snobbery) and the accusations they level at each other (hypocrisy or pettiness).

These different forms of high-income earners have effects on how they think others, particularly those richer and poorer than themselves, came to be where they are and by extension where they themselves think they sit. Earlier, we mentioned sociologist Rachel Sherman. In a study of high-earning couples in New York, Sherman wrote that her interviewees could broadly be divided into what she called the 'upward'-

and the 'downward'-oriented rich.[13] The former didn't think they were particularly wealthy, as their point of comparison tended to be people surrounding or immediately above their economic station. Since there will always be those who are stratospherically richer than the rest, the upward-oriented can rest assured they are somewhere in the middle. Sherman interviewed some respondents in their own homes and recounts one such interviewee commenting "everyone's so busy that you don't think about [the underprivileged]" while a member of staff was cleaning in the next room. The downward-oriented, on the other hand, tended to emphasise their own privilege and declare awareness of their luck. In Sherman's study, many of the downward-oriented rich concentrated in high-status professions such as academia and generally had liberal views (in the US sense of the term), while the upward-oriented were much more likely to be found in the upper echelons of the corporate sector and leaned to the right politically.

Put this way, Brahmins would be much more likely than Merchants to be receptive to ideas that highlight their own privilege and urge them to make greater efforts to help those less well-off. However, these days, you do not have to look very hard to find laments about the massive and growing distance between the values, views and life experiences of highly educated professionals and the majority of the population. We all remember Brexit, and we all know a columnist or politician or two who have made a career out of lambasting Brahmins.

In the previous chapter, we cast a light on the sharp sociological differences of high-income earners when compared to the rest of the population, especially in terms of education and occupation – and via those variables, also in terms of their networks and worldview. In other words, much has to happen for a Brahmin to be raised and equipped for the role: investment in their cultural capital, in time not working and in cultivating themselves. This puts Brahmin status out of reach for most people, especially in countries where access to education is increasingly unequal and mediated by debt. David Graeber once wrote that conservative voters in the US 'tend to resent intellectuals more than they resent rich people, because they can imagine a scenario in which they or their children might become rich, but cannot possibly imagine one in which they could ever become a member of the cultural elite'.[14] In that broad sense, both Merchants and Brahmins share (as to an extent, we all do), a certain unawareness of how many people lead very different lives from themselves. To paraphrase Nietzsche, we are furthest away from ourselves.

On (not) knowing where you stand

Interestingly, none of our interviewees considered themselves rich. Neither Merchants nor Brahmins, neither doctors nor City of London professionals, neither the upward- nor the downward-oriented, regardless of where they sat within the top 10%. This was partly because many of them were ignorant of their own position in the income distribution. Indeed, most interviewees were way off the mark: most said they sat around the middle or top 30%, though a few, quite diligently, looked up the data ahead of interviews. But not even they, conscious of where they stood, *felt* rich.

More importantly, however, we would argue that richness is not generally understood in relative terms. If it were, most people in Britain would be considered so. According to the World Bank, in 2018 around half of the world lived on less than USD$5.50 a day.[15] Richness is, in some sense, absolute. It evokes private jets, gold, power, the fulfilment of every whim and limitless bounty. Few overtly call themselves rich, and those who would sit in a particular cultural space: think of Donald Trump's garish taste in interior design, think of the characters in *Succession*, the famous HBO TV series. These are not the high-income earners we spoke with; not even the most affluent among them could compare. And even if they could, they wouldn't want the label (if nothing else, to avoid producing resentment). In the words of William, the Canary Wharf management consultant who was just in the top 1%, he has a 'sensible' German car and, after school fees and all other monthly expenses, ends up feeling 'cash poor', even though he knows, in the abstract, that he earns well.

However, when we asked interviewees if they felt privileged, most said yes. They were appreciative of the fact they had a well-paying job, a relatively secure economic situation, opportunities to study and develop themselves, and that they lived in an advanced economy with access to healthcare. The only ones who said no were the ones most invested in meritocratic discourse, who told us nothing had been given to them. They were, however, a minority. Most people acknowledge luck as part of their trajectories: having parents who could provide, a mentor, or a 'break' somewhere. A few uneasy sentences often followed that admission. In *Success and Luck*, Robert H. Frank pondered on the role of luck in society and the extent to which the lives of the 'successful' are marred by it.[16] He reflected that our lack of acknowledgement of luck in our own lives is harmful to society and perpetuates dangerous myths about others, but also about the uneasiness that the admission of luck often produces for the lucky.

Whenever that uneasiness appeared, a reference to hard work frequently followed suit. This was particularly the case with Merchants, who often think their position is down to grit and hard work. Their world is a fast-paced one where remaining competitive is key. Hence, their position within it always remains precarious. Roy, the CFO, told us, "I am where I am because I work very hard. I'm not a brilliant person so I have to work hard." This discourse also appeared among Brahmins. Jonathan, a semi-retired barrister, told us "Hard work? Yes, a hell of a lot. I work harder than anyone I know. Historically, eight days a week and 26 hours a day." It appeared especially in reference to a certain ethic of responsibility and professionalism: the satisfaction of a job well done and knowing you have helped others. However, it is difficult to tell whether these appeals to their industriousness were an 'ex-post' rationalisation of privilege. In other words, is privilege the consequence of hard work or is hard work something they do to justify their privilege? While many respondents did acknowledge that there are many in society who work incredibly hard but struggle to make ends meet, the comments of high earners still often seemed a world away from the reality of those who work the hardest in physical labour and have a shorter life expectancy.[17]

The fact they felt privileged but not rich, we believe, speaks to the interesting position they occupy in the income distribution. As the graph is steeper the closer you get to the top, those in a relatively advantageous place may still find themselves quite far from the very wealthiest. This means that there may be many luxuries or privileges that those at the bottom of the top 10% may not even dream of. Nevertheless, they know at least theoretically that they have had important advantages in life, particularly in the educational and professional realms. How to make sense of this? Are they 'posh' for example? What even are the boundaries of the posh?

Another way of understanding this quandary is through what sociology refers to as the primacy of either 'structure' or 'agency' and the concept of the 'sociological imagination'. In a 2017 article, sociologist Daniel Edmiston wrote that people in poverty have a better 'sociological imagination' than the rich.[18] By that he meant that they are much more likely to be able to put their private experiences in a wider context: how constraints and opportunities shape where people end up. The less well-off, in that sense, understand that not everything is down to drive and individual action (agency), but that much is determined by the place from which one begins (structure). By contrast, the rich tend to exaggerate people's capacity to influence their lot in life through their own actions rather than attributing it to 'luck', 'destiny', or wider societal forces.

Edmiston interviewed people in the lowest and the highest income deciles. He presented them with 'scenarios': hypothetical individuals and their economic circumstances to see how his interviewees would interpret their situation and the degree to which they deserved it. In Edmiston's account, 'limited exposure to, and awareness of, financial management in a low-income household appeared to inform the judgments of affluent participants'.[19] High-income participants often blamed the hypothetical people for becoming pregnant, for relying on benefits, for having too many children and for falling into debt. In their estimation, they shouldn't have done any of those things because it is irresponsible to do so without the necessary financial means. Low-income participants were much more sympathetic to the plight of the people described in these scenarios, to a great extent because they could see themselves in the same situation. They had a clearer view of how broader structures can force people, through no fault of their own, in certain directions and towards poverty.

Similarly, a study by sociologist Serge Paugam and others, titled *What the Rich Think of the Poor*, finds that the wealthy in Paris,

Delhi and São Paulo often engage in strategies that are both symbolic and practical to distance themselves from the less well-off in their cities.[20] Crucially, according to the authors, it is not only that the rich are separated from the poor as if by accident, but that this separation is enforced through policy, custom and architecture, and justified through stigmas related to peril and even 'dirtiness'. In other words, it is not only that the rich are ignorant of the plight of those in poverty because they simply do not share the same experiences, but that they often do their utmost not to have anything to do with them.

Put this way, the privilege that most high-income earners admit to does not stop them from judging the life choices of the worse-off. Indeed, this privilege is the sign of their membership to a group that cannot be justified in terms of race, gender, national origin or any other categorical variable, so instead the behaviour of the excluded is pathologised. They are lazy, unintelligent, feckless, lacking in aspiration, and so on. Privilege for high earners is both the result and the cause of their hard work – it is a prerequisite and a consequence: they work hard because they are privileged; if they weren't, they wouldn't. Much like, in Max Weber's famous account of the Protestant work ethic, predestination, far from producing indolence, impels believers to continually demonstrate that they are part of the chosen ones.

To be sure, this logic was much more common among 'upward-oriented' Merchants, but it was not completely absent from the Brahmins. Although they tended to be much more aware of the structural constraints low-income earners face and were much more sympathetic towards their plight, they rarely had contact with those living in very different social circumstances. We asked interviewees whether they tended to engage with people whose socioeconomic background was substantially different from their own. The high-earning and highly educated tend to mostly network with others like them; as their most important networks outside their families are linked to work and education, it is perhaps unsurprising. Most of those who experienced upward mobility answered that they did know people who were significantly less wealthy, as they were often living in the place from which they had 'escaped'. Gemma, for example, a consultant with a top 3% income, who moved from the north of

England to London, says: "You don't know what people earn in London. My closest friends tend to be people I've worked with, that's just how it's turned out, so you're meeting people at around the same economic level. At home, I know what people do and how much they earn."

The more that work and education are valued, the more time we are compelled to spend in them and hence to associate with people of broadly similar social status (especially in increasingly unequal countries). The fewer opportunities we have to meet others of a different social class, the more we depend on simplistic explanations, common tropes and the media, to try and understand them. And the more our own position is based on being able to distinguish ourselves (be it through the accumulation of money or 'cultural capital'), the less incentive there is to meet others who cannot meet our criteria of what is valuable. This also affects Brahmins, who often spend much of their time with other highly educated people (definitely the case in academia and the world of think tanks, in our experience). Interestingly, Adam, 39, who does not have a degree, was one of the few to reflect on people relatively close to him who ended up in a very different place. In the context of thinking of the role of work and luck in people's success, he said:

> 'I think it's not just hard work, I think it's also luck. I could still be working hard on the checkouts in Sainsbury's. My friend has just turned 40 and is doing exactly that. There's an element of luck and being in the right place at the right time.'

The effects of this social distance cannot be exaggerated. It is one thing to be aware in the abstract that others are worse off, to see homeless people in the street on your way to work. It is something else completely for them to be part of your life, with a voice and agency in the world you inhabit.

Income and status are always insecure

Despite their high incomes, our respondents conveyed a surprising degree of insecurity or 'fear of falling'. The majority of those living in London and south-east England, and in the financial and corporate sectors, are upward-oriented. While their employment provides independence and status, their workplaces, for those employed in the private sector, tend to be hugely unequal and hierarchical. Their frame of reference is with those higher up in their sector or the top of the 1%, who seem a world away. Roy, the CFO, commented that: "[h]aving £2 million isn't rich, but maybe £20 million, because people don't need that kind of money". Similarly, William, a management consultant, sees himself in the middle of the income spectrum, despite earning over £170,000 per year, which puts him in the top 1% of income earners. He is aware of this, though: "I know I am in the top 1% but I also know that I am a million miles from the super-rich."

Ben, a young IT consultant, told us he did not consider himself as high earning when approached for this research project. He had "self-selected himself out of the potential pool based on that [...] and it might be worth rewording [the Facebook recruitment post for the research project]". Dan, a head of client services at a marketing agency in his early forties with a top 6% income, thought he was in the 10–15% income bracket. We asked him if he finds his relative income position surprising: "Yes. It hammers home that there are a lot of people who earn a lot less. When you walk into work from Waterloo, I look around and presume everyone earns the same or more. The reality is not the case."

Little contact with those from other socioeconomic groups makes it hard to assess what 'normal' could be like for other people. In addition, the high cost of living, especially in relation to housing, contributes to high earners not feeling especially affluent. All but two respondents own their own homes or have a mortgage, with some having two. Jonathan, a 70-year-old, semi-retired barrister living in London still earns £170,000 but is nevertheless concerned about the possibility of losing his house if a mansion tax is introduced. He is angry to be even included in the 1% income band, which he finds a "nonsense bracket" as there "are very few [in the 1%] saying they're comfortable [...] you're going from £170,000 to £100 million or more [...] a ridiculous bracket [...]; it ignores assets. Plus, there are landowners."

Louise, a 44-year-old sales consultant living in London with a top 1% income, tells us that stamp duty is "too punitive", but that is "probably because I'm living in a very expensive area of the country". We heard from William, who, reflecting on the fact that he never has any cash left by the end of the month even though he is in the top 1%, comments "it must be very hard for vast numbers of people to make ends meet".

Contradictory isolation

High earners, like all human beings, are contradictory. When we asked Louise about inequality, the plight of those in poverty and whether the rich should do more, her answers were broadly the same as we would give: inequality is detrimental to society and not inevitable; those in poverty struggle because of circumstances beyond their control; the rich should make much greater efforts to address inequality. However, when asked which political party she voted for in the last election, she responded: "The Conservatives." The obvious question we should have asked next was 'Why?' but for some reason we simply let the silence linger. Louise's voice cracked slightly. "The tax issue. Protecting high earners," she said.

Like all our interviewees, Louise did not think of herself as rich. She agreed that there should be more redistribution and more help for those worse off in society, but she didn't agree it should come out of her taxes. She is sufficiently informed to know there is a problem that should be addressed and that she is privileged, but that does not necessarily mean she would support action that would directly affect her pay. Once, in describing the book we were writing to a Merchant acquaintance, we mentioned that many found the threshold for the top 10% surprisingly low. The person responded, "Yes! the top 10% doesn't earn that much! They should be taxed much less!"

High-income earners' tendency to speak of the well-off, the elites and the rich in the third person is due partly to a lack of experiential knowledge of the lives of those in other social classes and little incentive to find out. But it's also due to their particular circumstances. Whether justifiable or not, the more you earn the more expenses tend to accumulate. The more onerous it becomes to maintain your position, the less time there is to develop relationships outside your income bracket, networks or status.

This creates a situation whereby those who should feel 'well-off' do not because their frame of reference is those who belong to the same income level or above and because of broader economic pressures, which we explore further in the coming chapters. A certain contradiction (or if we are feeling less charitable, hypocrisy) thus appears, one we all partake in. Most of us may know global warming is an urgent issue, yet we continue to take flights and eat meat. We may believe public education should be strengthened to give everyone a fair shot but, if we can afford it, we send our children to private schools. We may not like rampant consumerism, we may even be against capitalism, yet we still wear trainers made in Bangladesh. Academics may know university rankings are a sham but will still prioritise the Russell Group universities. According to the 2022 World Inequality Report, the top 10% of income earners in the world produce 47.6% of all carbon emissions, even though interest in environmental concerns grows with income and education.[21]

We believe that to understand this duality (*knowing* but not *feeling* their place) and the contradictions that come out of it, we need to start thinking about high earners' isolation from others and how it is due, to a surprising extent, to the role work plays in their self-definition and their lives.

3

'Work is life, that's it'

This chapter looks at how high earners perceive work and shape a worldview in which their jobs and effort are the basis and justification of their status. Unsurprisingly, when they talk about work, they mean employment and are not talking about activities that have to be carried out and on which society depends, whether someone is paid to do them or not, such as cleaning or caring for older people. We have already established that high earners are sociologically distinct from the rest of the population, and implicitly see themselves as such. Work is fundamental to their self-understanding in two ways. First, although as individuals they might be quite different from each other, the high proportion of professionals and managers among them identifies them as a group – discounting a few exceptions in technical jobs such as railway drivers and pilots. Second, hard work loomed large in their accounts. This is crucial, as the fact they consider themselves hard workers is used to justify their position and validate their relatively high salaries. In their view, they neither belong to the idle rich (who do not need to toil) nor those in poverty (whose toil, if it exists, is lower down the rung).

Good jobs and the top 10%

As we were interviewing this group, it became clear just how much moral and social worth high earners gain from paid employment. Work to a great degree defines a person; it is key to how they evaluate themselves and others. As urban sociologist William Whyte wrote back in 1943, 'For a man to think about his job is to see himself as others see him, to remind him of just where he stands in society.'[1] Indeed, many social scientists have argued that a fundamental characteristic of modern societies is the primacy of work over other types of status such as kinship. Even the importance of gender, sexuality, ethnicity and other crucial dimensions of identity are often evaluated to the degree they are constructed as enablers or barriers to 'good' jobs. We are so used to this that we hardly notice. When adults meet for the first time, one of the first questions they ask is 'What do you do?', and the answer is rarely concerned with anything other than employment. This is also why the phenomenon of unemployment (and its associated stigma) only makes sense in modern capitalist societies.

Work, thus understood, generally means formal and paid employment or self-employment. This kind of work has a status that other forms do not, the recognition of being engaged in something 'worthwhile'.[2] Self-respect is thus felt through fulfilling the social norm of engaging in a paid job but not through, for example, unpaid care, which is often associated with women. Besides prestige and material rewards, formal employment also offers high-income earners benefits such as private medical insurance, life insurance, pensions and stock options. This drives their interests even further away from universal public services, which they believe they rely on to a much lesser extent than those who earn less.

Such formal work grants our respondents not only status but also 'independence' and autonomy. Meanwhile, informal work is frequently conceptualised as being 'dependent', in the traditional gendered model of the male provider and the female homemaker. Feminists have long argued that viewing formal employment as guaranteeing self-reliance while informal or unpaid work is secondary is a misleading model of human behaviour and damaging to policy decisions. In fact, the economy is predicated on unpaid labour, which has its fingerprints all over paid work.[3] In 2020, the International Labour Organization valued this unremunerated work at 13% of global gross domestic product (GDP), 75% of which is estimated to be carried out by women.[4]

Regardless, considering how the economy is organised, informal work cannot at present provide the economic security that formal employment does. The status the latter also carries is often crucial for our self-definition and determines not only material returns but the esteem by which each of us is rewarded. It is perhaps unsurprising, then, that talk of social mobility immediately means talking about the jobs that a person has had over their lifetime and those of their parents: ideally, always better paid, onwards and upwards. This is also why many of our interviewees emphasise their support for equality of opportunity over equality of outcome, which generally means equal access to educational and training opportunities so people from all backgrounds can compete for the best jobs. In this view, worth and deservingness are always implicitly connected to these jobs, and they are valuable because it takes effort to get them and not everyone does.

Even so, social mobility does not occur in a vacuum. Sociologist Lauren Rivera has shown that, at every step of the hiring process, elite employers in the US favour the upper classes: they tend to recruit most strongly from Ivy League universities where the children of high earners are disproportionately represented. CVs are screened according to the prestige of the institutions candidates attended, while the interview process itself is biased towards applicants from the same social strata as the recruiters.[5] Earlier we showed how Friedman and Laurison found similar patterns in the UK.[6]

Despite new diversity and inclusion targets encouraging companies to recruit employees from working-class backgrounds and the increasing number of larger employers that have stopped demanding applicants with Russell Group degrees, analysis of ONS data shows that those from better-off backgrounds are 80% more likely to land a top job than their working-class peers.[7] Of those from working-class backgrounds who do become professionals, 17% earn less than colleagues whose parents had professional jobs. Working-class women in professional jobs earn 36% less than men from a professional background in similar posts, compared to a 17% gap between men and women who are both from professional backgrounds. Polling finds that British workers from ABC1 occupations are more likely than those working C2DE jobs to have asked and been successful in asking for a pay rise.[8] Women from working-class occupations (69%) are considerably more likely than women from middle-class occupations (55%) to have never asked for a pay rise.[9] For the first time, in 2018–19, the Social Mobility Commission began to look at the interaction between class, gender, ethnicity and disability, finding that women, people with disabilities and minority ethnic groups from working-class backgrounds generally experience multiple disadvantages in occupational outcomes.[10]

There are also substantial differences at a local level. Where you grow up makes a difference in how much your family background affects your life chances.[11] People from privileged backgrounds and who have university degrees are much more likely to move. Those who do move do far better financially than those who remain. They earn 33% more and are more likely to end up in professional jobs.[12] Moving out is often necessary to move up.

Regardless of those systemic-level differences, education and effort continue to play an important part in respondents' narratives about how they attained their position. The people we spoke with, especially those who had been the most socially mobile, were keen to give a meritocratic description of how far they had travelled socioeconomically. Tony was one of them. A senior manager with a top 1% income in his fifties, he came from a working-class background. Thanking his stable and supportive parents for his success, he also spoke of following his father's example – joining the army at 17 and rising to the rank of captain, which was "quite an achievement from his [father's] humble stock". Tony reflects: "If my mum and dad were alive, I'd say they'd be proud of where I ultimately ended up."

Christopher, one of only two respondents under 35 already in the top 3%, worked for a global IT service and consulting company. He knew he was "massively privileged" to have been able to study and questioned the degree of equality of opportunity in the UK: "I don't believe in meritocracy. If you work hard, you can improve your baseline. There are two classes in Britain: those born in opportunity and those born in disadvantage, who would need to work incredibly hard."

Like Tony, Christopher also thanks his upbringing for his upward trajectory, in his case one that was "middle class [and] valued education". Louise, a 44-year-old sales consultant living in London with a top 1% income, does too: "It's [...] having a system around you, including your parents, that are going to help you identify opportunities and nurture you. The problem is if the parents haven't had those opportunities, then it's hard for them to give them to their children. It's a vicious cycle."

Interestingly, however, as these accounts imply, education means not only having access to institutions that can provide it to a reasonable standard, but also coming from a home life where education itself is valued and there is an understanding of the type of education that could help someone succeed. This suggests that some of our respondents believed poverty could be explained by 'low expectations'.[13] In other words, the onus is put on the underprivileged for undervaluing education. It's not that opportunities don't exist, but that some people cannot identify them.

Education, in these accounts, operates at the meeting point between individual and structural explanations for poverty but doesn't solve them. The less well-off may – or may not – be to blame for not getting a good (generally meaning middle-class) job and moving upwards, because poverty understood in this way is ultimately due to ignorance. While such views came across as patronising, they were also ambiguous about where they lay blame. Was the misfortune of not earning enough the fault of an individual's characteristics or was it down to being brought up in the wrong family and failing to escape from it?

Explanations emphasising an individual's role in their social mobility soon tend to return. Upbringing is not everything, and talent and graft in adult life play a key part. Educational ability is often cited as a key factor in social mobility because it is an acceptable, undebatable attribute that reinforces the belief that social mobility is deserved. Many respondents mentioned their intelligence, degrees and good grades, especially the Brahmins. Few acknowledge their luck in not having had any significant structural barriers impeding their social mobility, such as health emergencies, caring responsibilities or having to work to put food on the table. Gemma, a management consultant in her late thirties in the top 3%, does, however. She mentions that although gaining a place at university did kick-start her successful career, her "very supportive family" helped with rent during a degree internship in London. This opportunity allowed her to pursue a structured career in a large corporate firm, providing the stability she did not experience growing up.

There is also little distinction between educational qualifications and the networks and social capital (private) education can provide. Twenty-three of our 29 UK respondents were state educated. This might be as you would expect if you considered that well over nine out of ten children attend state schools in Britain, but more than you would expect if you took into account the overrepresentation of the privately schooled in highly paid jobs.[14] As the Social Mobility Commissions have concluded, the small elite who rise to the top in the UK today looks remarkably similar to those in the same position half a century ago. As former Conservative prime minister Sir John Major put it, 'in every single sphere of British influence the upper echelons of power are held overwhelmingly by the privately educated or the affluent middle class'.[15] This is seen, for example, in the monopolising of senior roles in law, the armed forces and the civil service by those who attended private schools.[16] As the commission pointed out:

> Of course, the best people need to be in the top jobs – and there are many good people who come from private schools and who go to top universities. But there can be few people who believe that the sum total of talent resides in just 7 per cent of pupils in the country's schools.[17]

However, despite this overwhelmingly obvious dynamic of working life in the UK, only one high earner we spoke with, a state school headteacher, suggested that bringing education under the state sector was the key to properly addressing inequality.

Few interviewees mentioned labour market inequalities either. Whether due to a skills gap, a rapid expansion of graduate labour (and the associated credential inflation), decreased union membership or the increased participation of women, the UK's occupational structure has changed dramatically in the last decades. Today, the British labour market has an hourglass shape, polarising at the top and bottom ends in terms of occupation and earnings, with few jobs in the middle.[18] This amounts to a two-tier system where employment growth is concentrated on high-earning workers pursuing seamless career progression at the top while others are stuck in dead-end, insecure jobs at the bottom.

Some careers that in the past guaranteed secure, white-collar employment, are increasingly precarious at the entry level – and many people are kept there or forced to jump ship. Increasing precarisation of jobs and the over-reliance on insecure part-time employment seems to be expanding in many walks of life, as illustrated by striking criminal barristers, a profession traditionally considered to be elite.[19]

Many respondents were aware of these trends. Some acknowledged that young people today do not enjoy the same opportunities they had growing up (all but one had been to university or a polytechnic). When we asked them what role luck had played in their life situation, they acknowledged that having had the means and opportunity to attend university without facing crippling debt or having to compete in a labour market experiencing credential inflation was crucial. However, the acknowledgement of that luck is qualified; some pointed out that a person still has to apply themselves and make good decisions to make the most of it. Hard work is indispensable.

Work is hard

Hard work is a consistent trope, particularly for Merchants working in the private sector or who started their own businesses. They often tended to emphasise the need to remain competitive in the market, and that the market itself is the best arbiter for societal outcomes. Nevertheless, Brahmins put great importance on hard work too, if sometimes with a different emphasis. This was manifested in their endorsement of providing good-quality service (for instance to students or patients) and of the effort needed to attain a certain level of expertise and credentials in their line of work. Education, understood this way, is a trial by fire that validates those who went through it (though the commodification and expansion of higher education can undermine this narrative). Even so, high earners are increasingly acknowledging that hard work does not always guarantee success and that some must work much harder than others for similar rewards. Hard work, after all, is not valued solely by high-income earners. Louise, a sales consultant, tells us: "I'm sure there are a lot of people who are hard-working who are just in low-paid jobs."

It tends to be those who work outside the corporate structure, with experience in or with the public sector and working with colleagues and clients from different income groups who discuss in detail the structural barriers preventing social mobility. They not only refer to the realities of low-wage work but also may compare their salaries to those of workers fulfilling essential roles for little remuneration. Sociologist Katharina Hecht describes such respondents as 'critical evaluators' who 'question evaluative practices based on money as a metric of worth, do not view market outcomes as necessarily fair and are concerned about top incomes and wealth shares'.[20] In our study, they tend to be at the lower end of the top 10% income band.

When we asked our respondents the question 'Do you think that, broadly speaking, if you work hard you will succeed [in the UK]?' they expressed strong feelings about inequality and referred to the realities of low-wage work. Duncan, in his late fifties, a director of a non-departmental public body, living in Scotland, right at the margin of a top 10% income, comments:

> 'I struggle with the idea that if you work hard, money will come to you. If you're on a minimum wage in this country, working 16 hours a day, you'll only get a certain amount of income. Irrespective of what you do with it, that's all you'll get. In theory, being in work means you can build networks and relationships and move on and earn more. But frankly, if you're working for minimum wage in McDonald's, you're not meeting many people.'

Stephen, a professor living in Manchester with a top 6% income, spoke of people who have to take two jobs to make ends meet, who are "working hard, but not exactly flourishing". When asked whether he thought hard work had a role in determining his current status, Paul, an architect working with the public sector, just in the top 10% income band, who splits his week between London and Liverpool, felt strongly that it was not: "People who clean hospitals – they work hard. No, that is a terrible suggestion to make. People who think they work hard because they earn hundreds of thousands of pounds are not working as hard as they believe."

Hannah, a 44-year-old occupational health consultant, earning just above the 10% threshold, tells us in relation to the statement 'The richer the rich, the more all of society benefits': "No! I don't agree, because I think the rich getting richer benefits themselves and I'm not sure how much of that is passed down because I think some people get rich at other people's expense."

Such respondents also confirm the importance of networking for social mobility. Claire, a teacher, living in Manchester, with an income just above the 10% threshold, speaks of the 'old-boy network': "Opportunity comes from having money, contacts, knowing people in places, work experience and connections." Wang, an under-35-year-old former doctor who now runs his own start-up, observes that he gets to meet many wealthy entrepreneurs who mostly come from wealthy backgrounds. This, in part, he thinks is what made them successful, as they were able to take risks without having to worry about their financial security.

Several respondents comment that while hard work may have been the route to upward mobility in the past, this was no longer true. They felt it had the potential to contribute to economic security, but would certainly not guarantee it. Maria, a marketing director in her forties with a top 3% income, comments:

> 'This was true 50 years ago [...] even if you were working class, if you worked hard you could earn enough to get your kids through school and then to university, and then they could potentially break out of the working class and make the middle class. It's only just starting to hit the middle class that it doesn't matter how hard you work, you may not earn enough money to break even, let alone make it out of your social class. And that is key – that change.'

Peter, a young IT consultant with a top 1% income, tells us: "I disagree with the idea that if you work hard, you'll do well. It used to be the case. But that plays back to when career paths were designed and the way to progress was to show that you worked harder than anyone else."

Presenteeism was another feature in discussions about work. The UK labour market is characterised by increasing work intensity with the second-highest average weekly working hours in Europe, only after Greece. Still, we have the second-lowest GDP per hour worked in the G7. Evidence suggests that there seems to be no direct link between hours worked and the strength of the economy. The opposite seems to be true: higher productivity is associated with fewer hours per year spent at work.[21] The pandemic exacerbated this trend. Some of our respondents described the transition to working remotely as characterised by an 'always on' culture and an extended working day, to an even greater degree than used to be the case. Women who had been working and carrying out childcare at home were more likely to report increased psychological distress during the pandemic.[22]

Perhaps aware of these developments, some also raised the need to work 'smart'. The emphasis on individuals' responsibility to ensure their employability is also seen in how respondents – particularly those working in the corporate sector – talk about the importance of embracing risk in an uncertain global marketplace. This implies the belief that upward mobility is possible solely through the cultivation of human potential, as sociologists of late modernity such as Beck and Giddens argued.[23] Peter, one of the youngest respondents – the head of his own IT consultancy and with a top 1% income – provides an example of an over-individualised sense of his trajectory. He believes that good decision making has led to his current position, knowing "[w]hen to pursue opportunity, to balance risk with reward." He reflects that "this might be related to upbringing and being encouraged to pursue risk". This includes a willingness to be flexible. It is closely associated with making good decisions and leveraging the skills that you have: "These days it's about working smarter. We have to see what technology is doing. Why work hard as a taxi driver if you might be replaced by a self-driving car?"

Later in the interview, we asked Peter if he thought there should be a space for people who are not necessarily good decision makers, such as the taxi drivers he spoke about. He responded:

'If someone cannot recognise [...] the demise of an industry, then that's a problem that needs to be addressed, maybe through re-education and empowerment. But it's ultimately their choice whether they do something about it or not. However, I believe there should be a general understanding of future-proofing jobs. [...] Reskilling and retraining are important, but there needs to be self-motivation and self-drive there. The government shouldn't do everything.'

This commitment to flexibility implies remaining competitive against a global workforce, being prepared to move from job to job and relocating if necessary. In these meritocratic accounts, the right attitude and self-motivation are crucial, and in turn, affect opinions about inequality and local communities. For Peter, the taxi drivers threatened by automation are at least partly responsible for their economic misfortune; they need to have self-motivation and initiative. Sean – a 40-year-old with a top 1% income who did not have much parental support growing up and was one of the staunchest Merchants in our sample – tells us his own motivation and hard work are the reasons for his success: "Nobody coached me to go to university or to do well for myself."

Though hard work was key, the end of that work seemed to be less important. The high earners we spoke with rarely thought about the role of their jobs beyond the workplace. We asked them about their career progression, where they've been the happiest and the most discontented work-wise, and what they thought the effect of their work was on society, if any. A few times the question was interpreted as an accusation (particularly by those working in the City). Peter, from the previous example, left the corporate world and now works for himself, employing five people. He says of the move: "I've been the happiest now because everything is under my control. I have full autonomy over the decisions that I make; I can change the work-life balance."

Respondents who have been working for corporations for a long time, even those like Peter who have moved on to set up their own companies, are not used to even being asked what wider role their work or organisation plays in the economy or society. His response was typical: "I don't think my current job has a huge effect on larger society." Susannah's answer in particular astonished us. In a very senior position at a major international bank, she seemed surprised even to be asked the question:

> '[laughs] Not much really. Society at large [...]. Well I suppose you could say that I'm helping to make sure [the bank] are efficiently spending [...]. They've got a huge customer base globally [...] so we're helping deliver them products at a more affordable price and the customer service they get around that is better. So I suppose you could say that, but/if I compare that to my husband's contribution as a police officer, his is way more.'

This is worth underlining. Susannah is a highly educated, high-achieving woman at the top of her career working in a senior position in banking in one of the financial centres of the world. And yet she doesn't think her work makes a massive difference to the lives of others. Would we be right to disagree, considering she is the one actually doing the job? Anthropologist David Graeber famously argued in his 2018 book *Bullshit Jobs* that an increasing number of employees do not believe society would be worse off if their jobs did not exist. This applied even to the private sector (35% of its employees in the surveys he cites), which is supposed to be driven by efficiency and where useless jobs would supposedly be driven out by the bottom line.[24]

Only a few respondents in the private sector conveyed a sense of purpose in or motivation for their work beyond material gain and the narrow, direct satisfaction of the needs of their clients. These tended to focus on acquiring knowledge, being part of a good team, and producing something technically sophisticated that does its job well. Ben, an IT consultant earning just over £100,000, told us:

> 'I am happiest when I'm learning new things. So, in the nineties at the software company that was being acquired, I suddenly had a bigger responsibility and it

was an opportunity to learn and get involved. That was a nice place to work. But, after a while, when they got rid of everyone, it felt a bit empty. Before that, it was a great bunch of people and I enjoyed working there.'

He described his motivation as:

'To keep doing the best you can and it's the way forwards and upwards. You may not like what you have to do, but by doing it you can move on to bigger and better things. The other half of it is that you have a mortgage and bills to pay.'

And he had pride in his role of making something: "I think the product we're selling and implementing is helping defend people against hackers and other cyber security attacks. It does it very well."

Ben, and a few others, were the exception to the rule. Their main motivation was learning, improving and delivering, and they were proud of their accomplishments. This is an enviable and commendable position, to be sure. However, we would argue their situation was predicated on possessing specialised expertise in areas that haven't yet suffered a dramatic loss of status (IT, for instance), and on remaining at a certain distance from the very top of management. They tended to concentrate on technical occupations and were not necessarily at the top of the hierarchy. Michael, a 49-year-old engineer, told us he is the happiest he's ever been at his job at the minute. He's "near the top of the tree. Above me, it gets political."

Other respondents working in the corporate sector who had views about its broader societal effects tended to have experience outside it. Luke is one example. A 27-year-old strategy consultant with a top 8% income who attended private school and Oxbridge, enrolled on the Teach First programme before joining one of the 'Big Four' accounting firms.[25] When asked what effect his work had on society he replies "currently very little [...] and if it does it's probably negative". Asked to elaborate on what that role is, he replies: "Essentially to help big companies and make rich people richer."

Some, such as Maria (whom we introduced earlier), had left the corporate world for more socially minded positions. When we first interviewed her, she was working for another Big Four firm, but in the follow-up interview she had joined an organisation focusing on the underrepresentation of women in boardrooms. When asked what she thought the effect of her work is on society at large, she replied: "For once I'm doing something that does make a difference. [laugh] But that [...] hasn't really been the case in my previous jobs. My previous jobs have been about me making money."

Meanwhile, those in the public sector, much like their counterparts in the technical occupations described earlier, tended to say that they were satisfied with their jobs and were clearer about their benefits to society. This was particularly the case for those in healthcare and education. Douglas, who had a lifetime's career in the public sector and social enterprise told us that in his view people working for large organisations do not feel that empowered in them and allude to their unattainable echelons. He very much preferred the current organisation where he works, as he is working with "a good bunch of people" where you are able to "run your own show".

Nevertheless, many in the public sector also had apprehensions about the pressures they were under and conflicting views on their management. Jonathan, for example, a semi-retired barrister, but still in the top 1% income bracket, looked back at an extensive career, originally built on legal aid, but local authorities "bled out" with consequences for his practice.

What both Brahmins and Merchants had in common was that being busy tacitly provided status. Lack of time was cited as a key barrier to not doing more outside work. Stephen, a law professor, pithily told us: "Work is life, that's it." Meritocracy, corporate culture and organisational hierarchy loom large. All of these reward (or seem to reward) keeping apace in a competitive and fast-moving world, in which everyone knows they can be replaced by younger, more technically skilled candidates (or even software) at short notice. That means more and more time invested in work, staying afloat and honing new and old skills. This confirms previous research that speaks of pervasive uncertainty and chronic insecurity about the future of jobs, housing and relationships, which is present even in the top decile.[26]

One consequence of this sense of anxiety is overwork. Maria, when asked whether she would say she is generally happy with her career progression, said:

> 'Yeah, very happy. In some ways, I would have liked to be more senior at [company] but I was put off by the people above me because they weren't great role models and they were quite stressed. I worked very long hours [...] and I thought if I got more senior it would be even worse.'

Maria seems to reflect on the fact that many companies reward talent that 'goes above and beyond' and delivers value (through achieving projects, securing clients or managing people) in addition to their prescribed job. Just fulfilling your job description is not necessarily seen as enough to get promoted or obtain a good, in-line-with-inflation pay rise. These practices reinforce the perception that getting to the top echelons of the company would require too much effort and negatively shift the work–life balance.

Furthermore, the pressure to keep moving up in a career often involves being mobile, which meant most of our respondents didn't volunteer outside work. Christopher, an IT consultant with a top 3% income, when asked about his social/civic behaviour, replies: "As soon as we settle down – we're quite nomadic at the moment – I would like to do something hands-on, something that makes a large societal shift and helps lots of people." Others spoke of a working culture, particularly in large private corporations, that made it more difficult to develop connections with their community as less value was placed on activities such as volunteering.

We also asked our respondents whether they thought the private sector had any responsibility for reducing inequality. Most Merchants were surprised by the question and most emphasised creating jobs, paying tax and earning profits, not much more. Gemma, a consultant in her late thirties, was one of a few who spoke directly to this, precisely because her job was to help drive organisational change: "Get businesses to do things better – impact on society, their culture, reputational risk, making institutions more stable. Treating customers more fairly. Not messing up the economy. Keeping an eye on big business. [Businesses] would do whatever they like if there was no structure in place."

Louise, whom we introduced earlier, works for a global tech company with a household name. She acknowledged that societal benefit was not a priority: "So, you do see private companies do things like apprenticeships. But I can't think of any private companies that are really investing in society. You do have corporate responsibility programmes, but they are not top of the agenda."

While the women, especially those with young children, tended to feel that they ought to do more in their local community, the men we spoke with rarely questioned their level of interaction in the same way. It was considered something their wives did or that they could do when they were older. They rarely volunteered and left school commitments mostly to their partners. William, a management consultant in the top 1%, tells us:

> 'My wife has chosen to work in the charitable sector […] a residential school, to look after children. She could be doing something that pays more but is very important in our local community, it's one of the largest employers there. What I do here [at work], enables my wife to do something there, as a partnership.'

The exception to this tendency was when volunteering or donating was sanctioned by their employer. Respondents were more comfortable talking about corporate responsibility. Luke, the 27-year-old consultant we introduced earlier, thought that while there was more appetite for corporate responsibility, there was very little action. One example he cited was Barclay's scheme to train customers in financial management skills.

Maria thought similarly: "there's got to be something around a more sustainable outlook [as] people are interested in giving something back". In her follow-up interview, she repeated that companies have "got to give a reason for them to go back" and that they "now have to have 'purpose' – this is the new buzzword!" Worrying that we might be returning to Victorian times, she also commented that "The private sector would have to plug that gap, particularly in healthcare […] If employers don't have healthy employees and […] we have another pandemic […] well."

Even those who were relatively senior in the corporate sector made similar comments. William, in the top 1%, told us that charitable giving is encouraged in the Canary Wharf firm where he works: "Trustees, boards of governors, contribute […] being a citizen has become more prominent. The business is much more aware of how it's perceived." Peter, a young IT consultant with a top 1% income, also told us:

> 'We are looking at how to give back. We do open source [coding]. Also, the consultancy wants to contribute to marine aspects, such as beach clear-ups. […] I like to do this and it resonates with me, but also a lot of aspects are due to PR [public relations] / marketing of the consultancy. I also like that I have the flexibility to do this via the consultancy.'

However, as the last example implies, volunteering organised by corporate responsibility is quite different from contributing on an individual basis to your community outside the remit of paid work. This is because corporate objectives include the status of being busy and helping the organisation position itself. Many large established companies allow employees a number of hours per year to dedicate to volunteering. These hours go largely unclaimed because most employees would rather spend additional time on activities that further their careers within the company. As long as volunteering does not further one's connections and interests, it is not an interesting enough proposition. In the best-case scenario, such initiatives could be compared with the extracurriculars carried out by the young of the top 10% in the hope of improving their chances of gaining a university place or their first job.

Perhaps unsurprisingly, few of those we spoke with contemplated any reform to their workplaces. Their perspectives were mainly individualised, focused on their sense of control, and started from the position of the job they do. Their workplaces were also mostly hierarchical, and workplace democracy was rarely mentioned. This, we believe, is at least partly because of the long-term decline in union membership and the individualisation of the sense of worth in the workplace. Many of the individuals we spoke with worked for organisations where appraisals and performance reviews were regularly conducted, where their work was increasingly monitored and where perceptions of how hard they worked had a direct effect on their status, economic situation and career progression.

Nevertheless, research shows that employees often dislike how they are ranked and scored. According to a survey of Fortune 1,000 companies, 66% of employees were strongly dissatisfied with their performance evaluations.[27] A later study showed HR executives were equally disparaging of performance management programmes; 70% believed such reviews did not accurately reflect employee contributions. Two thirds said performance management practices were easily distorted and misidentified who were the high-performers.[28] Performance management has also been identified as a potential source of employee anxiety.[29] Far from being a catalyst for improvement, such reviews are often met defensively, resulting in an atmosphere of competition that stifles innovation, transparency and collaboration.[30]

Despite these obstacles, the current crises are bringing the contradictions of the working world to a head and won't be solvable by past strategies. As of 2016, only 16% of the UK's private sector workers were covered by collective bargaining agreements. While the UK's overall trade union density is considerably lower than many European countries, there have been green shoots in the movement recently with high-profile cases of employment rights not being protected, such as the fire and rehire policies of P&O Ferries.[31] As the cost of living crisis unfolds, trade unions have seen a recent rise in membership, among women in particular.[32]

Even Sean, one of the most solid Merchants in our sample, said in his follow-up interview that the pandemic had "made me reflect on what's important in life. So, I'm no longer running my own company and don't have to work all the time." Michael, a 49-year-old engineer just in the top 10% and living in the south-west felt that people's attitudes as a whole had changed during the pandemic:

> 'You can't eat money. When you can't get food or fuel or whatever you need to live. A lot of people are less money-centric, more lifestyle focused. Difficult to measure. A lot of people have started saying "What's the least amount of money I need to live contentedly?" Not many people were asking that [before].'

Taking a breather

When we were thinking about potential titles for this book, we considered 'never good enough'. However, it had already been taken by a few other publications. Among those, we found an evocative ethnography by Laura Alamillo-Martinez, which explored feelings of anxiety among students and parents in a Spanish upper-middle-class secondary school.[33] She describes how children who, in many respects are privileged, seem to have a fairly precarious view of their future security, one that depends on their performance. If they do not measure up, they have no one but themselves to blame. Though certainly, the road from good school grades to a high-paying job is long, winding and marred by uncontrollable factors, this does not detract from the seemingly ever-present dread, stress and anxiety these students have when thinking of their future. Reports on the high rates of mental health issues among elite university students – even before the pandemic – suggest this is a widely underreported phenomenon.[34]

Reading about such issues made us reflect on our own upbringing and on the hard-working ethos both Brahmins and Merchants share. Both of us were brought up in families where grades were overvalued. For Marcos, it has to do with his family history. His paternal grandfather lost his job as a journalist after Pinochet's 1973 *coup d'état* and could never work again. This experience of sharp downward social mobility made his father concentrate all his energies on attaining a well-earning professional job, in which he succeeded. But it also meant that Marcos was raised to believe having perfect grades is the only guarantee for a good life and that, even then, history may happen, so to speak. Gerry was raised the same way. Her mum had been left without financial support at a young age when her parents divorced acrimoniously while she was taking her A-levels. Not having been able to attend university herself, she had ambitions for her daughter to be the first person to do so on her side of the family. There was a lot of pressure to aim high.

Similarly, our respondents define themselves largely through hard, smart work, through their competitiveness, flexibility and their achievements. An underlying meritocratic 'common sense' justifies their own position and their aspiration to move up the ladder. This 'common sense' is also the rationale for legitimising inequality, a cultural logic based on deserving a lot in life as the reward for effort and talent. From this worldview, moral and social worth is derived from paid employment and measured by income, educational attainment and professional status (which are also, interestingly enough, the variables that distinguish this group sociologically). Such pressures may also explain, for example, the 2019 US college admissions scandal, where wealthy parents had been colluding to guarantee access to elite universities for their children.[35]

Nevertheless, and seemingly independently of the importance of hard work, most people we spoke with only rarely thought more broadly about the place of their companies or the effects of their work in society. They reflected Kate Soper's view that the more caught up you are in work, the less time you have to imagine, let alone believe, that alternative ways of living are possible or to look into how the existing system might be improved because: "Through its theft of time and energy, the work and spend culture deters development of thinking and critical opposition [...] those suffering most from time scarcity are unlikely to be spearheading the revolution against the work practices that create it".[36]

This logic of over-emphasising work as 'position' and 'graft' also affects Brahmins. Despite their left-of-centre views, high-income earners who hold their position based on claims of expertise and educational credentials can come across as hierarchical rather than egalitarian. They implicitly accept an unspoken meritocratic truism that the public conversation and decisions over the public purse should be made by those with the most career achievements and educational credentials.

What is needed, we argue, is greater emphasis on a third, often neglected dimension of work: the result of an action which changes the world in some way. David Graeber said that today's world seems to be ruled by "the general principle that the more one's work benefits others, the less one tends to be paid for it".[37] In other words, he argues, many believe a job that is purposeful and beneficial to society should be its own reward, while work that nobody would do unless they were getting paid for it should be better remunerated. This, from Graeber's viewpoint, explains the difference in earnings between nurses and corporate lawyers.

Still, losing sight of that ultimate purpose risks turning work into a perennial chase for status that has few, if any, effects beyond giving workers a respectable 'job' and granting the status that comes with being perceived to 'work hard'. Neglecting the end results of our work risks fostering both overwork – and the neurotic need to be always on call and always at your best – and apathy towards its effects on the world, which often are limited to making those who are already wealthy wealthier. To tackle that dimension of our working lives, politics is unavoidable.

4

Don't rock the boat: politics and the well-off

High earners have political clout. That is one of the main reasons we wrote this book. Compared with other income groups, they are more likely to feel more engaged in politics, to believe they have a say, to vote and to have higher levels of trust in government.[1] Because of those reasons, they are arguably among the demographic groups that are most courted by political parties.[2] They are also overrepresented in elite positions of authority including the 'Westminster bubble'. Every MP qualifies, as well as many of the most influential civil servants, journalists, lobbyists and policy experts. This also applies in Brussels, Washington and most centres of political power.

Still, our respondents frequently showed unease with politics and misgivings towards much of the electorate. During our first round of interviews, following austerity and the Brexit referendum but before the 2019 general election, they expressed fears about political instability, populism and the erosion of democratic norms. Most were cynical about the current state of politics and political parties. And it was clear to see how that cynicism expressed itself in the 2019 elections. Of the 20% least deprived constituencies in England, 1 elected the Labour Party, 7 elected the Liberal Democrats and 98 were won by the Conservatives.[3] During our second round of interviews in early 2022, they were mainly apathetic and pessimistic. In the aftermath of Boris Johnson's 'partygate' scandal (where he was shown to be in flagrant violation of his own COVID-19 rules), the opening salvos of the Ukraine–Russia war, and a looming cost of living crisis, even the most Conservative among them had few reasons to be cheerful about the state of British politics.

Our interviews confirm that many people do not have well-worked-out political ideologies, and their values have a stronger influence than any identification with political parties. These guide their choices across public and private spheres and 'have come to play an increasing role in [their] political choices [...] as older group-based loyalties have lost their power and structural roots'.[4] The majority of high earners we spoke with were conservative on matters related to social security, income redistribution and taxation. Though they were in principle supportive of public services such as the NHS, quite a few were concerned with how they were run, referring to 'mismanagement' and 'inefficiency'. Many were quite supportive of means testing rather than the universal provision of public services, even if the latter would allow them to tap into services currently unavailable to them, such as care for older people, healthcare provision and higher education.

These views have been under strain. The populist waves of the 2010s, from both the left and the right, came to challenge the centrist, liberal consensus that has held sway at least since 1990. 'Billionaires', 'the rich' and 'metropolitan elites' were decried more frequently, and what high-income earners often saw as 'common-sense' politics became increasingly unpopular with large parts of the electorate. With this context in mind, this chapter explores what we know about our respondents' politics, their degree of political participation and the political tensions among them. But before that, we provide some of the contexts behind the crisis of the post-Cold-War consensus.

The state of the British polity

When we began this research in 2018, the UK was the fifth most unequal country in Europe. The top 10% took 28% of the country's total income, around half of which was captured by the top 1%. Indeed, since the 1960s, inequality has increased between the top 1% and the 99%, but fallen within the 99%.[5] After the 2007–08 financial crisis, a temporary reduction in top incomes meant that inequality declined slightly, but by 2017 the average CEO's pay was 145 times that of the average worker.[6]

The 2008 financial crash was partly caused by unsustainable household debt in the US and beyond; in other words, the increasing dependence on credit of large parts of the population and the incentives faced by financial institutions to offer loans to those unable to repay them. This credit-driven growth is connected to decades of runaway incomes at the top and stagnant wages at the bottom.[7] Half of the UK population had barely gained from the previous four decades of growth, with a declining share of national income going to salaries and a rising share going to capital. Today, 60% of those in poverty have someone in their household who is employed, which is 20% higher than in 1995.[8] With sluggish household earnings at the bottom, average weekly earnings have mostly decoupled from GDP growth. The UK has been getting richer but most people are not noticeably better off. This has been particularly true outside the capital. Average weekly earnings among full-time employees in London are a third higher than the UK average and nearly two thirds higher than those in the north-east.[9] At the same time, though London is one of the richest regions in northern Europe, 27.7% of its inhabitants live in poverty.[10]

After the financial crisis, the UK government, instead of tackling the root causes of the financial crash – an economy over-reliant on an over-leveraged financial system whose proceeds mostly benefited one city – found scapegoats; initially welfare recipients and later, immigrants. In 2010, Labour was replaced by a Conservative-Liberal Democrat coalition whose main policy response was to cut public sector spending while relying on the Bank of England to provide quantitative easing,[11] which was 'originally conceived to enhance productivity and wages by bringing down borrowing costs and encouraging investment. Instead, it has pushed up asset prices (which favours wealthier asset-owners) but without the investment.'[12] Money ended up in the coffers of banks rather than generating more loans to individuals and small businesses. In parallel, spending cuts were presented as necessary for reducing the deficit, but were also a bid to dismantle what the coalition saw as an over-centralised, ineffectual and overbearing state and to 'discipline' a population that was framed as idly taking advantage of the largesse of hard-working taxpayers. Economist Simon Wren-Lewis has shown that, although by 2013 the government had stopped its most ambitious spending targets, the restructuring of the welfare state and the vilification of its beneficiaries remained.[13]

With £12 billion of unspecified welfare cuts promised during his campaign, David Cameron said in a speech a month after securing his re-election in 2015: "if you want to work hard and get on in life, this government will be on your side."[14] It was all about *getting on* and *working hard*. Benefit claimants as a whole were often implied to be deadweight. But among those not in work, some of the sharpest cuts were aimed at disabled and young people, while state spending on pensioners – a crucial constituency for the Conservatives – was ring-fenced.[15] In the words of Brown and Jones: 'Single mothers, the unemployed and recipients of disability benefits were blamed for depleting the country's financial reserves through claiming state welfare, while the actual architects of the financial crisis in the City of London were never mentioned.'[16]

Tens of thousands of disabled people are estimated to have died from the combined impact of cuts in social care, working-age benefits, healthcare and housing, as well as from regressive tax increases. Disabled people are 8% of the population but took an estimated 29% of all cuts, including the Personal Independence Payment for people with the highest personal care and mobility needs. Around that time, there was a noticeable slowdown in the growth of UK life expectancy.[17]

Austerity also undermined business confidence and the investment required for growth. Since 2010, the economic recovery has mostly been driven by increasing public and private debt. In tandem, quantitative easing – although explicitly designed to supply banks with liquidity to lend at low interest, instead boosted the assets of the richest while lending to UK businesses was negative.[18] Credit instead flowed to an overheating property market, fuelling property prices. This affected harshly those who do not own their homes but created a boon for sellers, landlords and the real estate sector.

Meanwhile, technological change, automation, offshoring, and the tension between globalisation and the nation-state continued to threaten the local labour market and create a sense of economic insecurity, while there was little to no improvement in productivity, investments, exports, or manufacturing.[19] After decades framed by a narrative of progress, many in the UK faced the prospect of living in a country that was going backwards, where children would be poorer than their parents and where working was much less profitable than owning.

Two social movements sought to give answers to this malaise: Brexit and Jeremy Corbyn's Labour leadership. Both sought to convince disaffected voters to join their ranks, either by blaming immigrants and Brussels (Brexit) or billionaires and media barons (Labour) for the despair and disconnect engulfing us all. Brexit relied mostly on votes from those aged 50+ (60% of voters aged 50–64 and 64% of those aged 65+ opted to Leave), with a GCSE or lower qualification, and living in the countryside.[20] In contrast, Corbyn was supported by the young, the university educated and those living in urban areas.

The first succeeded; the second did not. In its success, Brexit left a deep scar in Britain's body politic that is unlikely to ever heal. Indeed, though the referendum result is not as widely contested as it was before the 2019 election, today most Britons believe it was the wrong choice.[21] That election also marked the unceremonious end of the Corbynite project which, whatever faults it may have had, was the last political movement to represent young precarious workers in any significant manner. And all of this was before the pandemic and the Ukraine–Russia war.

Are the top 10% politically active?

Nearly all our respondents vote regularly and all are interested in politics. As we have said, the higher your income, the more likely you are to vote. Talking about individuals' civic responsibilities, Gemma, a young consultant, said that "voting is part of it". Similarly, Tony, a senior IT manager in his early fifties with a top 1% income and living in the north comments: "If you want to get involved, then you have to vote, take part in the democratic process." The few who hadn't always voted explained that it was due to work relocation and not being based in any one place for long.

For the majority, this is the extent of their political involvement. We asked if they were part of a party, political group or trade union, or if they protested or participated in politics in any other way. Only a couple of respondents answered affirmatively to any of those questions. While some had signed online petitions, only two had been to protests. Adam, a professional services consultant, comments that while he hasn't ever been on a protest, he had "intended to go to a pro-Europe march, but my wife wouldn't let me". Jonathan, a 70-year-old, semi-retired barrister just in the top 1% bracket, comments, almost proudly: "I'm not really a joiner."

Among our interviewees there is a curious tension: while as a rule they vote and follow politics, most do not participate in politics in any consistent manner. Their relative passivity, however, should not be equated to the disaffection of those who believe politics is not for people like them.

Three reasons were immediately apparent for this relative lack of participation. Not enough time is the first reason cited. Interviewees are much more likely to prefer using their waking hours with their families or advancing their careers, in much the same way that they are more likely to donate to charity than to volunteer. Second, the decline in civic engagement has been well documented by sociologists such as Robert Putnam and Nina Eliasoph in the US.[22] The third reason is that many high-income earners are wary of the oppositional, factionalist, and in their view, populist and extremist character that politics has taken in the past few years.

While some in the top 10% may consider joining a national party, few would go out of their way to participate in their local party, certainly not for personal interactions. While we are reminded that there never has been a golden age of political engagement, Putnam and others confirm that there has been a rise in anti-political sentiment, including towards local government.[23] And there is no corresponding positivity towards informal politics to compensate for this trend. In terms of participant numbers, alternative forms of political action – from demonstrating to donating and volunteering – do not seem to be on the rise. They also appear to be minority forms of action practised mainly by citizens who already vote and join parties.[24]

In 2019, for the first time since the mid-1970s, more than half of British survey respondents were dissatisfied with democracy in the UK.[25] While dissatisfaction with democracy has risen across many countries, it is striking that the developed countries worst affected are those with majoritarian electoral systems. That dissatisfaction increases when economic inequality increases, and has an even stronger impact geographically, with some areas of the country feeling neglected – in gerrymandered or safe seats.[26] While levels of trust and confidence have risen back to pre-Brexit levels, 44% of British people still say they almost never trust politicians to tell the truth, down from 51% in 2019.[27] People tend to keep up with political news nationally, but few take an active interest in how their local area is run.[28]

The proportion of the UK electorate that is a political party member has fallen from around 1 in 12 citizens in the 1950s to around 1 in 50 today. The UK has one of the lowest party memberships in Europe.[29] As Berry and Guinan chart, the local voluntary and community sector, which could sit at the heart of participatory politics, was hollowed out during austerity with grassroots organisations 'struggling to survive, competing for what money is available and with less and less capacity to give disenfranchised citizens a voice'.[30] Changing the electoral system would:

> breathe new life into campaigning by moribund local parties in historically safe seats, and would give party supporters a reason to be politically active in areas where the voting system had previously made their votes worthless. It could also encourage a less negative campaigning style, which has greater potential to engage turned-off voters.[31]

Gerry's experience of joining her local Labour Party in a safe Conservative seat confirmed a formal top-down bureaucratic relationship between local and national parties with, locally, a small executive of long-standing members and rules and procedures which could be off-putting to a newcomer.[32] And, at least until the pandemic temporarily changed the pattern of some people's working lives, there was very little interest in or knowledge of local politics by the community with many members of the public believing that local parties are run by paid officials rather than volunteers. Labour Party members make up 1.1% of the voting public[33] and are not a very representative slice, either, with members being on average much older, whiter, more male, and better off than the UK population average.[34]

Even if there were a renaissance of local politics, local councils have faced devastating cuts to their budgets for over ten years, leaving many on the brink of collapse. This includes a long-term reduction in the number of councillors, with 500 losses since 2014.[35] As an Unlock Democracy-commissioned report on the past 40 years of local government describes it: "the erosion of local democracy has been substantial, putting into jeopardy local government's ability to continue providing a vital democratic link for the communities it is elected to serve." What is more, the role of the councillor has been increasingly 'managerialised' and 'depoliticised'. As a result, 'accountability gaps' have emerged, with local government being bypassed by a 'new magistracy' of unelected bodies.[36] It is therefore unsurprising that there is little public interest in becoming local councillors.

On the whole, local councils only come to mind when the bins haven't been collected or when making a planning application. It is certainly not an area most would entertain spending their time in. Running for elected office is on the decline and this has been Gerry's experience when trying to encourage members of her local Labour Party to come forward and nominate themselves for local government.[37] The lack of remuneration (only expenses are paid) is also a barrier for people who might be interested, especially those on lower incomes or with family responsibilities. Although much depends on the local ward, candidates tend to be older and male. A lack of confidence and being put off by the potential experience is also a key factor, no doubt not helped by our polarising media and the combative and elitist nature of national politics.

One noticeable tendency, however, is the influence of more liberal voters moving from cities into affluent suburbs, which has only been hastened by the pandemic. Since 2019, this has been part of the explanation for the growth of progressive politics in the 'blue wall' (a set of parliamentary constituencies in the south of England where Conservatives have historically dominated). In contrast to the relative lack of interest in local formal politics, local pressure groups have grown, often set up about a specific issue such as a planning application and they exist predominantly online. Similarly, local branches of national pressure groups such as Extinction Rebellion or Make Votes Matter have sprung up. It has been Gerry's experience that members of such groups then move into formal politics as a result of their campaigning on local issues.

Given this, the lack of trade union or party membership among our respondents is also noticeable yet unsurprising. The two clearest exceptions to the rule are staunch Brahmins such as Paul, an architect just in the top 10% income band living in London, who is the only respondent to currently be a party member (Labour) like both his parents before him. Only one respondent, Duncan – a director of a non-departmental public body who votes Green – is a lifelong trade unionist and charity volunteer.

Other partial exceptions include Gemma – a consultant in London who had briefly been a member of the Liberal Democrats as part of an internship in parliament, but left once it finished, and Maria, who joined Labour only to vote against Corbyn's leadership. Maria's views also speak to the third reason many high earners have for not participating actively in politics: they do not like what it has become. Most respondents were, as predicted by the literature, quite progressive when it came to 'cultural' issues but less so on economic matters, which situated Labour supporters to the right of Corbyn and Conservative respondents to the left of every Tory leader after Cameron. Most felt short-changed by both parties in terms of both the ideology and the behaviour of its leaders. Many were likely to vote for the Liberal Democrats or speak approvingly of Tony Blair, and even David Cameron. Ben, 39, working in IT in the south-east, describes his relationship with the Conservative Party:

'I have been a Conservative Party member in the past. But there's no way with the current lot. I left the Conservative Party not long after Theresa May came in and the direction of Brexit was becoming clear. I also became disillusioned with people like Boris Johnson. He was previously MP for Henley, not far from here.

Him and Michael Gove in particular seem interested in helping themselves rather than fixing anything or running the country. That comes across bluntly in their case.'

Even when respondents identify with a party without being members, most have caveats. Roy, a 66-year-old finance director with a top 3% income, says that the Liberal Democrats probably best represent his views, but that he won't necessarily vote for them as he doesn't see what difference it will make. Jonathan, the 'non-joiner', semi-retired barrister we mentioned earlier, tells us he has always been a Labour supporter but he often doesn't vote for them. Claire, a teacher living in the north with an income just above the 10% threshold, describes herself as a "floaty voter". Maria, similarly, votes tactically either for Labour or the Liberal Democrats without belonging to either:

Maria:	I have been a member of a political party. I've been a member of Labour so I could vote for Jeremy Corbyn not to win.
Interviewer:	So you're not a member anymore?
Maria:	Yes I left. I felt quite bad because I'm between LibDem and Labour, so I thought I'm not going to keep it up in case I want to join the LibDems in the future.

Caught in the middle

Many respondents felt that political parties had been moving away from the typical centre ground. That comment was mostly levelled at the Conservatives, but similar views were expressed about Labour under Jeremy Corbyn. Many who had voted for Labour in the past felt it was no longer for them; it had veered towards socialism, a 'dirty' word for many. They much preferred the pragmatic, centrist politics of the New Labour era. Christopher, an under-35-year-old, working for a global IT consultancy, in the top 3% and one of the few who doesn't vote, says it is because "there's no party that I feel totally affinity to". Tony, introduced earlier, tells us:

'Everything's "far" – what's happened to the centre group? It's not just in politics, it's in every area of life, there's nowhere everyone can meet [...] the age of debate is disappearing. The age where you could persuade people of your opinion has gone. Everyone sets off down a track. I don't know when it happened [...] they became polarised.'

Maria as a marketing director with a top 6% income, has similar views:

'You know [...] it's too kind of ideological and now it's getting even further [...] the ideology is too far to one side. And the centre won't work either because [...] sometimes the centre can be quite weak, trying to keep too many people happy and they don't actually come out and say "This is what we're going to do," [...] that's not gonna work either.'

Our respondents' unease with current politics and predilection for previous centrism was clear. Perhaps this is why the Liberal Democrats represent the affluent voter's protest vote. Most interviewees said they would be voting for the same party in the 2019 general election as they had voted for in 2017, and parties' different stances on Brexit were the deciding factor for those contemplating changing their vote. Most intended to vote for the Liberal Democrats, primarily because of their pro-Remain stance. One mentioned that the unfairness of the voting system needed to be addressed. While we asked no specific question on Brexit – we preferred it to arise naturally – respondents spoke of the divisions it had revealed, such as Hannah, the occupational health consultant, earning just above the 10% threshold, who said: "If you look at the ways the country was divided in terms of areas, you see the more deprived areas broadly speaking voted for Brexit as opposed to more affluent areas that voted Remain."

Dan, the head of client services at a marketing agency in his early forties with a top 6% income, described the turmoil in April 2019:

'Brexit is on everyone's mind. A few weeks ago, it felt like the country might tear itself apart. It questioned friendships, political standing, democracy as a vehicle for governing, and that's quite scary. People seem hellbent on destroying what was a democratic process. MPs are not acting on behalf of the public. The whole thing is an abomination.'

When asked during the first round of interviews whether she thought inequality had had an impact on British politics in recent years, Louise, a 44-year-old sales consultant living in London with a top 1% income, replies: "Yeah, absolutely. Brexit is the stand-out one. The fact that people like Jeremy Corbyn are still leaders. No one ever thought originally that he would stay so long. Maybe that's due to, in part, the inequality across the nation. Yes, it's definitely played a part."

Ben, 39, an IT consultant in the top 3%, also commented on inequality and polarisation: "There's more polarisation in politics, perhaps because of inequality. You become not so happy with how things are organised and you either follow Jeremy Corbyn or the Green Party route, or you blame it on foreigners and get into UKIP."

Our research spanned Brexit, the governments of Theresa May and Boris Johnson, the pandemic, and the beginning of the post-pandemic recession. The lack of effective opposition was a concern throughout the process. Respondents mistrusted Jeremy Corbyn's ability to handle the economy and saw Keir Starmer as ineffective. In our follow-up round in early 2022, we asked whether they thought the country had been changed politically by COVID-19. Michael, a 49-year-old, engineer just in the top 10% living in the south-west, who spoke with us a few months before Boris Johnson's resignation, responds:

'[W]hile the current incumbent is untrustworthy, corrupt [...] you could not accuse them of doing nothing. This country is in a better situation than most. Puts us in an interesting situation. Left with a government that is not trustworthy. During Covid, the quality of the opposition is so weak, that the system is untenable. The opposition is supposed to put the counterargument [...]. It's not functioning. So we have one party with free rein. We get benefits off of that: they make decisions quickly and choices go through unopposed, rather than everything getting talked about; but we also get corruption.'

Tax: the glue in the social contract

Regardless of the distress about polarisation, Brexit and the radicalisation of political discourse, the overwhelming majority of wealthy constituencies in Britain went to the Conservatives in 2019, a party that had just purged most of its Remainer MPs. Though we suspected more, only four respondents openly told us they consistently voted Conservative. They did so mostly because of taxes. All four had young children, three worked in the corporate sector, and all were near the top of the ladder. Three were surprised by their position on the income distribution. Upward-oriented, they all thought they were placed much lower down the scale.

Louise, a 44-year-old sales consultant living in London in the top 1%, is one of them. She worries about the high cost of living and does not feel particularly wealthy. Nevertheless, as we described earlier, she gives taxation as the reason for voting Conservative: "as I've started to earn more [...] and worked hard for it, I care more about the tax I pay. Didn't think about it when I was younger [...]. Now I'm more aware of it and how it's helping society." While she agrees that those with the means should actively care for those with fewer, she thinks she pays enough tax already and therefore believes increasing taxes wouldn't solve the problem.

Susannah, another 1% income earner with young children living in the south-east, is similarly concerned about taxes. She feels that the existence of stamp duty and inheritance tax amounts to an unfair 'double taxation'. In terms of inequality, she feels there has to be a 'gap', a certain level of inequality for the economy and businesses to run: "people won't strive for anything different [...] if everyone has the same". At the same time, she thinks there is a duty to "make sure people at the lower end of the gap can live well and healthily".

Merchants, especially those with the highest incomes, tended to feel their duty to provide was already being carried out by paying tax, but many also recognised the need to provide for those on the lowest incomes. However, the lack of exposure to different income groups by those working in the corporate and financial sectors is a significant barrier to their understanding of the lives of those well below them, affecting their beliefs on the extent of inequality and the role of redistribution and welfare. Even before the 2008 crisis, Toynbee and Walker had found an increasing disconnect between the financial engine of the country in the City of London and the lives of the majority.[38] Considering the economic and political tendencies that followed, it is unlikely that this distance has been bridged.

Others, especially Brahmins working in the public sector, disagree. With jobs in healthcare, law and education, they were more likely to vote Labour, more likely to mention the negative effects of austerity such as the surge in food bank use, and more passionate about the need for public services. Jacqui, a state school headteacher, in the top 6% income band, felt that living in the north of England gave her a more grounded perspective on inequality, which informed her work: "Inequality is something to be concerned about: you want every kid to have the opportunity to succeed." Claire, another teacher living in the north and just above the top 10% threshold, comments: "The rich shouldn't be rich at the detriment of the poor. There should be a basic standard. [The rich] should have a duty." Concern with society's duty to care is consistent with European Social Survey (ESS) data showing an increase in the percentage of people in the top 10% who agree that the government should strive to reduce inequality (see Figure 2.1, Chapter 2). However, what that concern means in practice and the extent to which it would open a space for more redistribution is open to debate.

How to make sense of this primacy of right-of-centre voting based on an economic anti-tax rationale over any other factor, especially considering that the economy hasn't been performing especially well? A centralised parliamentary system and concentrations of elites in our politics, government, academia, media, law and other areas of public life have created a society in which 'economic change is currently done to people rather than by or with people'.[39] We found this to be true for high earners too. Despite being part of the elite – well educated, informed about current affairs and regular voters – they are as much in thrall as the rest of us to an economic 'common sense' that legitimises political power and underwrites the social contract.[40] Our respondents tended to accept a mainstream version of our economy, society and politics described as 'realistic to the extent that it approaches what already exists'.[41]

This version of economics – which operates more as a set of maxims than as a positive social science – has been used as a crucial prop for political authority for some decades. It has been propped up by, among others, right-leaning think tanks that traverse the worlds of media, academia, politics and economic interests. Many of its senior members are also part of the top 10% and, at least until recently, have been mostly insulated from the effects of the policies they propose.[42] Since the 1970s, their work has contributed to commodifying spaces that once seemed beyond purely financial considerations, such as public health.

One consequence of this process is that politics is reduced to questions of managerial competence (which party or leader will be most efficient?) or to bitter partisanship, where each party attacks the other regardless of the result. An example of the former focus on how the state is managed and its (in)efficiency rather than focusing on politics with a capital 'P', is provided by Michael, introduced earlier, in his explanation of what determines his vote: "My preference has always been for competence and rational behaviour. Who's more rational?"

The erosion and hollowing out of institutions – and the subordination of democracy to a certain vision of economics – has seen the worlds of politics, media and finance collapse into each other. A world in which vested interests stop reforms being made that would hit the wealthiest the most, as that would go against 'common sense', regardless of how many experts argue the contrary. Economist Simon Wren-Lewis, for instance, has argued that there is an increasing distance between the discipline of economics and what is broadly understood in politics and the media as 'the economy' and 'basic economics'.[43] Maria, the management consultant we quoted earlier, compared the crippling effect of business taxes on high street businesses with global tech firms: "And yet you don't get the same application of tax to technology platforms. That has to be looked at. Basically, they don't want to upset all their friends so that's why they don't do anything."

If high earners were to ask more often who has the power and why, when considering high prices for food and fuel, for example, they would see how deeply the market has entered every facet of life. Increasingly, no area of social and political life can avoid 'the gaze of a blanket financial audit'.[44] Finance is placed above legal mechanisms and determines which policy pledges will be kept, to the point where it is no longer clear that contemporary capitalism requires a norm-based legal model of the state. Only one respondent, a barrister and expert in housing law, reflected on the history of our state infrastructure in his lifetime: "You've got to start with Thatcher. Demunicipalisation of gas, water, electricity, railway, [...] housing [...] with the right to buy [...]. A mass transfer of stocks. A mass depletion of what the state, what public services, provide."

Conflicted views on the role of the state

Many respondents working in the private sector distance themselves from the welfare state, for at least two reasons. First, there is a certain status in thinking that they are not dependent on public services. If welfare recipients and state spending are blamed for the recession, it is perhaps to be expected that paying taxes while 'going private' becomes a reason to feel proud. Nobody in our sample describes having to make frequent use of public services, living in social housing or needing social care. Where respondents have children of school age, they are either in private schools or in state schools in relatively affluent areas. Framed like this, state spending commitments by one government or another seem much more abstract, and much less applicable to this demographic compared with the rest. They see no concrete benefit to their lives from further state spending, and if they did they would consider that a sign of failure, so the consequences of austerity feel foreign. The only partial exception is healthcare, which is more easily framed than most other policy areas as an issue beyond individual control. However, most of those that mention health problems have private healthcare 'for emergencies', often as part of their employment contracts.

Second, public services are considered inefficient and sub-par compared with the private sector, the NHS among them. For many, the state is almost by definition overweening, elephantine and prone to corruption. This belief in government inefficiency is often paired with low trust in the state's role in the economy. Ben, 39, an IT consultant in the top 3%, was one of many who justified not wanting to pay more taxes because:

> 'A lot of government initiatives are woefully inefficient. Where there is a new scheme or project, it seems they end up paying hundreds of millions or billions more than what it should have cost. Outside government, if you put £10 worth of help into inequality you may get £10 worth of effect. But putting that same £10 through the government will give £2.50 worth of overall effect.'

This sense that the government overspends and that it is not a question of spending more but rather 'spending better' is widespread among those working in the private sector. It is also consistent with ESS data from its rotating modules on welfare attitudes in 2008 and 2016, which show an increase in the percentage of British people who agree that social benefits and services place too great a strain on the economy (Figure 4.1).

Nevertheless, three quarters of those we spoke with felt that inequality was increasing. When asked how it was noticeable, they spoke of the more visible elements of poverty, such as homelessness on their way to the train station, and the rise of food banks and donation boxes in supermarkets. Nearly all were concerned about it at its most extreme and felt that people should not be struggling on the breadline. They saw providing for those with fewer resources as a moral duty, if sometimes a reluctant one. We have mentioned that the top 10%, while less favourable to redistribution than other parts of the population, are becoming less reticent. As we showed in Chapter 2, in 2018 the top 10%

Figure 4.1: Agreement with the statement 'Social benefits and services place too great a strain on the economy' in the UK, 2008–16

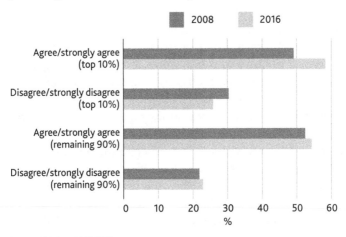

Source: ESS data, 2010, 2018

were more open to the suggestion of redistribution than they were in 2008. Most feel that 'in the fifth richest country in the world' the system is not working.

However, those working in the private sector, and those earning above £100,000 in particular, are conflicted as to the role the state should play. Jonathan, a 70-year-old, semi-retired barrister in the top 1%, starts by being clear that it is the government's duty to address inequality of outcome, then mid-interview argues instead that its role is only to ensure equality of opportunity, and from there concludes that its duty is purely to ensure people's basic standard of living: "Its duty is to provide education and opportunity and a basic standard of living. A basic standard of living – adequate, at least."

Sean, a 40-year-old with a top 1% income, who owns a recruitment company, is clearer:

> 'I hate these questions about the government because I don't know if the government should fix anything in this country. They have a duty to make sure that people are not living below the poverty line and they have a general duty to keep people safe and protected.'

Interviewees also discussed the relative importance of cash transfers as opposed to services and infrastructure. Michael, for example, a 49-year-old engineer earning just above the 10% threshold, is not alone in thinking that the emphasis should be taken away from universal benefits and instead make them means-tested. In his view, policy should focus on investing in the "infrastructure [that is currently] missing for better education, council housing, childcare".

Support for universal services as they are organised now (for example, the NHS) was weaker from those respondents working in the private sector, with little reference to the social solidarity function a universal system provides. Even the few who refer to the tradition of universalism, often end up arguing in favour of means-testing. Dan, head of client services at a marketing agency with a top 6% income, argues that if services are partially paid for by their beneficiaries, they will improve through customer demand for better quality: "If you pay a contribution to your son going to school then there's an expectation of what you're getting back. If you pay council tax, you expect bins to be collected and local services to function."

Ben, 39, an IT consultant in the top 3%, argues that people can't be trusted not to abuse the system. "Part of the problem is that [the NHS] is universal and absolutely free, and some people abuse that. If you give people a free resource, there's no reining in demand for it. [I] think that should change to slightly more means-tested."

However, he then makes clear that this does not mean he favours a US-style health service:

> 'If you've been run over and are taken to hospital you shouldn't have to show payslips before they operate. I'm thinking [introduce means-tested payments for] primary care. A bit like dental care, in certain situations you get it completely free and the same with prescriptions. I think we ought to do something like that with GPs as well.'

Duncan, a director of a non-departmental government body, refers to the erosion of the political consensus on universalism:

'It's quite frightening because it undermines all of the principles from after the Second World War, which were about caring for everyone and a communal approach to life based on people's experience. The creation of the welfare state and the NHS were two of those which society generally accepted. A lot of that has been eroded in the past 20 years, so it seems a bad thing instead of a good one. It's seen as unaffordable [by] the rich. Not the super-rich, just those with income – there's more an attitude of "I'd rather pay for myself than pay into a pot." It would be good to try and reverse some of that.'

The relatively weak support for universalism – especially from those working in the private sector – and the few references made to austerity, are to be expected. They can even be framed as a progressive impulse not to support the well-off with the taxes of those on low incomes, and fit perfectly also with the stigma associated with public service users and welfare recipients. Instead, a 'rights and responsibilities' discourse runs through many respondents' accounts.[45] Michael, a 49-year-old engineer just above the 10% threshold, was one of a few to concede that benefits only provide a minimum standard of living. This may stem from his experience of living in relative poverty as a child:

'Any one of us can find ourselves in a situation where we really haven't got any money and it can happen really quickly […] although unemployment is low at the moment, it can still be difficult because there's a lot of choice out there. You can easily find yourself with no income for a while. If you do go onto welfare then it's a very, very difficult situation. The welfare state will give you really not quite enough money for what you need. It might give you enough to live on. But things like maintenance, anything that requires any kind of upkeep – you quickly will find you can't run a car, and then […] you can't get a job […] so, there's a divide, a watershed point, at which if you go beyond an economic line, it all decays, the whole situation collapses very quickly.'

Where will the political tide take high earners?

High-income earners occupy an interesting position. They dominate politics and most institutions of political importance and yet they feel unease: not mainly because they think politicians live in a different reality from theirs (like many others feel today), but because they are fearful of the current political tides. It's an attitude reminiscent of Barack Obama's response after Donald Trump's win in 2016: of disbelief at the perceived irrationality of others, a fear that passion has overtaken reason. Small 'l' liberal views seem to be going out of fashion on the economic and cultural fronts, discredited by figures such as Bernie Sanders and Jeremy Corbyn on the left and by Nigel Farage, Marine Le Pen, Jair Bolsonaro and the like on the right. Famously, Theresa May said in October 2016 "if you believe you're a citizen of the world, you're a citizen of nowhere. You don't understand what the very word 'citizenship' means." That seems to us like an almost direct critique of the subjects of this book.[46]

Although elites are rarely popular, the 2010s have seen anti-elite discourse become increasingly commonplace. Perhaps this is unsurprising after an economic crisis mainly caused by a financial system populated by unaccountable high-income earners, highly educated experts who were not capable of predicting it or dealing with its fallout, and growing concentrations of wealth. At the same time, the concept of 'elite' is murky, and we do ourselves a disservice if we think it is homogeneous or easy to identify. Nevertheless, it is not cavalier to assume some Brahmins and some Merchants are part of it.

David Goodhart, a journalist and think-tanker who started his career on the centre-left and has moved steadily to the right in the past years, has written two relevant books on the matter.[47] In *The Road to Somewhere*, he argues that the 'anywheres', those whose economic situation and outlook are directly influenced and benefited by globalisation, have dominated politics for too long. In the process, they have cast aside the 'somewheres', those with more local attachments and more small 'c' conservative mindsets. In *Head, Hand, Heart*, Goodhart states that in the last decades, society has tended to value the kinds of non-routine jobs that require credentials and specialist knowledge, prioritising the academically oriented. In other words, we have overemphasised the 'head' (expertise) over the 'hand' (manual labour) or the 'heart' (care), and the 'anywhere' over the 'somewhere'. In such a system, the top 10%, populated as it is by highly educated professionals and managers, has done well, ostensibly at the expense of those who are now leading the backlash against their values.

Goodhart's analysis is compelling if betraying a sometimes unhealthy animosity towards urbanites, which puts him in dubious company. However, this diagnosis does not answer why the most affluent constituencies in England voted in huge numbers for the Conservatives after Boris Johnson purged the party from moderates and populated it with Brexiteers, or why Trump voters in the US were more affluent than the national average.[48] The left-of-centre ideas on culture and right-of-centre ones on the economy that high-income earners seem to favour appear to be under attack. Yet, when they had to choose, a majority seems to have chosen the economy. Why is that?

We would argue that 2019 was a watershed. In front of the country and high-income earners were Jeremy Corbyn and Boris Johnson. Corbyn was portrayed as a radical left-winger and irresponsible on the economy, though his programme would have been considered a normal social democrat one in much of Europe – indeed, his spending proposals were almost identical to Germany's in 2019.[49] Johnson is an openly mendacious politician who opportunistically positioned himself on the right of the right wing of his party and, while pursuing Brexit, seemed to propose little to no change on the economic front. High-income earners sided mostly with the latter, at least based on results from the least deprived constituencies.

From a purely materialistic standpoint, it was an unsurprising choice. However they are understood, elites are in some sense defined – not illogically – as likely to be negatively affected by redistributive policies. Any such change risks impinging on their privileges and their capacity to reproduce their elitism and bequeath their resources to their children. That is, after all, how tax hikes are commonly framed among high-income earners. If pushed, we would say that many in the top 10% resent the left for promoting policies in the run-up to the 2019 general election that in their minds were irrational and harmful, forcing them to vote with the far right. In the conflict between their economic interests and their sociocultural inclinations, the former took precedence.

Meanwhile, in the background, Brexit, one of the most impactful and radical policies of the last decades, continued to disrupt huge swathes of the economy, and trickle-down economics continued to drive concentration at the top. Most far-right parties propose precious little to avert these trends and instead espouse a Darwinian view of the economy, where those 'out' are punished for the benefit of those 'in'. Most of the relatively affluent are generally considered 'in', but as the history of far-right movements shows us they are driven by the exclusion and scapegoating of one segment of society after another, and at some point they may find themselves the target.

High-income earners are, in the main, not delighted by this turn of events. A majority do remain small 'l' liberals and resent being ruled by governments that are allied with right-wing European administrations such as Orbán's Hungary, under a programme and a discourse that is not too distant from those of Trump, Bolsonaro, Meloni or Le Pen. Brahmins are the most worried; they fear not just polarisation and populism, but also the loss of democratic standards and the legitimisation of bigotry in the public arena. This often prompts them to become apathetic and ever more distant from the political process. The attitude of many Merchants can be encapsulated by a *New Yorker* cartoon from 30 January 2017, days after Trump officially became president (Figure 4.2). Two male figures in suits look down on the city from what seems to be a swanky office in a skyscraper. The caption reads: "Part of me is going to miss liberal democracy."

Whatever you may think of the proposals coming from the left, it is clear that neither the Conservatives nor any hypothetical centrist programme has answers to the structural crises that are beginning to affect everyone in this group. This gives us some indication of the fragility of our society and economy: even the top 10% is feeling wary. In less unequal countries, the same group is far more secure and has much less to worry about. The next chapter further explores some of the crises and tensions that our respondents and many of our readers now face.

Figure 4.2: *The New Yorker* cartoon, by Barbara Smaller

"Part of me is going to miss liberal democracy."

Source: Barbara Smaller/The New Yorker Collection/The Cartoon Bank

5

Business class tickets for a sinking ship

Whether they know it or not, and through whatever means, high earners have a disproportionate influence on policy. Since they are more likely to vote than most, political parties court their opinion, and they are often sociologically similar to the elites of these parties.[1] In Europe, research shows a similar pattern.[2] Nevertheless, and despite their relative political dominance, politics doesn't seem to be working for the top 10%. Holes are beginning to appear in their meritocratic narrative. Access to housing, jobs, opportunities for career advancement and places in elite universities for their children are becoming scarcer and competition fiercer. Many are also becoming increasingly aware that a catastrophic event such as an illness or accident could derail their until now upward trajectories.

As a rule, high-income earners are relatively pessimistic about their country's future but less so about their own. They are, in the main, quite optimistic about themselves, which betrays a tacit distance between how they see their lives and the fate of the rest. However menacing challenges such as climate change and inequality may be, many are confident they will still do well. Politics happens to others, so to speak.

At the same time, intergenerational inequalities are becoming more accentuated, as Millennials and Generation Z find the transition to adulthood increasingly difficult and many are unable to maintain the economic status of their elders. Housing is becoming nigh unaffordable without parental support, especially in metropolitan areas where salaries tend to be highest. At the same time, education does not seem to guarantee a comfortable living as it once did, as income and status are becoming closely linked to inheritance and wealth. Our respondents' optimism was less pronounced when asked about the world their children will live in.

As we write, and in no particular order, there seem to be record highs in all the wrong things. Just to name a few: global temperatures; inequality; inflation; the cost of energy, food, transport and housing, and the profits of privatised companies supplying those resources; excess deaths; turnover in key essential services; and waiting times for emergency services and hospital operations. And there are the corresponding record lows in all the wrong things too: life expectancy; real earnings; productivity growth; income growth in the lowest deciles; and the state of public services.

This chapter explores how critical events (Brexit, the pandemic, the Ukraine–Russia war, the cost of living crisis) and the structural crises of our times may affect the top 10%. As much as their situation is more secure than most, they are finding it harder to ignore these crises, especially in the long run. It is clear that the factors behind their anxieties are sociological and structural, and affect far beyond the top 10%.

Critical events

Brexit

The 2016 referendum for the UK to leave the EU was followed by a further four years of negotiations. During this time, other social and political issues were crowded out of the policy agenda, even those often reported to be behind Brexit itself. As Sean, the owner of an HR consultancy, put it: "Brexit has overshadowed everything political." High earners acknowledge the inequalities exposed and aggravated by Brexit, and the fact it has many causes and facets. Not least, Brexit exposed the cultural and socioeconomic divides in the country, many of which criss-crossed the Conservative versus Labour divide.

The Brexit vote has often been characterised as largely working class and English, driven by older, socially conservative people living in declining areas and feeling increasingly powerless to face the pressures of globalisation.[3] Another theory on the motivations of Leave voters was that they tended to be old enough to remember more equitable times and might have associated the UK's EU membership in 1975 with a decline in living standards because during roughly the same period economic inequality has taken a marked turn for the worst.[4] Whatever the motivations, five years on, Ipsos polls showed that Brexit identities are still stronger than party identification.[5] Most high-income earners we spoke with were against the whole thing. They told us they no longer felt represented by politics; they feared polarisation, populism and their economic impacts. Ben, 39, an IT consultant living in the south-east in the top 3%, explains to us why he voted Liberal Democrat:

> 'Brexit is a big thing for me and they seem to be the most pro-European party. I think their views are closer to my own. The Conservative Party has taken a lurch to the right following the departure of David Cameron and I don't feel the party is even close to representing my views anymore. I have been a Conservative Party member in the past. But there's no way with the current lot.'

Other people's lack of concern for the impact of Brexit also troubled our respondents. Alan, a 50-year-old director of a logistics company in the south-east, when asked about what worried him about his country and his own future, replied, with reference to Brexit, that the British need to have a greater "ability to respond to misinformation". Claire, a headteacher living in Manchester with an income just above the 10% threshold, commented: "people felt they were going to get more money into the system. People who voted Leave thought they would be better off. They were lied to." International onlookers, such as *The New York Times*, wrote about the corrosive impact of Brexit on British politics and 'the readiness of the political right in particular to lie and peddle obvious untruths, to place their party politics and party unity over and above the national interest'.[6]

COVID-19

The UK has one of the worst Covid records in the world. The country was ill-prepared for the pandemic after more than a decade of disinvestment and privatisation of public infrastructure. Adult social care was particularly vulnerable. Despite being warned, the government downplayed the importance of care provision at the beginning of the pandemic, neglecting to supply it with further funding. The first confirmed COVID-19 cases in the UK were on 31 January 2020.[7] On 25 February, Public Health England issued guidance for social care settings, advising that 'it is [...] very unlikely that anyone receiving care in a care home or the community will become infected' and 'there is no need to do anything differently in any care setting at present'.[8] From an initial £5 billion emergency response fund, £1.6 billion was allocated to local authorities, but they were not legally required to spend that money on social care, and it was therefore not always received by the sector. NHS England asked hospitals to urgently discharge patients who were medically fit back into social care settings, and 25,000 patients were.[9] It was only midway through April 2020, almost a month after social distancing measures had been put in place, that an adult social care action plan for controlling the spread of infection was finally issued. This delayed and uncoordinated response failed to protect an already vulnerable sector.

On 27 April 2022, the High Court ruled that the government had been reckless in moving Covid-positive patients back into nursing homes from hospitals and that this led to thousands of unnecessary deaths.[10] At the same time, government spending elsewhere, such as the £37 billion pound test-and-trace scheme – which according to the Public Accounts Committee, achieved none of its aims and failed to make 'a measurable difference to the progress of the pandemic'[11] – amounted to double the central government cuts to local authorities over the last 10 years.[12] Meanwhile, the pandemic highlighted the poor pay and working conditions of many essential workers in society. A third of care workers, for example, are paid less than the real Living Wage.[13]

Covid may also have been the first time many high earners experienced being direct recipients of state cash transfers through the furlough scheme and business loans. In 2020, COVID-19 benefit claimants were much more likely to be highly educated and younger than before.[14] At the same time, high earners were also insulated from the worst effects of the crisis, as a higher income was strongly correlated with the capacity of a job to be carried out from home and with savings on non-essential goods and services such as eating out and leisure travel.[15] Apart from a reminder of the importance of key workers and public healthcare provision, this relative insulation from the most severe economic effects of COVID-19 may well contribute to a forgiving attitude towards the government's management of the pandemic, as well as relative ignorance of its broader social consequences.

Ukraine–Russia war

According to the OECD, the UK will be the major economy to be most affected by the Ukraine–Russia war. It will be the slowest growing in 2023 due to a combination of factors, including higher interest rates, reduced trade, rising energy prices, and the fact that, in 2019, the UK imported around 13% of all its fuel from Russia.[16] Nevertheless, disruption to the supply of energy to Europe will affect wholesale prices in the UK to a greater extent than implied by direct trade links. Traders buy gas in the UK to avoid higher prices in Europe and then export it to the Continent, both reducing UK supply and causing prices to rise in the Continent.

Inflationary pressures on households from soaring food and energy prices, cutting household disposable income and living standards and lowering consumption as the book goes to publication, mean that consumer spending continues to shrink and confidence is low. Recovery, as the Institute of Government predicted, looks likely to be delayed by the uncertainty holding back the UK economy as firms and consumers 'adopt a "wait and see" approach, cutting back on investment and consumption plans'.[17]

Energy costs and market failures

Paul Johnson, Director of the Institute for Fiscal Studies, described Kwasi Kwarteng's September 2022 budget as a 'complete reversal of policy compared with the government only a few months ago, this was like an entirely different government coming into office'.[18] Within three weeks, without having won a general election, Liz Truss had announced the biggest unfunded package (over £50 billion) of tax cuts in 50 years, bigger than any introduced by Margaret Thatcher. These included cuts in the basic rate of income tax to 19p; a reversal in the rise in corporation tax and national insurance; abolishing the cap on bankers' bonuses; and lowering the tax rate on incomes above £150,000.[19]

Markets unsurprisingly reacted, concerned at the potential for rising inflation, without a serious plan from the government to pay the debt back, so sterling was sent 'spiralling down and gilts soaring, costing the Bank of England £65bn to prop up pension funds'.[20] Two of these tax cuts (the top rate and corporation tax) were subsequently rolled back due to public and market pressure. However, even with the quick U-turn on two taxes, the richest 5% of households will still gain almost 40 times as much as the poorest fifth of households by the measures announced.[21] Crucially, Rishi Sunak's government is still planning public spending cuts and further austerity. With the need for additional borrowing and no fiscal plan in place, the government has undermined the Bank of England's attempts to tackle inflation and led to interest rates spiking on government debt, volatility in sterling and market uncertainty.[22]

Described variously as 'disastrous', 'a fiscal and moral outrage', 'a reckless mini-budget for the rich' and 'At last! A true Tory budget',[23] what's surprising about this episode is the confluence of three phenomena: the brazenness of the proposals, which married tax cuts for the most affluent with spending cuts for the most vulnerable; the effect of the markets' reaction to the government's sudden lurch to the right, reflecting their increased power as quantitative easing starts to be reversed; and that all of this is happening in a context where the fallout of previous and ongoing crises (not least 2008, Brexit, COVID-19 and the Ukraine–Russia war) still afflict the UK economy. Ultimately, this represents a rift between the markets and their most die-hard advocates and the end of the idea that tax cuts are per se a responsible proposal to spur growth and address government debt. If we are lucky, this might be the end of the idea that 'trickle-down economics' brings benefits to anyone other than the already wealthy.

Still, British people face mortgage rate rises, the costs of which will pass on to both owners and renters; rising costs of food, of which 50% is imported, and which in the context of a falling pound will continue to go up; and an estimated 80% increase in energy bills this winter.[24] The effect of these cost rises, in combination with long-term wage stagnation and no uprating of benefits in line with inflation, means that many millions of people will be in ill health and food, energy and fuel poverty. Communities around the country have already set up 'warm banks' as well as food banks.[25]

While we've been led to believe our markets are competitive and consumers can shop around, COVID-19 and the energy crisis have exposed the role of monopolies. In the case of both gas and electricity distribution networks, six companies have a market share of 94%. Among the gas networks, one operator has close to 50% of the total market share. It also has higher profit margins than any other sector in the economy.[26] Large oil companies are making huge profits in 2022 – a year that saw energy costs rise 23 times faster than wages – and are distributing these profits to shareholders rather than investing in decarbonisation.[27]

This doesn't have to be the case. Some of the owners of energy companies operating in the UK are foreign governments, such as French-owned EDF. In France, energy bills went up by 4% in spring 2022, while in the UK, they went up by 54%. While EDF made £106 million in the UK in 2020 alone, that was followed by overall losses, partly due to reduced nuclear output and to the cap imposed by the French government to shield consumers from soaring energy prices.[28] In contrast, the UK economy remains dominated by monopolistic practices, with some of its biggest corporations using the cash generated from profiteering to maintain their position, buying up or pricing out smaller rivals, and, increasingly, investing in financial markets. Indeed, some of the world's largest international monopolies are behaving like banks, using their cash to buy up the bonds (debts) of other corporations.[29] Meanwhile, in August 2022, then-chancellor Nadhim Zahawi stated that those earning £45,000 may need support for their energy bills; that is, over the top 20% income threshold of £43,700.[30]

There is little regulation of monopolies. The House of Commons Committee for Business, Energy and Industrial Strategy on the regulation of the energy sector concluded that the government had 'prioritised competition over effective market supervision, failing to recognise the fundamental importance of energy supply and maintain sight over Ofgem's actions'.[31] This failure of regulation has left the energy supply market and taxpayers more exposed to the global wholesale energy crisis. Not even the private sector is immune, as thousands of pubs and other venues face closure without immediate support.[32]

Market failure is affecting all essential areas of life in the UK. This is seen only too starkly in care provision. It is not a coincidence that there is little to no public conversation on the topic. The sector is monopolised by a handful of private equity firms. HC-One, the UK's largest care home operator, received an additional £18.9 million in government payments for Covid costs, while its owners, in the year 2020 alone, continued to siphon £47.2 million in tax-free profits to the Cayman Islands.[33] All the while, care homes are in a continual crisis, with the sector now losing one third of its staff every year.[34] Under-investment, coupled with demographic pressures, mean that an increasing number of people need adult social care and support but fewer are getting it, with many having much less than they need.[35]

Structural crises

Precarious work

Precarity has become an increasingly salient issue, especially for young people just joining the labour market. The rise of the gig economy, degree inflation, the casualisation of previously secure occupations such as academia and law, high housing costs and automation threaten the livelihoods and security of many.[36] Certainly, these pressures are more strongly felt lower down the income distribution; however, the top 10% is not immune, not because they are feeling the effects of these processes now, but because of the looming sense of fear for the future they elicit. Indeed, the threat of automation seems to be increasingly patent among high income earners, as artificial intelligence software such as ChatGTP threaten to render many professions obsolete.[37]

Few high earners we spoke with had experienced significant disruptions in their careers. While some had been directly affected by the financial crash, others remembered feeling only its 'ripples'. Nobody who started an ambitious upward trajectory had to change their career path due to, for example, health or family reasons, though to be sure, there may be a certain 'survivorship bias' in our sample, as we considered those who were in the top 10% at the time of being interviewed. Men in their forties or fifties, in particular, described uninterrupted career trajectories; most had stable upbringings, often with their mothers staying at home while their fathers worked. They often seek to replicate that model for their own families.

Nevertheless, at an age when their parents would have been moving into comfortable retirement, having paid off their mortgages and seen their children become independent, those in their fifties who had been recently divorced instead found that their upward trajectory wasn't as upward as they expected. Alan, in his fifties, whose interview we referred to earlier, talks about the prospect of continuing to work into his sixties and seventies, as he had recently been through an expensive divorce. Paul, an architect in his late forties, also divorced, imagines himself competing with younger versions of himself: "[you] find yourself back in the twenty-something's situation, but with less potential".

Younger high earners spoke with a similar insecurity in the face of a fiercely competitive labour market. Gemma, a management consultant in her late thirties, and one of the few respondents with no dependants, said she felt insecure about maintaining a sufficiently high income within the corporate sector. Having initially been drawn to the rigid structure of working in a large accountancy firm, she began to feel she was on "a treadmill" and left to become an independent contractor. However, she now finds this "a scary move", partly because there's no structured progression and her income "may go up and down a little". This relative insecurity is made worse because the amount of money she needs to sustain herself is increasing: "my stable bar gets higher all the time". She even explains that her decision not to have children is partly due to not wanting to feel "trapped financially [...], coming from a volatile economic background, where money was always really tight". When asked whether she has savings, Gemma says: "I have to keep a pot [...] because my job's really unstable". This chimes with recent research for the Economy 2030 Inquiry, which found that high earners fear losing their jobs, partly because they do not think the benefits system 'has their back'.[38]

The sense that those in the private sector must always be moving on, moving up and cannot take their position for granted is a striking yet common feature in their narratives. This contrasts with greater job retention and security in the public sector, if at lower earnings. In sum, insecurity and anxiety are prevalent for those in the private sector, particularly in the City of London, and those who live in London and the south-east. There, the cost of living is highest and they are more likely to be living near the super-rich.

Given this, many in the top 10% worry that their children will not be able to climb the ladder as they have done. The meritocratic rationale for the distance between those who do well and those who do not is the reward for effort, whether in the form of hard work or attaining educational credentials. Respondents such as Susannah, a top 1% earner, were starting to see that this link was weakening as middle-class jobs are being hollowed out:

> 'I worry about my kids. I don't know what they're going to do because of all the jobs [...] and I say this from a financial services background [...] a lot of the entry-level jobs have all been moved offshore. So, where I started, when I started my job at [accountancy firm] is now done in India and has been done in India for some years [...] So it's harder to break into those industries.'

Stephen, a law professor in his early fifties and in the top 6%, when asked if he agreed with the statement 'Broadly speaking, if you work hard, you will succeed in the UK', replied that there was "no guarantee of that at the moment, based on the number of graduates who find themselves in so-called dead-end jobs".

Housing

Perhaps unsurprisingly, research shows that the top 10% is more likely than the rest to have a mortgage.[39] In our sample, nearly all own their homes or are paying a mortgage, with some having two. Many of them have done well from the rise in house prices. The value of land has increased fivefold since 1995. Nevertheless, many among them feel the cost of housing and would like to see council tax and stamp duty replaced with a proportional property tax.[40] Over half of the UK's wealth is now locked up in land, dwarfing the amounts vested in savings. Britain's broken housing market and housing crisis is in fact a land crisis, as Guy Shrubsole demonstrates in *Who Owns England?*:

> Politicians can talk all they like about building more homes, or slashing planning regulations to free up developers. But fail to tackle sky-high land prices, and all you'll end up with is a bunch more unaffordable houses. Housing developers are often accused of land banking to bolster their profits, but in reality all landowners have a propensity to hoard land – and to demand as high a price as they can get when they come to selling it.[41]

Older generations have benefited from rapid rises in the value of their homes, generous occupational pension provision, decades of healthy wage growth, free university tuition when they themselves studied, tax breaks for pension saving and capital gains on main homes, and the 'triple lock' on the state pension.[42] The young, meanwhile, spend an increasing percentage of their earnings on rent, all while real wages have stagnated. Considering this, it's unsurprising that a growing number of young adults are living with their parents. In 2018, a third of those privately renting in the UK only had £23 to spend on anything else each week after paying for their rent, gas, electricity, and food.[43] And this was before COVID-19 and the cost of living crisis.

The housing market continues to move further out of reach for many young people. The stamp duty holiday introduced in July 2020 to kick-start the housing market, together with increased demand for larger properties due to homeworking, has contributed to the fastest rise in house prices since 2005.[44] The average age for owning your first home is now 33 and a third of those first-time owners will have had help from 'the bank of mum and dad', partnering or government support.[45] After more than a decade of low interest rates and rising house prices following the 2008 financial crisis, the 2020s are now seeing interest rates *and* house prices increase – and sharply so. This could have serious political repercussions if highly indebted homeowners – having been sold the idea of home ownership as a rite of passage and ploughed hard-earned savings into their deposits – were to see mortgages become increasingly unaffordable or unavailable, as indeed we saw in the market response to Truss's 2022 mini-budget.

Paul, the architect in his early forties whom we introduced earlier, lives in London, and reflects on the ability of his children to buy houses, particularly in the south-east. He advised them to stay up north, where they studied: "I have told my three children, who've been to university in Birmingham, Keele and Manchester, that they should consider staying in the north to have a higher standard of living."

The importance of inheritance in transmitting inequality is evident in housing. It presents a challenge not only to meritocratic views but also to the ideal of modern life, what in the US is called the 'American Dream'. Paul continues to ponder the relationship between housing and inequality:

> 'It's intergenerational, isn't it? My children will be able to pay their rent, but don't know what will happen, there's no gaining any security as it stands. [...] It's Thatcher's effect on Britain, to make people insecure and greedy. People grab enough for themselves. They have to be all right. But there's a loss of belief in the community, a divergence between those who've got

it and those who haven't. The property market is an indicator. [...] It excludes a lot of people. For a whole generation [owning a home] won't be taking place. It matters where and when you're born.'

The prospects for the financial reforms needed to change the housing circumstances for young people are unlikely in the short term. There is little political will in the ruling parties.[46] What this will mean for the top 10% is uncertain; it could mean further attempts to shore up their assets, but also resentment if they cannot do that. As we found in our follow-up interviews, many older children are remaining in the parental home, with pressing consequences for the quality of life, family formation, mental health and career progression.

Wealth inequality

In most countries, and certainly in the UK, wealth inequality is much greater than income inequality and getting worse at a faster rate.[47] Globally, unrecorded offshore wealth has grown exponentially since the 1980s, significantly more than recorded onshore wealth; and in the case of the UK, it is valued at 15–20% of GDP.[48] Net private wealth has risen from 300% of the national economy in the 1970s to over 600% today.[49] This increase has been driven by growth in the price of property and the value of private pensions. A recent Resolution Foundation report describes the extent of wealth inequality:

> Wealth gaps have not just grown over time, they are also extremely high from an international perspective. The share of wealth held by the richest 10 per cent in the UK is in line with the OECD average, but the gap between these rich families and the poorest 40 per cent of the distribution (measured as a multiple of median earnings) is the second highest in the OECD – only the US is more unequal.[50]

'Extraction capitalism', as Stewart Lansley has termed it, is 'the latest incarnation of the collective monopoly power of the nineteenth century'.[51] However, while this form of capitalism and its resultant inequality has become the norm, it is unlikely that the country will improve economically while we continue to ignore the effects of wealth growing so much faster than income, partly because any corporations and individuals sitting on income-generating assets will not be motivated to innovate or invest in new businesses. Low corporation tax even encourages working individuals to move labour income into companies and, as share ownership is concentrated in the hands of the wealthy, these tax incentives on corporate profits benefit almost exclusively those who are already well-off.

Despite what right-wing think tanks would have you believe, low taxes at the top disproportionately benefit those with savings and assets, which produces economic stagnation and inequality. The wealthy spend a smaller percentage of their income on simply getting by than those who need to work to survive; they are, increasingly, the only ones who can save. This decreases overall demand and limits who is able to save. In this context, monopolies are inevitable. Employees can't negotiate the wages they receive related to output and neither can they – along with consumers and regulators – influence the markup of selling prices over costs.[52]

Furthermore, modern wealth is largely dependent on wealth accumulated in the past. As Piketty puts it, wealth grows more rapidly than the rate of growth of income and output,[53] 'capital reproduces itself faster than output increases. The past devours the future.'[54] This can be seen in the historical injustices of legacies that have started to gain salience. Movements such as Black Lives Matter have begun to put a spotlight on how the wealth of the truly wealthy in the UK is based on a long history of exploitation of non-White people.[55]

The dominance of capital in the UK isn't only useful for wealthy Brits. According to Oliver Bullough, in his celebrated book *Butler to the World*, Britain 'operates as a gigantic loophole, undercutting other countries' rules, massaging down tax rates, neutering regulations, [and] laundering foreign criminals' money'.[56] We are now seeing the consequences in sectors including energy, banking and care of having become a 'paradise' for disaster capitalists. Not only that, but as Bullough reminds us:

It's not just that Britain isn't investigating the crooks, it's helping them too. Moving and investing their money is of course central to what the UK does, but that's only the start: it's also educating their children, solving their legal disputes, easing their passage into global high society, hiding their crimes and generally letting them dodge the consequences of their actions.[57]

Climate change

Tackling climate change will require a profound transformation that will have a massive impact on households and their consumption. Individual carbon footprints will have to be cut from 8.5 tonnes to 2.5 tonnes by 2030, which will require huge change and disruption. The gaps between environmental targets and actual footprints show that high-income countries need to reduce their emissions by 91–95% before 2050.[58] However, lead author on the Intergovernmental Panel on Climate Change (IPCC) Lorraine Whitmarsh warned that 'we are going nowhere'.[59]

This is unsurprising to many commentators. Stewart Lansley points out that business as usual has long been 'bad for livelihoods, resilience and the environment, while big business has mostly eschewed any sense of wider responsibility to society, the workforce or the planet'.[60] Equally unsurprising, given its track record, is that the UK government has not signalled much urgency on the matter. Instead, it hints that British people shouldn't need to disrupt their behaviour or lifestyles. This is despite the fact that, for example, climate objectives will not be met without a major improvement in UK housing.[61] How can sustainable homes be made affordable? Are the workforce and the housing sector ready to deliver the changes needed? How can policy help drive this change? How can we avoid the costs of transition landing unfairly or its benefits being unfairly distributed?

While research shows that the higher your income, the more likely you are to worry about climate change, the topic rarely appeared in our interviews, and when it did, it did so only cursorily when respondents were asked about their fears for the future. Carbon-intensive luxury consumption is globally responsible for half of all emissions. Each member of the top 10% of global emitters produced on average 27.7 tonnes in 2019.[62] The equivalent from low-income groups is significantly lower: the top 10% produces 48% of all emissions, while the bottom 50% produces only 12%.[63] Plus, let's not forget that a disproportionate share of people from wealthy countries will be included in that 10%.

These figures demonstrate that the main driver of climate change isn't overpopulation or birth rates in poorer countries. The rich emit more carbon, not only through the goods and services they consume but also through their investments. This means that high earners will have to make a greater effort at curbing emissions, but the opposite is happening. Lower-income groups are shouldering the burden as recently happened in France, where the government raised carbon taxes in a way that hit those on low incomes in rural areas, kick-starting the *gilets jaunes* (yellow vests) movement. One of the few interviewees who spoke at length on the climate was Jonathan, a barrister near retirement. On a gloomy note, he said:

> 'The world's collapsing. We're at the end of our days. Global warming, rising seas, floods [...] I see no remission in that. [I am] not convinced my daughter will see out her natural life [...] In another 50 years there will not be a world in recognisable form.'

Social reproduction under threat

Healthcare

Before the pandemic, indicators of health inequality in the UK were already getting starker. From the beginning of the 20th century, Britain experienced continuous improvements in life expectancy but from 2011 these improvements slowed dramatically, almost grinding to a halt. In 2020, for the first time in more than 100 years, life expectancy failed to increase across the country and for the poorest 10% of women it declined.[64] The year 2015 saw the largest rise in mortality since the Second World War.[65]

Powerful evidence on health and wellbeing inequalities – and how these are reflected in education, employment, income and quality of life – has been published since the well-known 1977 Black Report (*Inequalities in Health*) and later in the 2010 and 2020 Marmot reviews. The latter illustrated how the 2010s austerity has affected the social determinants of health in the short, medium and long term. These range from rising child poverty, declines in education funding, increased precarity and a housing affordability crisis, to a rise in homelessness and increasing reliance on food banks. Darkly, the reviews suggest we will see many of these impacts only in the longer term when austerity's children are adults.

COVID-19 reminded high earners that the NHS, public health and social care are crucial for the wellbeing of us all. However, pressures relating to public sector pay, austerity and a cost of living crisis have presented an unprecedented threat to the health and wellbeing of the UK.[66] High earners are fearful that waiting times and beleaguered service provision will not provide for them and their families. Several spoke to us about 'going private' when they could. Indeed, the UK now pays almost as much as the US in out-of-pocket healthcare, with the number of people resorting to crowdfunding campaigns to pay exorbitant private medical expenses rising 20-fold in the past five years. It is also the people who can least afford them who are paying the most. Between 2010 and 2020, the portion of UK spending that went on hospital treatments increased by 60% overall, but more than doubled among the lowest-earning fifth of the population. The poorest now spend as much on private medical care as the richest, in relative terms.[67]

The extent to which higher earners will continue to be insulated from the worst of inequalities is debatable. Marmot warned a focus on the poorest and the very richest is obscuring more widespread health inequalities, with 'middle class people [...] missing out on an average of eight years of full and active life because of deep-seated inequality'.[68] Conditions that lead to marked health disparities are detrimental to all members of society, with some types of health inequalities having 'obvious spillover effects on the rest of society, for example, the spread of infectious diseases, the consequences of alcohol and drug misuse, or the occurrence of violence and crime'.[69] Economic inequalities, for example, were shown in the US to be closely related to the frequency of deaths from external causes such as homicides and accidents.[70] Put this way, reducing health inequalities would benefit all of society by reducing the incidence of spillover effects. Woodward and Kawachi conclude: 'A society that tolerates a steep socioeconomic gradient in health outcomes will experience a drag on improvements in life expectancy, and pay the cost via excess health care utilisation.'[71]

All of the health inequalities described and their spillover effects will have significant impacts on social care, which has been an ongoing national crisis for decades. This has been compounded by an ageing population, a declining number of hospital beds and the responsibility having been shifted from hospitals to cash-strapped local authorities. It has been made worse by devastating losses to local services from cuts in central government funding, at a time when demand for services has soared. Austerity cuts have also forced responsibility for social care to be shifted onto families. Cuts were more severe in deprived areas while spending in fact increased in more affluent ones, which means our respondents were unlikely to notice.[72] However, it's crucial for high earners to understand that the crisis in social care has a direct effect on the speed at which acute hospital services can meet patient needs. A collapsed healthcare system slows down the discharge process, which in turn leads to fewer available beds and increased waiting times. Marmot warns: 'if health has stopped improving it is a sign that society has stopped improving. Evidence from around the world shows that health is a good measure of social and economic progress. When a society is flourishing, health tends to flourish.'[73]

Education

Millennials are the first generation not to achieve the progress their predecessors enjoyed, on a number of living standard measures, including pay stagnation, a shift towards less-well-paid and precarious employment, lower home-ownership rates and higher housing costs (spending a quarter of their income on housing).[74] Since 2012, there has also been a noticeable decline in real terms spending on education, falling by about 14% to its

2005–06 level, with the biggest drops found in education for 16- to 18-year-olds.[75] Higher education funding has also been erratic, with cuts to the sector offset by the tripling of tuition fees after 2011. This has given the UK the second most expensive higher education system in the OECD, only after the US. Nevertheless, spending specifically on higher education has little effect on educational achievement. At best, higher education institutions can only partly compensate for the effects of inequalities that start early in students' lives. While Millennials are the best-educated generation in history, the cohort-on-cohort gains experienced by Generation X have not been reproduced. The 37% increase in degree attainment recorded between the 1969–71 and 1972–74 cohorts fell to just a 7% improvement between those born in the early and late 1980s. And as the Intergenerational Commission pointed out, 'non-degree routes have not picked up the slack'.[76]

Despite acknowledging their luck in having access to a university grant, avoiding the levels of educational debt seen today, and joining the labour market before the current credential inflation, our respondents nevertheless underplayed the importance of networks and social capital accessed by attending top universities and private schools, which seem to be ever more important. Many seemed to retain a belief in meritocracy and education as its vehicle.

Whenever we asked for the drivers of poverty, education was at the forefront, regardless of the fact that we have seen declining real wages and casualisation in parallel to increasing educational attainment. In a recent poll by *The New Statesman*, 60% of British people believe that an individual can change their social class in their lifetime, despite only 25% saying they have themselves changed class. The poll results also demonstrated that young people in the UK are becoming less confident about their future: 'Many worry they will never be financially stable, a rising proportion don't feel in control of their lives, and nearly half feel hopeless because of unemployment.'[77] Jonathan Mijs, assistant professor of sociology at Boston University, who specialises in perceptions of meritocracy and inequality, attributes this to a gap between aspiration, belief and lived experience. 'Perhaps they believe they will climb the ladder at some future time, or maybe their belief stems from the many stories of upward mobility that reach them through social media, TV and film; the exceptions to the rule that keep their hopes alive.'[78]

While some of our respondents might be able to afford private schools and save for their children's university fees, they were aware that it was getting harder to gain admission and pay for university education, and to get a well-paying job on the basis of your degree after graduation. The extent of elitism in our education system is illustrated by the 48 out of 211 sixth formers from Eton who got Oxbridge places in 2021, roughly the same number who got in out of the UK's estimated 33,250 state school sixth formers claiming free school meals.[79] Unsurprisingly, top private schools' alumni go on to monopolise senior positions in elite professional, financial and managerial jobs.[80] For example, only 7% of children attend private schools, yet 70% of judges went to one. In the US, something similar applies. Lauren Rivera's *Pedigree: How 'Elite' Students Get 'Elite' Jobs* demonstrates 'that the way in which elite employers define and evaluate merit when hiring strongly tilts the playing field for the nation's highest paying jobs toward children from socioeconomically privileged backgrounds'.[81] This includes recruiting primarily from a select number of universities, themselves accessible to a privileged few.

Crisis of democracy

Between 2016 and 2022, Britain saw one historic referendum, two general elections, five prime ministers and a chaotically handled pandemic. A large percentage of the population are disillusioned by British democracy and unsure whether 'business as usual' can simply continue. Just as monopolies have become the norm in the economy, so too in our democracy. Without fundamental change, many foresee the alternative will be either greater xenophobic nationalism or a privatised technocracy (or both).[82]

The continuity of a well-functioning democracy requires safeguards designed to ensure that a government cannot do too much damage during its term of office or subvert the democratic process to prolong itself. These safeguards are under threat or already becoming weaker and, if we are not careful, there is nothing to prevent the UK from turning into a 'managed democracy'. In the past years, parliamentary scrutiny has also been under threat. A clear example is the unlawful prorogation of parliament to avoid its scrutiny of Boris Johnson's plan to leave the EU without an agreed deal on 31 October 2019. Another is the resignation of two of Johnson's ethics advisers within two years, due to being unable to support his breaches of the ministerial code.[83]

The integrity of our democracy is also maintained by regulatory review, most importantly by the Electoral Commission, the formerly independent body that is meant to ensure that elections are free and fair. However, in 2021, it was announced by the government that the commission would be stripped of its powers to propose criminal prosecutions, and be overseen by a Conservative-dominated committee of MPs.[84] This attack is seen partly as a result of the commission calling the Conservatives to account for irregularities in the Brexit referendum.

The Conservatives have been in Number 10 for 63% of the time since 1950, despite receiving 41% of the votes cast throughout this duration, compared to Labour's 40%. Most votes went to parties to the left of the Conservatives in 18 of the 19 general elections in this period.[85] In 2017, under our current voting system, only 11% of constituencies changed hands: the remainder were 'safe' for the incumbent party. Under the current first-past-the-post system, 70% of votes are not counted and therefore wasted.[86]

In 2019, the Conservatives gained power with less than 44% of the vote. On average, 38,264 votes were needed to elect one Conservative MP in the last election, while that figure was 50,835 votes for Labour, 336,038 for the Liberal Democrats, and 865,000 to elect Caroline Lucas, Britain's only Green Party MP (2.7% of votes returning 0.2% parliamentary seats). Those campaigning for a more democratic voting system refer to this pattern as the 'inverted pyramid of power'.[87] Voters are starting to question how democratic our electoral system is and the possibility of reforming it is increasingly becoming 'a doorstep issue', certainly among younger voters.

Speaking one's mind, critically challenging government decisions and protesting peacefully are a vital part of a healthy free society. However, the pandemic has been used as a moment to, as Mark Thomas says, 'chip away' rights and silence dissent.[88]

In 2021, in just 48 hours, the Policing Bill, the Elections Bill, and the Nationality and Borders Bill were introduced with the government at risk of turning the UK into one of the only countries in Europe without a right to peaceful protest.

At the same time, three quarters of the UK press is controlled by three people: Lord Rothermere, Rupert Murdoch and the Barclay family. All of them present a consistently right-wing view of public events and issues, 'that of a handful of wealthy individuals based outside the UK, whose personal objectives bear no relationship to those of 99% of the population'.[89] On top of this dominance of the right in the press, the party that has been in power for 12 years is now consulting on plans to stifle whistle-blowers and journalists who might embarrass the government by leaking details of its activities.

The 1998 Human Rights Act, the main piece of law that protects freedoms and human rights in the UK, is also being replaced with a British Bill of Rights. With this new Bill, the duty to ensure that legislation is compatible with rights and freedoms will no longer exist. Public bodies will have no obligation to respect such rights and neither will the courts have to follow European judgments. This has profound implications for the devolution settlements, which legally require active compliance with the European Convention on Human Rights, especially the Good Friday Agreement that has guaranteed peace in Northern Ireland. The politics of devolution is already fragile. In May 2022, Sinn Féin won the most seats – and first preference votes – in the Northern Ireland Assembly election, becoming the first pro-reunification party to win an Assembly election in Stormont, while the Scottish National Party and the Scottish Greens enjoy a healthy pro-independence majority in Holyrood. In short, as Stephen Gethins puts it: 'The UK is in trouble. Voters have backed an independence referendum in Scotland and a Northern Irish party seeking Irish reunification. But you would never know it if you listened to debate and discussion at Westminster.'[90]

Our respondents tended not to mention any of these ways in which democracy has been undermined, although they did discuss the relationship between the press and the right wing of politics. They were not activists and did not attend protests so they were unlikely to be aware of the freedoms being curtailed.

However, they did feel isolated from politics, and did not think that they were represented. Those in Scotland conveyed an added lack of identification with British politics. Post-pandemic, they were also aware that Boris Johnson's position had repeatedly been undermined by scandal, but there was a sense that there was no alternative.

We can't solve collective problems individually

Data tell us that while economic development and rising living standards are important drivers of wellbeing in the developing world, having more makes less of a difference to wellbeing in richer countries.[91] The weight of evidence also shows that economic growth in the UK has slowed markedly and that the fruits of whatever growth we had went overwhelmingly to very few at the top.

Despite being concerned about the societal effects of inequality, few if any high earners can envision how to make Britain's economy and politics more equal, robust, resilient and free. Nevertheless, it is clear the most serious problems we face are too big for any one segment of society, or perhaps even one country, to deal with. The climate emergency has been aptly described as 'a collective action problem on steroids',[92] and one that will have to be navigated by the whole of society and even the whole global community.

Problems such as climate change are too big for any one group in society to address, no matter how influential that group might be. And crucially, solutions designed in isolation won't work. Designing policies to tackle climate change, for example, without corresponding policies to address inequality, will not work. Reducing inequality, on the other hand, will increase the wellbeing of entire populations, which will in turn lessen their environmental impact.

In other words, those in positions of power in government and political parties need to formulate policies that work not only to improve life for their own demographic, but for their children too. Even if Labour forms a future government with a huge majority, it is unlikely to set out a programme of sufficient structural change to enable this to happen. Nowhere is this starker than in the need for collective agency on climate change. This requires both that we think again about what governments can do for us and that those in government rethink their own role. Why and why now? Because, regardless of their shortcomings, only states have the capacity to bring about the scale of change needed to address a problem the size of climate change. They can and should take on the strategic leadership role in living a cheaper, easier, more tranquil life, moving towards net zero. Part of this means bringing stakeholders together across the economy and civil society, part of it means providing better education and awareness to signal the extent of behavioural change that will be needed in schools, businesses and organisations.

Nevertheless, most responses to recent and ongoing crises have been personal rather than collective. Rather than cumulative, concerted action on the environment, individual actions such as recycling have tended to be prioritised. This is especially the case among high earners, a group that feels increasingly isolated, living by an ethos that prioritises hard work, mobility, individual responsibility, flexibility and accumulating resources to improve their own circumstances. The next chapter looks in more detail at those strategies.

6

Jumping ship, but where to?

This chapter explores what respondents told us about their experiences of weathering shocks in the past: the financial crash in 2008, Brexit and the pandemic. We reflect on how they might act when facing similar shocks in the future and whether these approaches will remain effective. We begin by talking about the ability to be mobile and competitive.

Mobility

High earners see being flexible enough to move as a means of ensuring they continue to thrive, including relocating abroad. This 'brain drain' mirrors the capital mobility that is the foundation of the UK's financialised and internationalised economic model, explains the magnetic pull of the City of London, and underpins the view that any turn to the left would cause capital flight.[1] When we first interviewed Alan in 2019, a 50-year-old director of a logistics company living in the south-east, he was considering the benefits of higher tax countries: "A progressive tax system, not an outrageous tax system. Not a tax rate of 95% at the top that doesn't encourage wealth creation. There should be balances. We should be like Nordic countries. High taxation but high benefits as well." By the time of our follow-up, in early 2022, he had moved to Finland.

One consequence of this mobility is that, while high earners may anticipate a crisis, they almost never think that it will affect them personally. As Ben, a 39-year-old IT consultant living in the south-east explains, he can rely on his membership to a globally competitive and mobile workforce:

'For my own future within the UK, I'm pessimistic. Brexit is a big factor colouring that [...]. My wife is Bulgarian so my daughter can also have Bulgarian nationality. If things go badly, it's not too difficult to move. If it goes really badly in the UK, I can see us moving overseas.'

However, relying on mobility as a strategy to avoid crises in a post-Brexit, post-COVID-19 world may prove increasingly difficult. Some respondents expressed insecurity about the impact of Brexit: they saw it as an event that could affect them personally. When interviewed about his views on the future before the pandemic, Sean, the 40-year-old owner of an HR company in the top 1%, told us: "I feel pessimistic about the future of my country and optimistic about my future. However, depending on the outcome of Brexit that may change to both being pessimistic."

His fears were not unjustified. When we interviewed him again after the pandemic, his plans to move to Gran Canaria had been thwarted by Brexit. As immigration policies become more restrictive across much of the world – whether because of the pandemic, war, refugee crises or old-fashioned immigrant scapegoating – many in the top 10% may also see their capacity to move curtailed, even if their wealth and educational credentials are considered.

Mobility also has limited long-term value as a strategy against climate change. As we mentioned earlier, our respondents rarely brought up unprompted the issue of climate, and when they did, it was generally cursorily. However, the scale of the challenge cannot be ignored for long. Michael, a 49-year-old engineer, just in the top 10% living in the south-west and one of only a few to mention the topic, said: "We're all strapped to the same planet!"

Insulation

Not all high earners can physically move away from societal and economic shocks. They may not have the skills required in other markets, the capacity to simply pack bags and go, or may have dependants keeping them in place. So what are the alternatives? The first is to try and insulate themselves from the worst effects of such crises. William, a management consultant and a top 1% earner in his forties, found that even though his team had disappeared overnight after the 2008 crisis, the first salvo of this new era, he still kept his job. Maria, a marketing director also in her forties on a top 3% income, felt she had been "insulated" from the 2008 crisis as, while her department had been reduced, she had simply moved to another part of the firm. Alan, a 50-year-old director of a logistics company, also in the top 3%, confessed that the crisis had "bypassed him" but felt that "in services and its effects, it is not over for normal people".

This insulation from 'normal people' is worth teasing out. Luke, 27, spent the first part of his life in a private school, enlisted in the army, then attended Oxbridge. He was later a teacher in the Teach First programme before starting work as a consultant for a large accountancy firm. He told us that his background meant he doesn't really think about inequality on a daily basis. He comes from a privileged upbringing and all his friends do too. He does not interact with anyone outside his socioeconomic group, although he did when he was a teacher: "It was clear I was teaching kids with very different lives." Yet Luke was still surprised to find his income placed him in the top 8% of income distribution. He thought more people would be above him and, looking for a house to buy in London at the time, he didn't feel particularly affluent.

In addition, high earners were also insulated from the pandemic by being more likely to be able to work from home, thus reducing the risk of catching Covid while saving on commuting and other costs.[2] It also allowed them to save or invest in their homes. Amazon sales went through the roof at the same time as COVID-19 deaths tended to concentrate among the most vulnerable groups in society.[3] Michael, the engineer with a top 10% income quoted earlier, said that he tries to make his life "as bulletproof as possible, not too sensitive to global conditions or local ones". By the time of our follow-up interview, Paul, an architect just in the top 10% income band when we first interviewed him, had moved into the top 3% in 2022. While his practice had suffered initially, a government loan allowed it to stay in business. During the lockdowns, he had also taken a consultancy, "cashing in on his experience". As a result, when asked if the cost of living crisis had affected him, he said "I feel quite well-off. There has been significant improvement in my income."

During the lockdowns, better-off families reduced consumption to a greater degree than poorer ones, as they tended to spend a higher proportion of their income on social goods and services that were less available during the pandemic such as restaurants and leisure travel. Meanwhile, lower-income families deploy a larger percentage of their earnings on essentials that cannot be reduced, such as food, bills and housing. It was the same with the wealth of the richest. During the pandemic, 'a typical family in the richest 10% of families experienced an increase in the value of their wealth by £44,000 per adult'.[4]

If the pandemic had any positive potential, it was to bring to bear the importance of low-paid key workers and instil in us a greater sense of social solidarity. However, and more tangibly, it threatened to exacerbate the increasing inequalities of the past decades. It also risked insulating the top 10% even more than they were before: their only social interaction with those on lower incomes being their status as clients (of the gig economy and delivery services, for instance).

Some of the high earners we spoke with think inequality has diminished between the lower and middle classes, citing increased material consumption of cars and TVs as evidence. Nevertheless, they also think it's growing between the very wealthiest and the rest, though only a few, such as Maria, were explicit about the scale of inequality in the UK and its destabilising effects: "I think what is really key in the last 10 years, maybe 20 years, is [that] the difference between CEO pay and executive-level pay and people on the shop floor is totally ridiculous and unsustainable. And this creates a big sense of animosity."

Isolation

High earners are generally not tied to one local community: this in itself holds a status that extends to other areas of life, such as independence from public services. As Alan, a logistics company director in his fifties living in the south-east with a top 3% income, put it: "[I]solation from social context is something that only the very wealthiest can achieve." Respondents often commuted from areas largely segregated by income. If they live in a mixed-income area, long working hours, especially in the corporate sector, don't allow them to make time for their local communities. The rules of climbing the ladder are applied as much to parenting and to time spent outside work. Rachel, a treasurer for a multinational organisation with a top 1% income, when asked whether she mixes with people from different socioeconomic backgrounds, responded: "How much interaction are we talking about? Friends and family? No. But my kids go to the local swimming pool on a poor estate and I happily participate with other parents. My son goes to their houses to play."

These segregated realities are also true for high earners' online lives. If working from home, high earners tend to subscribe to networks of similar professionals. Our social media narrows down, reinforces and feeds back to us what we want to read. This phenomenon, which has come to be called the 'echo chambers', is as true for high-achieving, highly educated individuals who feel well informed as for everyone else. In fact, research has shown that the more political media people consume, the more mistaken they are about the other side's perspectives.[5] That is partly why election results seem to always take us by surprise.

One of the consequences of this isolation may be high earners' lack of sociological imagination discussed earlier. Douglas, who has worked in the public sector for most of his career, was one of the few, for example, to comment on the unequal impact of the pandemic: "Middle-class people were phoning for pizzas to be delivered by poorer people. [COVID-19's impact] very much depended on your occupation [...]. The people screwed were those not able to furlough whose wage rates had been squeezed."

The competitive pressures of work and the status of busyness, of not having time, of being quick on your feet act as a barrier to connecting with others. Hannah, a 44-year-old occupational health consultant, living in the south-east and earning just above the 10% threshold, reflected:

'We're all so busy running around, living our individual lives and I for one have such little time to do what I feel

I need to do, that I haven't got anything left. I think part of this is because of increased expectations [...] the hours that people commute, the hours they spend at work [...] we don't have the same connections.'

Hannah's comments chime with a pervasive sense of the increased pace of life among our respondents, something that sociologist Hartmut Rosa has written extensively about. Acceleration is one of the key features of modern society; changes in technology, social tendencies and the pace of life render our lives harder to predict and our commitments more fluid.[6] The desire for a simpler, happier past is shared across generations – with around 70% of people in each age category holding this view today – which may explain the appeal of those politicians who wish to bring back an imaginary view of the 'good old days'.[7]

Meanwhile, much of life outside work is reduced to what David Graeber referred to as 'compensatory consumerism': 'pumping iron or attending a yoga class at the local gym, ordering out from Deliveroo, watching an episode of Game of Thrones, or shopping for hand creams or consumer electronics'.[8] Similarly, sociologist Robert Putnam wrote that there's been a 'striking shift in how we allocate time – toward ourselves and our immediate family and away from the wider community'.[9] Besides the well-documented decline in involvement in organisations such as clubs, political groups, unions or churches, there may also have been a reduction in the amount of time spent informally interacting face-to-face with others outside our immediate circles such as our neighbours. This is happening in all groups, with a corresponding decline in the availability and quality of public spaces such as public libraries and swimming pools.[10]

All of these tendencies mean it's increasingly rare for high earners to get to know people outside their usual interaction with friends, family, work and education, especially when other networks (such as those based on religion or hobbies) either dwindle or move online. Considering this group's disproportionate political influence, this is not innocuous. In unequal societies, how people treat each other is affected by income differences; there is less social mixing, less social mobility and less respect granted to those from different social strata. Research on the wealthy in Paris,

São Paulo and Delhi has shown this.[11] In addition, marriages between people from different socioeconomic backgrounds are less common, with an increase in what sociologists call 'assortative mating'.[12] There is also more residential segregation. We are more separated from each other – culturally, socially and physically. We become increasingly worried about how people judge us relative to others and social contact is more stressful. As a result, everyone keeps more to themselves.

Unequal societies also have poorer mental health, with higher rates of psychotic conditions, narcissism, lack of confidence, low self-esteem, depression, and anxiety.[13] People trust each other less, and less trust means more stress. Although the top 10% may be floating away in their own socioeconomic bubble, that mistrust still engulfs them: it's both the cause and consequence of their isolation. Our respondent Hannah also told us: "The other thing that stops me from doing other things is also fear. We've also become much more fearful of being involved with other people and of putting ourselves out there to do something."

In highly unequal countries, which the UK is increasingly becoming, we are less likely to be helpful to each other; community life deteriorates and violence is more common. A vague but ever-present fear manifests itself in, among other things, the higher percentage of the labour force employed in guarding duties.[14] At their worst, these fears end up fuelling trends such as the increasing demand for bunkers for the rich in far-off countries such as New Zealand to prepare for a post-apocalyptic world.[15] Maria, a marketing director with a top 3% income, was one of several respondents to voice concerns about insecurity and civic unrest: "if you don't distribute that wealth then you get inequality and then there's discontent. Then, once you get discontent you get civil unrest and then, you know [...] slippery slope."

What these strategies of insulation, isolation and social distancing all achieve, however unintentionally, is a decline in trust. Even high earners cannot live without trust. It is a needed component of not only large and complex societies but also of the economy itself. Any transaction that's more than just a face-to-face barter of goods depends on trust, as the goods and services being exchanged will be separated in time and place. Trust is both more essential and more fragile in the modern economy where distances and chains of connections have been stretched even further and we will need to build appropriate institutions to strengthen it.[16] Figure 6.1 portrays a nightmare vision of what happens in a world of bunkers without trust and a functioning public realm.

Figure 6.1: 'Daddy!' by Peter Schrank

Source: © Peter Schrank/The Independent

Enabling the wealthy

Many in the top 10% have jobs whose purpose is to service, support and protect the wealth of the top 1%. Indeed, whole cottage industries have sprung up to supply the needs and whims of those with the most capital: from furnishers of high-end consumer products to family offices concentrated in London that provide expert services to manage the wealth of some of the highest-net-worth individuals in the world. As we saw in Chapter 3, quite a few high earners also see the public role of the private sector only as paying taxes, increasing value for shareholders and creating jobs. Wang, a doctor and entrepreneur, was very clear on this:

> 'The system is clearly engineered for the benefit of the wealthy. Skewed to the benefit of wealthy investors. I don't believe in trickle-down. It just leads to accumulation of wealth. Having integrated with the wealthy, society creates these structures to accommodate the desire of the wealthy to stay wealthy.'

However, this subservience to the wealthy does not only apply to accountants, corporate lawyers, hedge fund managers or other such professions. It is also true of us, the authors, and other cultural sector workers, academics, doctors, scientists and economists who facilitate the status quo. They make living in the capital more attractive, driving the concentration of talent and housing market speculation. Their parents have often sought to bequeath their children a fighting chance in a labour market where qualifications and expertise on their own cannot guarantee access to good jobs. And they work for organisations that are often owned, funded or overseen by the truly wealthy and well connected. For instance, anyone with experience in the charitable sector will know that many of those working or volunteering within it tend to be quite wealthy themselves and unlikely to challenge the interests of the top 1%.[17]

This enabling of the wealthy also applies to the way knowledge is produced in academia and extramural organisations. Be it because of funding priorities, disciplinary fads, or the pressures of peer review, much of the way that policy-relevant knowledge is produced has traditionally tended to speak to a narrow community of specialists or be critical in a way that allows access to a professional niche but doesn't achieve much else. Ghosh and Ambler put it this way for the case of economics: 'Much of the mainstream discipline has been in the service of power, effectively the power of the wealthy, at national and international levels. By "assuming away" critical concerns, theoretical results and problematic empirical analyses effectively reinforce power structures and imbalances.'[18]

One of the most successful things that the wealthy have done is, in the words of polemicist Owen Jones, to 'persuade the middle class that they're middle class too'.[19] When politicians talk about middle England, they are not always talking about people on median incomes, but actually about affluent voters in 'upper-class Britain' – they are the 'middle class' in the British sense of the term, after all. This is how tax rises on incomes over £80,000 can be presented as an attack on middle Britain, even though 19 out of 20 of us earn less than that.

However, while they often work for and with the wealthiest, the interests of the top 10% are and will become increasingly quite different. It's in the interest of the top 10% for education to provide genuine opportunities, for housing to be affordable, for work to pay well, for society to remain minimally flexible and open to new people and views, for there to be a functioning and transparent state, and for there to be a democracy at all. It's not difficult to think of modern authoritarian countries where the 1% is very well catered for, whether living in gated communities or free zones. Maria, quoted earlier, comments on the end result of a highly unequal distribution of income: "Even from an economic point of view if those people haven't got money they're not going to be buying your goods and services. So on a basic level, get with the programme [...] these people need to have a decent life [...] otherwise your circle's going to run out."

Notwithstanding the 'othering' evident in the reference to 'these people' in Maria's statement, she is one of the few to articulate that if those on a lower income don't have enough income then this affects the whole economy. Similarly, Paul, who as an architect was sensitive to housing trends, and living between Liverpool and London was able to contrast them, commented on the relationship between wealth and the unsustainability of extreme gentrification:

'It's not possible for a city to survive for any extended period of time if it only meets the needs of a small, wealthy minority. Even the most abstract financial service work depends upon an infrastructure of waged and unwaged care labour; even unoccupied trophy housing requires ongoing maintenance to keep deterioration at bay. A relative handful of high-wage jobs and so-called high-net-worth individuals cannot keep a city going, to say nothing about questions of justice.'[20]

Accumulating and hoarding

Inequality increases our concern with status and the importance of money. In her book *Get It Together*, journalist Zoe Williams states that 'wanting stuff is basically social' because it is a way of sending signals to each other about who we are. However, we can't simply flaunt our possessions. Signalling 'I can afford this thing, therefore I'm the best,' is an isolating, not a social-inducing act. The designer bag, or whatever it is, the purpose of which is to distinguish us from others, ends up also separating us from them. The satisfaction in owning it is therefore temporary.[21]

We saw how this 'compensatory consumption' took on a particular meaning as a coping mechanism during the pandemic, with online consumption, particularly for household items, as a means of spending unused income. When asked if his spending had changed during the pandemic, Paul replied "lots of online shopping". Sean, a 1% income earner and owner of an HR company, when asked the same question, similarly replied: "Everyone has been telling me how much they saved. I don't think I saved any money. Everything was online. Constant online purchasing – from basics, to gifts, to clothing. When the doorbell rang, and the Amazon man was coming, that was the most exciting part of the day."

Michael, a chief engineer, whose income had also increased from just below 6% to just above it due to an internal promotion,[22] also confirmed what national data tell us, that high earners had more disposable income and could save or replenish resources: "We have had much more disposable income than we have ever had. What we did, if anything needed repairing or replacing – a 'fortification mentality'. We kept a stockpile of food and wine and every bit of equipment or clothing that wasn't good enough, we replaced."

Improving wellbeing through consumption thus puts pressure on high earners' ability to keep up with an expected lifestyle and its costs. As money becomes ever more important, status anxiety begins to rear its head, which leads to longer working hours, more debt and more bankruptcies.[23] Paul describes how easy it is:

> 'People can think "If I had one million, I could buy [...] a flat in London [...] so maybe I need five or ten or 50 million." That is the spiral they're in [...] They want palpably more, but when you have had it taken away, it makes you realise you can live without these things, you think "What's important?"'

Some of the high earners we spoke to were starting to question consumption, not for its influence on their lives but for its impact on the climate. We know that their lifestyle choices and consumption patterns mean that high earners are responsible for a disproportionate number of emissions. Globally, the richest 10% accounted for over half (52%) of emissions between 1990 and 2015. The richest 1% were responsible for 15% during this time – more than all the citizens of the EU and more than twice that of the poorest half of humanity (7%).[24] What will happen if unlimited growth remains a national goal? Economist Kate Raworth points out that even the *Daily Mail*, perhaps the most influential right-wing tabloid, references a study published in 1972 that predicted business as usual would lead to a collapse of society by 2040.[25]

Social reproduction

Michael, a 49-year-old engineer just in the top 10%, living in the south-west, told us that "most rich people's time and money is spent maintaining status". This includes their children. However, as outlined earlier, access to elite education and housing is becoming ever more expensive. By way of illustration, the UK has the fourth highest childcare costs in the OECD. Net childcare costs for a working couple with two children, as a percentage of the average wage, and including benefits, are 28% in Ireland, 7% in Spain, 5% in Sweden and 36% in the UK.[26]

The correlation between economic disadvantage and poor educational attainment is particularly strong in the UK. One fifth of children in England on free school meals do not reach the expected maths level at age seven. The ability to choose schools is still a prerogative of better-off families. From the 1980s, the UK slowly introduced market policies into education (driven by consumer demand fuelled by league tables), ensuring that the middle class became the major beneficiaries of the best state schools. The education system continues to focus on 40% of students who take A-levels (the British non-compulsory qualifications usually taken after the age of 16). Furthermore, while the economic return to getting a degree has not fallen and the greatest social mobility gains come to people with degrees, not all such qualifications guarantee economic security.[27]

Seven per cent of children go to private schools in the UK, the majority of which have parents with a top 10% income.[28] They have three times as much spent on their schools than the average child in the other 93%. More money is spent on private education in Britain than almost anywhere else on the planet. Elite education is seen as the primary vehicle of upward (and protection against downward) mobility. From a very young age, the segregating and hot-housing of some children has a powerful and damaging effect on them.[29] In the UK, as less is being spent on the education of the majority, more are likely to drop out earlier. This is seen in the fall in the number of teenagers staying on in school and an increase in young people not in education or training.

Countries with bigger income differences have bigger differences in educational performance and lower average levels of educational attainment overall.[30] This is because differences in ability among people at different levels in the income hierarchy are produced by the hierarchy itself. Position in the hierarchy determines ability, interests and talents rather than the other way around. Each layer in the income hierarchy tends to do less well than those above it. In other words, this strategy is not just bad for those who don't do so well, it is bad for everyone, including high earners.

However, the ideas that anyone can get on, that differences in ability are the main influence on where people end up in society, believing that all those 'at the top' are naturally endowed with the 'right stuff' and that we should judge worth, ability and intelligence from a person's position are all potent.[31] This makes the chances of those currently at the top being open to alternatives to the status quo even more unlikely, unless they are presented with convincing and attractive alternatives (something that isn't happening at the moment).

Markets in everything

High earners continue to portray the public sector as unresponsive, slow and inefficient. Phrases such as 'you wouldn't get away with those inefficiencies in the private sector' were typical. This attitude is used as justification to use private services. Sean, a 1% income earner and owner of an HR company, comments: "I'll be honest, I have a private GP and any medical attention I've had the NHS has failed to deliver. So, I've gone private."

Some told us that they would rely even more on the private sector if its costs weren't out of reach. In our interview before the pandemic, Maria told us how she had defended her daughter's local state school from parents who had been complaining about it, by reminding them of the impact of funding cuts. In our follow-up, she told us that her daughter had now moved to a private school following the receipt of some inheritance. She rationalised the move by telling us that her daughter's potential had not been fulfilled at her previous school. She had been just a 'tick in a box'. The bureaucratic approach referenced by Maria and the corresponding reduced attention on children has partly come about, not just from under-resourcing but also by embedding competition into our social and economic institutions. In education, this has manifested in a preoccupation with Ofsted[32] ratings and performance league tables and associated distortion of housing prices that fall within certain schools' catchment areas. In turn, this creates 'sink' schools, with additional bureaucracy imposed on teachers already under pressure from class sizes and the challenges of under-resourced environments. High earners will have to question the assumption that public services can be resolved through further efficiency.

There is also an ongoing myth that government welfare spending is on those who are unemployed. In fact, in the financial year ending 2017, the single biggest item of spending was pensions, at 42%, while 1% went to unemployment benefits.[33] In 2020/21, of the £1,094 billion total spent by the government, £20 billion went to social protection.[34] At 28% of its GDP, the UK has the sixth highest ratio among the countries spending most on social protection in Europe.[35] Before the pandemic, there was a similar belief that spending on health was at runaway levels. As any cursory research will show, its increase as a share of total government spending is largely because of the UK's demographics and its health inequalities.

Research on the NHS demonstrates that it is under-resourced compared to other countries. In fact, it '[still] lags well behind other nations in a number of key areas that materially affect a country's ability to improve the health of its population'.[36] In 2018, the King's Fund found that the NHS has fewer doctors and nurses per capita than 21 other countries.[37] It also invests comparatively little in technology such as MRI and CT scans. While the media continues to cover the failures of emergency response times, and more than a tenth of the population is waiting for treatment (the highest since records began) the question that high earners should actually ask is 'not why doesn't the NHS perform better compared to other health systems but how does it manage to perform so well [...] when it is clearly under-resourced'.[38]

The NHS is of course also an interventionist system established to address problems *once they are there* in the population. Any preventive health systems have long been marginalised as was seen in the response to COVID-19. Studies of poorer but more equal countries with better health outcomes than the UK show that *equality is key to improving everyone's health*. Higher average material standards no longer improve wellbeing. Except under conditions of austerity, there is also little to no correlation between national income and changes in life expectancy.[39] What this research shows is that economic growth will not in itself reduce socioeconomic inequalities for developed countries.

Continuing with the individualistic, market-first, high-inequality paradigm that the UK has been stuck in, and which the government plans more of through deregulation, tax cuts and further austerity for public services will drive up inequality but do nothing to improve the lives of the majority.[40] Redistributing resources through environmental, economic and social intervention provides more plausible and popular answers to the country's challenges. This would include continuing to develop alternatives to big business, such as employee or public ownership, reinvigorating cooperation, and mutual organisations. Continuing on the same track will only give us more of what we already have: health inequalities and increasing long-term economic costs resulting from disability, ill-health and healthcare.

High earners also show little awareness of the consequences of private sector involvement in our public services, in the way that government itself has become financialised, whether through the privatisation of pensions schemes and our health service, the marketisation of higher education or through private finance initiatives (PFIs) — all taking liabilities off the public books and placing them with private investors. As a rule, for them, more private-sector involvement means less pressure on the public sector. In actuality, governments reduce their creditworthiness over the long term by having to show credit ratings to financial markets. Otherwise, they risk bond sell-offs and a run on their currencies, but, as Blakeley points out, this often doesn't matter to markets, as the time horizons of finance capitalism are shorter than at any other period in history.[41]

Collective denial

High earners' narratives often portray the belief that there is little that can be done about the crises we are facing. This is because they believe that impersonal forces create them, that they are driven by global or technical change out of our control, or they are governed by a 'natural' and inescapable economic logic. They do not factor in the political and ideological decisions and processes that have created a massive imbalance between employees and those who own companies and the extremely unequal distribution of income and wealth that results from them. Neither do they fully acknowledge what the financial crisis and then the pandemic have shown: that state-provided liquidity and full-on bailouts can be used effectively and are even necessary for the functioning of that logic.[42] The state has proven capacity to spend where there is the political will to do so, despite the persistence of pro-austerity interpretations of how governments work.[43]

Since 2020, some of the misunderstandings about government debt and the capacity of its spending are beginning to be demystified. Taking a look at how countries not far from us are handling the current crisis will show that costs are sky-high in the UK largely because of monopolies controlling key sectors, not least energy. Yet, there is still little recognition of – much less action taken on – the power that companies controlling our infrastructure have to design regulatory and tax policy in their favour. There is also little acknowledgement of the connection between that influence and increasing inequality. As long as high-earning voters do not recognise these connections, the obvious solutions will not be taken up. These include taxing excess profits, revising subsidies, or preventing share buybacks.[44]

Asking our respondents, in 2018–19, what public services they use, they would refer to having their bins collected or going to the park. Few mentioned social or physical infrastructure such as transport or public health. Most who had access to it (generally as a benefit from their employment) used private healthcare. Others asked what was meant by public services. Since the pandemic, the benefit of public goods and the cost of externalities – such as polluted rivers or air, or insufficient public healthcare provision – have been pushed to the top of the agenda. We are seeing more questions such as these on mainstream media: what happens when essential goods and services are in the hands of a few private companies? Should we spend more on long-term infrastructure projects? How do we make the nation more resilient to global supply crises? What are the effects of market failure in key sectors of our economy?

However, little has been done to encourage the electorate to think more radically and expansively about progress and prosperity, to talk about the purpose of wealth production and whether it really enhances wellbeing.[45] We are rarely encouraged to imagine alternative views to the mainstream consensus on how our economy is run – to do so is to be unserious. Markets have become embedded in our social and democratic choices to the extent that we have "drifted from having a market economy to being a market society".[46] This is especially the case for the top 10%. They often don't recognise market failures as they happen because they are the ones who often *give a voice* to these markets: as economists, as policy experts, as traders, as consultants, as journalists. And if all is kind of okay for them, all is good for everyone else. However, as Robert Reich has warned about the US:

> If the pandemic has revealed anything, it's that America's current social safety net and health care system does not protect the majority of Americans in a national emergency. We are the outlier among the world's advanced nations in subjecting our citizens to perpetual insecurity. We are also the outlier in possessing a billionaire class that, in controlling much of our politics, has kept such proposals off the public agenda.[47]

In other words, vested interests in highly unequal countries, such as the UK and the US, have a fear of enlarging the nation's sense of what is reasonable for the government to do for its citizens. And that is why, for example, the public have not been given any serious hopes about the government's role in investing in the UK's adaptation to climate change or to expect it to lead in a green industrial revolution in areas such as hydrogen, electric vehicles, decarbonising or renewable energies. Previous governments ended onshore wind projects, cut solar subsidies and slashed energy-efficient schemes, referred to as 'the green crap',[48] Truss's short-lived government even announced a commitment to extract 'every last drop of oil and gas' and lift the ban on fracking.[49] In the meantime, while we are in the slow lane, other European countries are moving ahead with adapting much more quickly. This will be to their advantage: the price of solar and wind energy, for example, is nine times cheaper than gas.[50]

High earners, as much as any other part of the British public, are used to putting their trust in elected representatives, the media and experts. In their case, this is perhaps even more natural, as these institutions are populated by people like them. They 'nod along' when politicians, media commentators and academics tell them that better wages for more people and a better-regulated financial system aren't possible because the country will lose competitiveness, jobs will disappear and they will suffer.[51] This is the version of events along the lines of, quoting philosopher Michael Sandel, 'whether we like it or not, the world is governed by neoliberal ideas, and that won't change. There's no point fighting the inevitable.'[52] What they are left with is the trickle-down argument that 'once the economy has picked up, living standards will improve'. This has endured for decades as common sense and is still pervasive, despite being widely discredited, even by US President Joe Biden.[53]

High earners need to push back on the related argument that we have to accept lower wages and everyone will have to accept cutbacks to important public services. The UK has enormous amounts of wealth (indeed, it lives off wealth; for instance, through a property market propped up by international investors); it is just very poorly distributed. Until these inequities are addressed, the country will continue to experience deficient demand, little productive investment and sluggish growth.[54] As Paul Mason put it, the 'six dials on the dashboard of the UK economy: inflation, investment, trade, debt, sterling and the current account [...] are all flashing red'.[55] We are at the end of what rising material standards can do for wellbeing and in the middle of the managed decline of a dilapidated economy. Only major improvements in our social environment can now increase our quality of life.[56]

The pandemic elicited a certain level of consensus, but that temporary sense of solidarity cannot compete with the influence of much more powerful long-term trends. The common factor in the strategies of high-income earners described in this chapter is the desire to distance themselves from these trends, even though nearly all of them inevitably will, if they haven't already, affect them and their children.

A more tangible future

One of the most interesting technological and financial developments of the last decade is the rise of cryptocurrencies – digital currencies that seek to do away with inflation and central banking through a decentralised registry system, the 'blockchain' – and NFTs (non-fungible tokens)[57] – which, in the simplest terms, are an attempt to replicate the logic of private property for online informational objects such as memes. Both are interesting economic and sociocultural phenomena; digital in nature but increasingly important for speculators. The most famous cryptocurrency, Bitcoin, began in January 2013 being traded at USD$13.30 and by January 2014, was worth $770. However, in the following years, its trading slumped sharply and then rose again, as competition started to appear and advocates struggled to make cryptocurrencies useful as actual currencies (or to seamlessly turn them into their nominal value). Cryptocurrencies then began to be used for trading NFTs, which operated like auction sales of images, tweets and other such online objects, now transformed into economic 'goods'. In 2021, that market trade was estimated at a nominal $17 billion.[58]

We mention these phenomena because they encapsulate many of the logics and strategies that middle to high-income earners may carry out in a context of increasing concentration of wealth. Both NFTs and cryptocurrencies have come to expand the logic of markets – in this case forcing scarcity on data that would otherwise be infinitely replicable. Even though they are virtual, they rely on physical resources and are astonishingly harmful to the environment: the carbon footprint needed to produce these goods has been compared to the emissions of mid-sized countries.[59] They rely on eager advocates to stimulate their demand, and are prone to create economic bubbles. Many investors have lost their life savings on the off-chance they'd see them multiplied by ten- or a hundred-fold off the back of other investors' eagerness. They are, in many ways, the 21st-century version of the tulip mania, but tulips at least are tangible (and beautiful).

Cryptocurrencies and NFTs are symptoms of awareness by those who trade them: that wealth and speculation drive economic outcomes much more strongly than wages and that early market access is everything. They are also predicated on an implicit libertarian philosophy that has only contempt for the welfare state: part of the reason cryptocurrencies and NFTs exist in the first place is to make taxation and central banking obsolete. These new markets, like other manias before them, promise their participants that if they enter early enough and convince enough buyers that they can become wealthy too, they'll win big, much like the winner of a Monopoly game is the one who buys earliest. Their very existence, in the words of filmmaker Dan Olson, represents "a turf war between the wealthy and the ultra-wealthy. Techno-fetishists who look at people like Bill Gates and Jeff Bezos, billionaires minted by tech-industry doors that have now been shut by market calcification and are looking for a do-over [...]. It's a cat fight between the 5% and the 1%."[60]

The popularity of NFTs and cryptocurrencies demonstrates a growing awareness that it will become increasingly more difficult to maintain our current standard of living through wages alone. The top 10% will find themselves increasingly confronting a number of myths about the capacity of markets to continue to provide their current levels of affluence. This includes the extent to which high earners rely on universal public services and the impact they have on their own life chances and social mobility. The arrival of the pandemic made it even harder for them to ignore the exposure of a significantly weakened healthcare system. It also showed how deepening inequalities directly affected the ability of key workers to keep essential public and private services going. As a result, inequality has become a more salient topic of public concern.[61] In the following chapters, we explore what will need to happen for the top 10% to back a stronger social contract. How can they be convinced that good-quality public services, available to all regardless of income, are more beneficial to them than lower taxes? What would life be like for the top 10% if they didn't feel the need to continuously apply the strategies we have discussed here?

We want to make a case that they shouldn't need to relocate to have a decent life, nor to insulate or isolate themselves from others. Not even to hoard or build the best post-apocalyptic bunker they can afford. In return, they would have better mental health and wellbeing. Not having enabled the exorbitantly wealthy and having lost the pretence that they will ever join their ranks, they would no longer sustain an economic system based on nepotism, the depletion of natural resources, and debt in place of decent wages. That is, a system, in the words of economist Diane Coyle, 'directed towards fending off the moment when the unsustainable can't be sustained any longer'.[62] Instead their taxes would provide more investment and infrastructure for high-quality public services and a safety net they would not be ashamed of using. There would be more funding for necessary collective changes such as bringing carbon emissions down. They would not feel the need to accumulate and consume to the same extent because, experiencing less status anxiety, they would interact with a wider group of people in a less divisive society. They might not be as well-off, but they would be better off.

7

Barriers to being comfortably off

We have been focusing on a group who, on the face of it, should be doing well for themselves, but who feel discomfort. This is manifested as anxiety about their jobs, as pressure to keep up with colleagues and neighbours, as nervousness about not being able to maintain their living standards, as fear of an uncertain economy, as not feeling attached to where they live. Previous research concludes that having stronger and more diverse relationships can improve wellbeing substantially.[1] Are then, high earners' primary concerns with themselves and their own economic future hampering their wellbeing? Could a more collective focus and addressing a range of barriers, which this chapter discusses, be at least part of the remedy for their individual concerns? This chapter explores high earners' perceptions of their own success and lifestyle. What might be preventing them from building social networks beyond their immediate circle and developing a wider sense of solidarity and belonging?

Barrier 1: Belief in meritocracy

A major barrier to developing a new social contract is how movements up or down the socioeconomic ladder tend to be explained. As explored in Chapter 3, many high-income earners emphasise their own part in their successes, explaining life outcomes as the result of their actions or factors they have control over: their skills, talents, willingness to work hard and the wisdom of their choices. This belief, that one's lot in life is and should be the result of one's abilities and graft, is often called meritocracy.[2]

In the words of Danny Dorling, with increasing inequality, the more widespread the opinion becomes that:

> It is, or should be, the 'fittest' who get to the top [...] that we are largely ruled by our betters, and that that is good for us. They think that almost all of the 1 per cent are very clever – much cleverer than most people – and that within the 1 per cent there are some exceptional geniuses.[3]

Dorling goes on to describe them as 'not part of an especially talented bunch and even those who are talented may not be that special'.[4] However, a number of those who do rule us believe they do so because they are special. We only have to look globally to see how meritocracy breaks down. By way of illustration, worldwide, the vast majority of those who score highest on IQ tests will be living in poverty.

Despite most of our respondents recognising the existence of deep inequities, a majority still believed that education was the main vehicle for moving up. It was seen as the route to opportunity. Following this idea, if more parents instilled in themselves and their children the importance of education and hard work, there would be more social mobility. However, widening access to education, laudable as it is as an aim, risks becoming a justification for inequality. This was seen in the views of those who did not necessarily come from privileged backgrounds. Gemma, a management consultant in her late thirties originally from the north-east and now living in London, is typical in citing her educational successes as the primary reason she became a high earner: "I was a high achiever. Teachers and family said 'You have to go to uni.' If I'd been an average student, that wouldn't have happened."

Emphasising her own attributes – equating status and respect with financial gain – makes her success seem acceptable, something she deserves. What this view ignores is that social mobility has often little to do with the educational system. Indeed, education in its current form arguably does more to enshrine social hierarchies than to subvert them. In the UK, more money is spent on private education than almost anywhere on the planet and it's also the home to the third most innumerate cohort of young adults in the developed world.[5] Graduates from a small number of private schools and elite universities dominate many top 10% professions, despite the fact that well over nine out of ten children attend a state school.[6] Moreover, decades of studies have shown that while school plays a role in socialisation, it is not as significant as the influence of peers, family and societal attitudes. As Peter Mandler has recently written:

> Middle-class and working-class kids today have the same educational experience, and yet the middle class still go into the top-paying jobs. One study showed that 30% of people from Class 1 backgrounds leaving school with no educational qualifications nevertheless end up in Class 1 jobs. It seems your class position is, mainly, inherited.[7]

Owen Jones wrote that aspiration, however commendable a goal it might be, has become a 'dominant atomised, consuming, acquisitive sense of self' sold as a means to individual salvation, resulting in the communitarian dimension of our lives being stripped bare.[8] This was evident among many of the members of the top 10% we spoke with. The route to economic success seems to begin with a geographical move away from the communities they grew up in – most often from north to south, in the case of the UK.

Barrier 2: Belief in the 'undeserving'

This is the counterpart of meritocracy: if the system is designed so that the best climb to the top, those who remain below do so for a reason. When some of our respondents talked about where they grew up, they made clear they were among the few who had 'made it out'. This was particularly the case for those who espoused meritocratic views and who had experienced upward mobility. They saw the places they were raised in and the people they knew there as 'others' in thrall to a culture of poverty. For them, deprivation, lack of housing, precarious employment, below-standard education and health inequalities are not understood as barriers to individuals succeeding, because those barriers had not stopped them. At most, what's needed are better role models and awareness of the opportunities offered by the market.

A belief that everyone in a meritocratic society receives their just rewards also runs the danger of estranging us from the experiences of others, exaggerating their chances of climbing the ladder and underappreciating how much current levels of inequality hamper those chances. Roy, a 66-year-old finance director with a top 3% income, told us:

> 'The less well-off are less well-off because of schooling, broken families, uneducated families, lack of control, blame everything on teachers [...] Where you have societies where some people are very rich, others very poor and no middle class, you're going to have problems. But when there are more echelons, when there's more of a spectrum, it's better, which is more or less where I think we are.'

This tendency to pathologise people and places runs deep in the British psyche.[9] As many social scientists have documented, it can be traced back to the division of the poor into deserving and undeserving in the workhouse. The latter were those who were able-bodied but seen as lazy and unwilling to take responsibility for their own lives. This put the idea that people experience poverty because of their own choices at the heart of British welfare provision, which explains the disciplinarian approach of many modern policies such as welfare-to-work schemes. Interestingly, although such attitudes were also present in other countries, we found that most interviewees in Spain had a more fatalistic view of poverty, seeing people living on low incomes as victims rather than as complicit in their own misfortune.

In addition, our interviews reflect a wider tendency to equate employment with independence and citizenship rights (such as access to social security). Being a full citizen thus means contributing through taxes and work. This view has an important communitarian element (the responsibility everyone has to 'contribute to society') but is unfortunately also often marked by cruelty towards those who are seen as failing to measure up

– and is predicated on what kind of work is considered valuable in the first place. The idea of an implicit charter of citizen rights and responsibilities – detectable in the discourse of all UK governments since at least 1979 – is an attempt to transform those who are perceived as passive recipients of social security benefits into active citizens engaged in public and economic life. This view hinges on (implicitly male) paid work, downplaying the importance of unpaid caring work and of key workers.[10] Despite being frequently reported and common knowledge in social policy and academic circles, our respondents rarely if ever considered the fact that the majority of those in receipt of social security payments in Britain today are in work. In their minds, they were a burden, while we would argue that those payments are actually subsidies supplementing the poverty wages in the private sector.

Barrier 3: Forgetting that 'no man is an island'[11]

Our research has shown that high earners often see their lives and experiences as mostly separate from the rest of society, in the sense that it was 'them' and only 'them' who drove where they ended up. Michael Sandel has studied the wider negative effects of elitism in universities in the US. Young people are sold the message that they have got their college places 'on their own merit'. This is of course mistaken and also means that if they fall short, they have no one to blame but themselves. If they continue to be 'successful', they often look down on those engaged in lower-wage work; people in such a situation are seen to have been judged by the market as less valuable and by educational institutions as less talented. And if they fail to remain in their position, high achievers risk anxiety and depression. This corrodes social cohesion. As Sandel puts it, 'the more we think of ourselves as self-made and self-sufficient, the harder it is to learn gratitude and humility. And without these sentiments, it is hard to care for the common good.' He continues:

> At a time when anger against elites has brought democracy to the brink, the question of merit takes on a special urgency. We need to ask whether the solution

to our fractious politics is to live more faithfully by the principle of merit, or to seek a common good beyond the sorting and the striving.[12]

Recently, COVID-19 exposed the assumptions still built into the design of our welfare state about the relationship between paid employment and independence, which were not true when the modern welfare state began in 1945 and are certainly not true now. For instance, that most 'proper' jobs are full time and permanent, pay enough to support dependants, and provide statutory sick pay and other protections from being part of a system into which each worker contributes. Nowadays the majority of those in poverty are in employment; many are precariously self-employed, with sick pay that does not cover their living and childcare costs, which are among the highest in Europe. Many are, in the words of Howard Reed and Stewart Lansley: 'piecing together a patchwork livelihood from multiple sources, not knowing from one day to the next if or when they will be paid. For creative workers, on whose innovations an increasingly knowledge-based economy relies, the borderline between unpaid and paid work is fluid and shifting.'[13]

The spread of COVID-19 raised questions over the necessary coupling of work and pay, where assumptions of what work is of the greatest societal value are being challenged. Many among us have looked at the rewards for different kinds of work and have begun to question why some earn so much more than others. Particularly, why are so many key workers, those we could never do without, paid so little? People who participate in the labour market should be able to earn a decent wage and those who cannot should be able to rely on a dependable and respectful benefits system[14] – precisely because, as the pandemic itself has shown, the fact that we can or cannot work in the first place depends on a myriad of factors beyond our control. The government's ability during the pandemic to provide an income floor for the population shows what is possible where there is the political will to do it. There was little backlash against the furlough and business support system, after all, and whatever existed was certainly less cruel than we are used to when dealing with benefits for those who are disadvantaged.

Barrier 4: Fear of falling

Although the top 10% are not in jobs we typically think of as precarious, many among them do not take their employment for granted. They exhibit, in the words of Barbara Ehrenreich – a formidable journalist and chronicler of the US's class system who died in 2022 – a 'fear of falling'.[15] This insecurity comes from being upward-oriented: comparing themselves to the 'super-rich' and as a result not feeling particularly rich themselves. The reverse of that orientation is that they don't really know what lies beneath – 'here be dragons'.

Gemma, without dependants and on a 3% income, who we introduced earlier in the book, was fearful of 'slipping down the ladder' and part of that fear was the implication it would be her own fault.

Much of the focus of our respondents' motivations was on keeping up with the cost of living, especially in London and the south-east where most well-paying jobs are. By December 2018, UK households had been net borrowers (had spent more than they received or 'lived beyond their means') for nine consecutive quarters (or 27 months in a row), with nothing comparable to that since 1987,[16] with a noticeable hit to family finances after the Brexit vote, and a sudden drop in the value of the pound. UK household savings are also very low and private debt – one of the key drivers of the 2008 crisis – is high. What is more, all of this was before the post-pandemic cost of living crisis.

Barrier 5: Consuming is all-consuming[17]

In modern capitalist societies, our lifestyles are inextricably linked to consumption, the goods and services we acquire and what this says about us. Material goods and the services we pay for take on a symbolic meaning, they are reflections of our position in the status order.[18] Symbols and the culture of elites trickle down to others, even while a mounting cost of living makes it increasingly difficult for most to keep up. Sociologist Shamus Khan points out that, while elites have opened up their institutions (such as their schools and universities) in terms of ethnicity and gender, income inequality has widened, leaving us with the 'puzzle of democratic inequality'.[19] There is at least a drive for inclusivity in gender and racial terms in elite institutions, but much less so on the basis of income or educational attainment.

Some of these consumption conflicts within the cultural position of our respondents were again illustrated by Gemma. She was aware of the difference in income between her home community and her network in London, and tries to reconcile this when her mother visits: "I'm very aware of different incomes when I go back home. [It's] very uncomfortable. When mum comes to visit, I pay for everything." At the same time, even though she has the purchasing power of her colleagues at work, she feels she doesn't 'fit in'. She encapsulated this in an anecdote from her first corporate job: "It was a very obvious difference [...] bit of a culture shock [...] people would say things like 'Do you ski?'"

Even if high earners can't copy the leisure pursuits of elites, they can try and imitate the consumption patterns of those just above them. Their 'ascriptive' identity (the personal, social or cultural identities placed on us by others) greatly influences the value of the resources they own. It's not enough that Gemma has the money to ski; she has to feel (and be seen as feeling) comfortable doing it, like a fish in water. This is a critical feature of the dynamics of inequality. Formal equality of opportunity, while essential, will never be enough. Ascriptive identities make up the foundations of durable inequalities and help us understand how elites can embrace opportunity without jeopardising their own advantages.

Groups are defined by who is excluded as much as by who is included. And this is not just based on people's characteristics, but also on food, music, objects, clothes, cars and so on. When one group seeks to distinguish itself, exclusion of others' practices becomes crucial. The field of culture, Khan writes, is not one that trickles down from top to bottom, but a struggle over who chooses and is able to like what kinds of things, and power is deployed by protecting or capturing a distinct way of defining oneself and one's group.[20]

Our interviewees were aware of this. For example, the age and type of car someone had featured in several interviews, even though we never raised the issue ourselves. Interestingly, this focus on consumer objects made them question whether inequality was in fact increasing. A senior executive at a major bank with a top 1% income told us:

Susannah:	I think inequality probably has increased but I don't know [...] whether it is more noticeable because people, and I include myself in this, place more importance on tangible items and being portrayed to have the best trainers, the best car, the best telly [...] so I don't know whether it's because it's risen or whether it's just because we have more access to those items and therefore it's become more visible.
Interviewer:	So, there's more competition at the level of consumption, of showing you have enough to spend on those things?
Susannah:	Yes, and it's become more of a status symbol – 'I'm doing well because I've got a new car,' or 'I'm doing well because I've gone on this holiday,' or whatever it might be.

However, while the increasing costs of living and maintaining a 'suitable' lifestyle are presented as problematic, none of our respondents commented on these problems as symptoms of something larger or questioned whether there should be 'a better balance between time and things'. This is because, as Neal Lawson says, this choice is never presented to them. "The option is never more time, it's always buying more."[21] The debt-driven, consumption-dependent growth model that has become dominant and which exerts such downward pressure on most people, including high earners, is interpreted as commonsensical, as a commitment to progress. There was rarely any reference to the shape of the recovery we have followed since the financial crash – how it has boosted the assets of those wealthier than they are and overheated the property market.

Barrier 6: Segregated lives

In the UK, the top 10% of income earners overwhelmingly work in professional, managerial and associated professional jobs, largely in the private sector in London and the south-east. It was similar for the other countries we looked into: in Sweden, they lived generally around Gothenburg or Stockholm; in Spain, it was Madrid, Barcelona or a handful of its other large cities; and in Ireland, it was overwhelmingly around Dublin, where most international capital is concentrated. These cities also tend to be among the most unequal regions in their respective countries. London itself is the most unequal part of the UK, with a high proportion of high- and low-income earners, and comparatively fewer in the middle.[22]

In addition, mathematically, there is more inequality within the 1% than within the 99%.[23] This concentration of capital income in the top 1% has left many high earners feeling vulnerable. Their colleagues at the very top seem a world away economically, although quite close in their minds. William, whom we mentioned earlier in the book, knows "theoretically" that he is in the top 1%, but at the same time feels like he is somewhere in the middle: in his immediate social world he's surrounded by people much wealthier than he is.

Little contact with people from other socioeconomic groups partly explains these distortions. High-income earners, especially those in industries like banking, just don't come across them – or at least not in a way that creates lasting social bonds. This 'availability bias' is a significant barrier to their understanding of inequality.[24] New research suggests that people's exposure to and interactions with other people across economic fault lines grounds their beliefs about inequality. As Jonathan Mijs describes it: 'When you look out from a bubble, you don't really see much inequality in your own network. Most people you know have the same kind of income, the same advantages and disadvantages, so the world looks meritocratic and more equal than it really is.'[25]

Earlier we mentioned Luke, a privately schooled and Oxford-educated 27-year-old consultant. He told us he had become more aware of inequality while teaching in a state school a few years ago. However, these days, even though he has read that inequality is increasing, he says "If you're in a privileged position, and all your friends are from a similar background, then you don't think about it on a day-to-day basis." His comment confirms what Mijs and others tell us – that people think about inequality by starting with their own experiences, from those close to them and then making inferences about the rest of society. We often overestimate the representativity of our context. Moreover, when 'bad' things happen to us, we attribute it to misfortune, bad luck or beyond our control, but when we look at others – for instance, the unemployed or victims of crime – we tend to think first about what they did wrong. We apply to them an 'individualising lens' – the exact opposite of our approach to others' successes and our own failures. This is known as the 'fundamental attribution error'.[26]

In countries where levels of inequality are increasing, people become less aware and less concerned about the issue, which affects how and the extent to which people learn about inequality in the first place. As Danny Dorling points out, numeracy levels display an almost inverse perfect relationship to economic inequality:

> [I]n places where the rich take far more, young people find it hardest to understand why there can be such a large difference in income between the median and the mean. In nations, in other words, where inequality is more of a problem, fewer young people will understand how it is measured.[27]

The more unequal a country is, the less likely there will be many bonds across income groups. The maintenance of the status quo is therefore in large part down to the effects of an unequal society. In such societies the class hierarchies are stickier: opportunities for children are uneven, marriages across social classes are less common, and residential segregation is higher. Referring to the US (but it might as well have been the UK), Mijs wrote:

> Increasingly, rich and poor Americans are living segregated realities: people's workplace, neighborhood and social network mirror their own economic circumstances and level of education, limiting the chances of rich and poor Americans sharing the same spaces and getting to know about each other's lives. This disconnect also means that neither can see their

unequal society for what it really is. That goes some way toward explaining why Americans underestimate inequality and overstate its meritocratic nature.[28]

Barrier 7: Work is not the new public square

Robert Putnam has been studying the decline in political, civic and religious organisations in the US for decades. In his acclaimed 1995 book *Bowling Alone* he documents how social capital in the shape of formal organisations has not increased to offset this decline; indeed, there has been a steep drop in union membership.[29] Unions and professional societies were once an important site for social solidarity in the US: "among the most common forms of civic connectedness" and a crucial precondition for economic collaboration. He questions whether people no longer like the idea of being a member of something or whether we have simply seen a shift 'between residence-based and workplace-based networks, a shift from locational communities to vocational communities. [...] perhaps we have simply transferred more of our friendships, more of our civic discussions and more of our community ties from the front porch to the water cooler'.[30] He describes modern-day US professionals and blue-collar workers: 'putting in long hours together, eating lunch and dinner together, traveling together, arriving early, and staying late. What is more, people are divorcing more often, marrying later (if at all) and living alone in unprecedented numbers.'[31] And from that, in one sense, '[w]ork is where the hearth is [...] the workplace increasingly serves as a sanctuary from the stresses of marriage, children, and housework'.[32]

David Graeber also studied the effects of spending so much time at work:

> Much of the day-to-day drama of gossip and personal intrigue that makes life entertaining for inhabitants of a village or small town or close-knit urban neighborhood, insofar as it exists at all, comes to be confined largely to offices or experienced vicariously through social media (which many mostly access in the office while pretending to work).[33]

Even so, Putnam points out that structural changes in the workplace have reduced the likelihood for much socialising. These include shorter job tenures, more part-time and temporary jobs, more self-employment, less unionisation, and threats of downsizing, automatisation and offshoring, all of which result in increased competition among colleagues and employee anxiety. In turn, this makes it likelier that most will keep their heads down at work to avoid getting fired, and thus less likely to form deep connections with colleagues as these would be so fleeting there would be little point. Putnam concludes that it is hard to accept the hypothesis that 'the workplace has become the new locus of American's social solidarity and sense of community'. Therefore, in his words, 'Any solution to the problem of civic disengagement in contemporary America must include better integration between our work lives and our community and social lives.'[34]

Work cannot be the new public square, Putnam concludes, because the ties we form there are mostly for instrumental, not social, reasons – and even conviviality is tainted in such a context. In addition, the more your clients and co-workers are of a similar social class – which is increasingly the case the higher your income is – the less likely you are to interact with those of a substantially different lot in life. A decline in our civil ties in our neighbourhoods and other areas of our lives can't be compensated for by work. Monitoring, hierarchy, competition, and lack of free speech and privacy all act as barriers to 'public deliberation and private solidarity'.[35]

Barrier 8: Rights and responsibilities

Prior to the pandemic, our respondents voiced what has been observed of middle-class individuals in the US, that the 'enormous complexity of society remained elusive and almost invisible to them'.[36] The absence of reference to "the structure that guides us all", as Hannah, a 44-year-old occupational health consultant earning just above the 10% threshold, puts it, includes an acknowledgement of interconnectedness and 'one's debts to society, that bind one to others, whether one wants to accept it or not. [This] is also the ability to engage in the caring that nurtures that interconnectedness'.[37]

Lack of solidarity is perhaps the greatest obstacle for the top 10%. Our respondents tended to believe public services were inefficient and, not coincidentally, had very low levels of trust in the capacity of the state. Apart from an enthusiasm for the state's role in providing at least baseline educational opportunities and healthcare services, support for redistribution was mixed. State inefficiency was often mentioned, as was the need to motivate people to work.

Our interviewees' attitudes towards the role of government were a world away from a vision of a social state outlined in recent European social democratic manifestos such as the Social Democratic Party of Germany's Programme for the Future. They made little reference to the British tradition of universalism (in the NHS, for example) and mostly argued in favour of means-testing. Dan, with a top 6% income, head of client services at a marketing agency, argues that if services are partially paid for by their beneficiaries, they will improve through customer demand for better quality: "If you pay a contribution to your son going to school, then there's an expectation of what you're getting back. If you pay council tax, you expect bins to be collected and local services to function."

Perhaps this preference for means testing could be explained by the fact many high earners prefer (and can consider) to rely on private healthcare or education if they can, as well as the fact that public services often operate as part of the background; they are unnoticed. Few of our interviewees declared they use public services frequently. Of those who mentioned healthcare issues, most accessed the NHS but also had private healthcare 'for emergencies'. Similarly, nobody lived in social housing or needed social care. Where respondents had children of school age, they were either in private schools or in state schools in relatively affluent areas.

Similarly, a rights and responsibilities discourse dominated opinions on the issue of increases in public spending. A slight majority of our respondents felt that the government should be 'helping people help themselves'. Michael, a 49-year-old engineer, just in the 10% threshold, was one of the few to concede that benefits only provide a minimum standard of living and this largely stemmed from his own childhood of living in relative poverty. For a majority of the others, a significant problem of more welfare provision was that it would discourage work. In relation to the proposal to have a universal basic income (UBI), for instance, they said: "I don't love that idea. I don't think it takes other factors like effort or drive into account"; "Pass"; "Not convinced. But I don't know enough about it"; "In the long term, benefit receivers lose the incentive to look for work." However, many also recognised that something like a UBI would be needed, as more jobs become threatened by automation. William, a Merchant (see Chapter 2) and a consultant well placed in the 1%, said on the matter:

> '[UBI is] an interesting concept, more relevant in a world with fewer jobs? But what do you do to keep those people busy, productive and leading fulfilled lives? How do you pay for it? It is becoming somewhat unavoidable, but I'm not sure how we pay for it.'

As this last example shows, the barriers that the top 10% face to developing greater 'sociological imagination' are not exclusive to them. After all, the fact there are fewer connections across social groups affects everyone. However, among high earners these barriers are perhaps exacerbated, considering how much their self-understanding is entangled with their views on work and their own position in the labour market. Like most of us, they live relatively isolated lives with little contact with those of very different means. And the less of that kind of contact there is, the more likely that judgements about people living in different circumstances will be preconceived. Nevertheless, the pandemic and the current cost of living crisis, not to mention the Ukraine–Russia war, have shown more clearly than ever how quickly individuals can get into difficulties through no fault of their own and how quickly financial reserves can be exhausted. With these barriers in mind, in Chapter 8 we explore how a different form of organising economic priorities and dealing with those in need could serve not just a majority, but also this group.

8

'When the facts change, I change my mind'[1]

'You have to face it head-on. You have to recognise what the tension points are and why people have them. Then you have to produce an alternative vision and deliver it. It's difficult to do that in small numbers. It needs a change of people who buy into that at the centre. It probably needs an opportunity to come out and that may be post-Brexit. If we end up leaving and everyone is further impoverished by it, which I think is 95% certain, that might be an incentive to say "It's not the thing you thought it was," and introduce a different narrative about how society can be delivered in a more equitable way.' (Duncan, director of a non-departmental public body with a top 10% income)

As a way out of the dilemmas we have described, this chapter suggests that high earners take a different perspective on their relationship with the state and their expectations of it. We don't want to offer a 'how-to' guide or tell them what to do; after all, that would be presumptuous and unlikely to have any effect. What we want instead is to put forward the case to those earning higher incomes that many of the ideas and policies that they think unfairly target them could actually be in their self-interest. What we propose here is mostly limited to taxation, redistribution, the state, the environment, and their social and economic lives because changes in those spheres of life are among the most urgent, actionable, tangible and far-reaching. However, many other policies could be explored; for instance, mitigating educational inequalities by addressing how they are reproduced by elite private schools.[2] Rather than dismissing such proposals as wishful thinking and not what 'the economy' needs, we argue instead that it is the status quo that does not make economic sense and does not benefit the lives of the great majority, not even of the top 10%. We also set out why and how high earners should have higher expectations of what the government can do for them. But first, we need to provide a reminder of why they are uncomfortable.

What high earners told us

The top 10% rarely know where they sit. They know they are not at the very bottom or the top but, interestingly enough, they underestimate their distance from both extremes. Our interviewees might be vaguely aware that the 1% are drifting away, but may not realise that they themselves are as far away from that 1% as they are from the median earner.

A belief that individual effort got them to where they are is pervasive, but waning. Working hard is a crucial part of their self-definition, yet many are surprised to be asked about the ultimate purpose of their work. Their priority, especially for Merchants, tends to be the bottom line, and this focus promises to allow them to lead a comfortable life.

They fear downward mobility, unemployment and economic downturns. Those currently at the bottom of the top 10%, with an income of around £60,000, may soon start to struggle to get on the housing ladder. If they don't have assets, their affluence feels increasingly precarious. As we mentioned earlier in the book, in late 2022, a government minister cited those just below them, people on £45,000, as likely to struggle to pay their energy bills.[3]

High earners know that it is now much harder and more expensive than it was in previous generations to progress through the rites of passage that they took for granted, such as finding a well-paid job, having a place to call their own and starting a family. In fact, for many of their children, these will be out of reach without family support. High-earning parents fear their children's downward mobility, perhaps even more so than their own.

Despite their relatively high income and status, those in the private sector find themselves in very hierarchical and unequal workplaces.[4] Even though many in the top 10% are managers and high-ranking professionals, they don't feel they have much power. While trade unions have been in decline for decades and their absence is rarely questioned, they are beginning to be sorely needed. Looking across the whole labour market, wages could be as much as 15–20% lower than they would otherwise be because of a lack of worker power. According to the Resolution Foundation and Centre for Economic Performance, this is equivalent to almost £100 a week for the average worker.[5]

High earners feel isolated and politically alienated but would be willing to pay more in taxation for better-delivered services, though they often struggle to trust the integrity and efficiency of the state. They support redistribution more than they used to, but want higher taxes targeted on those earning more than they do as well as on global corporations. This was nearly always the case when the issue of tax was raised in our interviews. It was others, the truly rich, who did not pay their fair share (though perhaps they are not wrong on this).

High-income earners have misconceptions about their relationship with the state and underestimate their reliance on it over their lifecourse. While they enjoy the status of using private services (often as benefits of their employment), if asked they acknowledge that there will be times when they'll need the public sector. Yet, understandably, they are frustrated with its current state. They fear that these services will not be there in an emergency. The question they ask themselves is 'Should we give more money to support a welfare state that isn't working?' The answer for many is 'no', because of the perceived inefficiency of the state, the undeservingness of its recipients or simply because they don't see the benefit in it for themselves. So, if high earners critique the value of public services in their own lives, do they approach their relationship with the economy and political system in the same way?

Question 'business as usual'

As we discussed in Chapter 6, we found that respondents were accepting of how the economy works to deliver profits to the top with excessive pay and bonuses for a few, rather than working to improve the wellbeing of the majority.[6] There was no reference, for example, to ten years of wage stagnation. Andy Haldane, a former chief economist at the Bank of England, has said that UK employees' share of national income has fallen from 70% to 55% since the 1970s, which is less than what they received at the outset of the Industrial Revolution.[7] Falling living standards should therefore come as no surprise, and none of this has anything to do with how hard people do or do not work.[8]

We, therefore, urge high-income earners to pause and consider why they think it is that the UK's economic and political system doesn't work for most people. How can they continue to be convinced by the argument that business as usual is best for our economy? The 15 years before the pandemic (2004–19) were the weakest growth period since 1934.[9] Per head, the economy is set to shrink. We have already been witnessing a 1930s-style drop in living standards.[10] The question is: who will be made to pay for rising prices? Without government intervention to ensure wages keep pace with inflation and strategic price controls in industries like energy, upward redistribution will continue apace.[11] Corporate profits are holding up; some raise prices higher than the increases in their costs. It's becoming even more difficult than it was to argue that these companies 'deserve' such profits.

The need to better understand the lives of others

Before the pandemic, quite a few of those we interviewed had already commented on social inequalities. Stephen, a former barrister, now a university professor, put it simply: "the taxation system. It works for the rich and doesn't work for the poor." He told us: "The way that society and economy has been managed post-crash, such as cuts to social services and the welfare state, there has been nowhere near enough redistribution of wealth."

Meanwhile, many of our interviewees, especially in the private sector, found inequality difficult to think about. This response by Sean, a 40-year-old owner of a recruitment company with a top 1% income, to the question of what has caused inequality in the UK is not untypical:

> '[Inequality is due to] lack of drive and effort. Nobody coached me to go to university or to do well for myself. I do understand certain situations mean people start off their life in a place where they don't have it. If I see a homeless person in the street, a child who's been kicked out, obviously I'll see them differently to a 40-year-old man who could probably get a job.'

We would argue this view underestimates current levels of inequality and how entrenched they are. Inequality is now of a completely different order from our respondents' parents' and grandparents' generations, a sign that jobs are no longer providing enough income to live a comfortable middle-class life. Current levels of inequality also raise the question of how the UK could continue to have a functioning economy if a majority of the population does not get paid enough to afford their bills or to live in the cities where they work.

During the pandemic, it became clear that many people in jobs that are vital to our society's survival have poor working conditions and are not paid enough to live on. Unions helped the public join the dots regarding the inequalities: wage depression, weak employment rights, real-term pay cuts, the high cost of living and crises in our public services.[12] This re-evaluation of key workers could lead higher earners to have greater respect for different social groups and the jobs they do. As high earners continue to move out of cities and work from home, there could be opportunities for more connection with a wider group of people and greater attachment to their local areas. It could lead to a softening of meritocratic beliefs. However, the pandemic could also have led to further isolation from the rest of society, in line with the increase in inequality after Covid, the change in consumption patterns and more time spent at home and online.[13]

High earners often don't acknowledge the extent to which inequality affects them directly because part of their status derives, after all, from how they differentiate themselves from others. Through a myriad of everyday ways, they avoid the stigma of being associated with people on lower incomes. As we have shown, these strategies will decline in value or become increasingly expensive. Two respondents, Douglas and Maria, were aware of this tendency and also what they gain from being influenced by people from different walks of life:

Douglas: For me, it's not role models, it's people that you meet that show you that good stuff is possible. [...] People collaborating together, making a good job of it. The influence of people.

Maria: I've tried to make myself read something else to get the other point of view but I've found it very difficult. [...] I'm quite lucky that I mix with a diverse group of people; maybe mixing with a diverse group has influenced me as well.

If high earners don't make connections with people who have different life experiences and continue to think of themselves as separate, they will continue to miss crucial dynamics about how society and the economy work. They'll be caught by surprise when the wave breaks.

Using public services without thinking less of yourself

The high earners we spoke with had a conflicted relationship with the state. Pre-pandemic, they saw public services as sub-par, slow and inefficient, fearing their decline. Paul, an architect, told us:

> 'Recently one of my children had to call 999. A burglar had got into the ground floor flat and was making his way up to the first floor. They didn't answer at first. Then, [the police] didn't come for 25 minutes. It's only until someone calls it [an emergency service] that you then feel it is lacking [...]. Until you need it, you don't know.'

However, few mentioned the impact of austerity on public services and on the people who provide them. Only Jung, formerly an NHS doctor, when asked whether he thought inequality had increased, replied:

> 'Yes, I think so, as a public sector worker I've seen little [in relation to] pay increases. Pay has been largely standard, not in line with inflation, while we hear bankers', CEOs' salaries [are] on the rise. So it does feel like the public sector is being shafted. You hear all the time of nursing staff, who haven't seen rises in pay for many years.'

The relationship of the top 10% with the state has seen some change since the pandemic, with many more aware of its support as a result – be it economic or health related. Despite this, high earners still have preconceptions about the extent to which they rely on and benefit from public services over the course of their lives. The idea that the welfare state is only for those lower down the socioeconomic scale reinforces the status that we discussed in relation to mobility (see Chapter 3) – of never being dependent if you can buy a service anywhere. It is also a way of imitating the 1% and their separation from the social context. Maria, for instance, though generally a centre-left Brahmin, said she had decided to go private to "give my space to someone else". Lamenting the situation, she said "The government wants us to do that, why else would they be advertising that there are no doctors?" Still, as Richard Titmuss is widely quoted as saying, 'separate discriminatory services for poor people have always tended to be poor quality services'.[14]

The belief that high earners do not benefit as much from the state as those on lower incomes is partly rational. When high earners need medical care, they can use private hospitals and they are economically sheltered by company schemes subsidising pensions and housing costs. Their children are more likely to attend private schools. They may not gain directly from the welfare system, but at the same time, they pay a higher percentage of their income for the taxes that keep those services running.

However, we have already argued in previous chapters that it is very much in high earners' self-interest and that of their children to support public services. This is because they gain substantially from the indirect benefits of the welfare state. For example, the doctor who treats a rich patient in a (private) hospital will most likely have been trained at public expense, and those who own businesses depend on the welfare state to care for the healthcare of their employees.[15] The public welfare system maintains the social fabric and prevents or minimises breakdowns of law and order. While this benefits everyone, it particularly does so for those 'with the most to lose'.[16] In 2022, criminal barristers went on strike for better working conditions, a warning against thinking that funding cuts will not be felt more widely. Barristers felt that politicians had supported cutting funding for criminal legal aid because "[B]y talking about slashing legal aid, it made it sound like they were being tough on criminals [...] there's no votes in funding defendants. Like I said, no voter thinks it's going to happen to them. But I'm afraid it does."[17]

Many more benefit from the operation of the benefits system than those who are directly targeted by it. Indeed, nearly all of us do; from public transportation and parks, to safer streets, healthier populations, a more educated society and the institutions that guarantee a more robust democracy. And while the pandemic momentarily reminded high earners of the importance of properly funding public healthcare, they tend to be unaware that most of them get back something at least close to what they pay into the welfare state. The majority will rely on it at some point during their lifetimes. The alternatives, either through private insurance or accumulating enough cash to see 'our families and ourselves through all eventualities are hugely expensive and out of reach for most'.[18]

When benefits are paid universally, irrespective of income, even if the amounts may seem meagre to a high earner, they can be important at a symbolic level. They strengthen the principle of being a citizen, part of something bigger, while decreasing the stigma from receiving them. As the late John Hills, an expert on income distribution and the welfare state, expressed it:

When we pay in more than we get out, we are helping
our parents, our children, ourselves at another time –
and ourselves as we might have been, if life had not
turned out quite so well for us. In that sense, we are
all – nearly all – in it together.[19]

Understand the cost of not investing

Part of taking a different perspective on what seems simply
common sense is to look at the role of government in other
countries. Globally, there is a clear tendency for states to
become more economically proactive.[20] Christian Lindner, the
federal finance minister of Germany, recently announced a draft
budget with the euro equivalent of £44 billion earmarked for
investments into 'climate protection, digitalisation, education and
research as well as the infrastructure required',[21] the goal being to
'transform Germany into a sustainable, climate-neutral and digital
economy' as part of a federal budget worth £401 billion.[22] In
Spain, train travel on large parts of the national railway network
is currently free. Even in the US, the Inflation Reduction Act of
2022 will pump hundreds of billions into low-carbon transition
and healthcare, including slashing the cost of prescriptions and
cancelling $10,000 of student loans for millions of graduates,
although this last item is being challenged in the Supreme Court.
This is in sharp contrast to the 'tax cuts for the rich and austerity
for the rest' recipe we have by now become used to.[23]

High earners will need to start pushing back on the fallacy that
the UK spends too much on inefficient public services and that
our financial problems stem from excessive state spending. Much
more significant to understanding Britain's economic woes is its
reliance on debt-fuelled consumption.[24] The well-worn truism
that 'there is no magic money tree', was used to drive over a
decade of cuts to benefits for the most vulnerable, while still
finding room for cutting taxes for millionaires and corporations.
Although reducing state deficits in normal times could lead to a
fall in the government debt-to-GDP ratio, doing so in a recession
is self-defeating.[25] This is not least because, as governments cut
spending and try to pay down their debt, money is taken out of

the economy, which has impacts on growth and tax receipts, all while increasing pressures on the welfare system.[26]

It is also crucial to understand that failing to invest in the social safety net actually increases the taxpayer's bill in the long term. After 12 years of austerity, the UK has not been able to significantly reduce its government spending and is set to increase it, largely due to our ageing population and inequalities exacerbated by austerity itself. Child poverty, for example, will cost an estimated £38 billion a year.[27]

On the eve of COVID-19, government spending was equivalent to about 40% of GDP – around the average for the post-war period. The single biggest item was pensions, while 1% went to unemployment benefits.[28] Following the pandemic, spending spiked sharply, rising to its highest level since the First and Second World Wars.[29] Of the £167 billion additional government spending in 2020, only £20 billion went to social protection, while the rest went to support businesses (over £122 billion).[30] The UK is way down the list in Europe on social spending.[31]

Since at least 2010, every government has made one of its central commitments to cut billions of pounds in public services, regardless of how the economy is doing.[32] It is time for high earners to decide whether to continue thinking that the NHS is ailing because the public sector is inefficient or to acknowledge that chronic underfunding is the cause. As state schools can't recruit teachers or refurbish their classrooms and one in five teachers have to spend their own money for school supplies,[33] are they going to continue to believe the UK is a meritocracy while elite professions remain dominated by the privately educated? Would they change their minds on the matter if suddenly they could not afford private education? Can they continue using the inefficiency argument for justifying further cuts to public services when many of those services are businesses in the hands of private companies?

If high earners continue to believe it is in their best interests to exclude themselves from the welfare state and rely on private services instead, they will have a strong incentive to avoid paying taxes. Some will go to great lengths to do so. If they do, they also have to accept that they are complicit in the deterioration of our public infrastructure and civic institutions, which will steadily make us an even more divided society.[34] Either way, for those seeking to foster social solidarity among high earners there is an urgent need to destigmatise public services. As we wrote in the 2020 TASC report, 'the top 10% should be able to use public services without thinking less of themselves'.[35]

Expect more from the private sector

High earners were generally silent on the political aspects of their work. They rarely reflected on its effects on society at large. To an extent that is unsurprising among those in the 'army of professional enablers, including accountants and lawyers who design new schemes to help their clients pay less tax'.[36] Envisaging change seems unlikely, given the level of monitoring, hierarchy, and lack of free speech and privacy that many refer to when describing their workplaces.[37]

Nevertheless, relationships between high earners and their employers are beginning to change. Many we spoke with wanted a better work-life balance and fewer hours, a 'well-proven intervention to improve wellbeing'.[38] According to a 2019 survey, 70% of employees believe a four-day week would improve their mental health and 64% of businesses supported the idea of adopting one. More than three million people in the UK would like to work fewer hours even if it would result in less pay, and 10 million would like to work fewer hours overall.[39] Crucially, again looking at international evidence in countries with shorter working weeks, reducing hours does not result in reduced productivity.[40]

Working fewer hours would also reduce high earners' carbon footprint. In the words of Stronge and Lewis from the think tank Autonomy, '[w]orking less not only reduces the sheer amount of resources being used as part of the labour process, but it also reduces the amount of carbon-intensive consumption that comes with what Juliet Schor calls the "work and spend" cycle'.[41]

Everything we do will need to change

One of the fundamental problems with the public and political debate on the climate is that inequality is rarely acknowledged as part of the issue, and therefore high earners don't recognise how much they are part of the problem.[42] Any meaningful change will thus be difficult for them, not least because improving wellbeing while consuming less is in tension with many aspects of their lifestyles.

Three quarters of the public agree with the statement 'If individuals like me do not act now to combat climate change, we will be failing future generations.'[43] However, the scale of behavioural change is not yet appreciated. For each person to reduce their carbon footprint to 2.5 tonnes by 2030 won't be enough to continue with small, relatively unobtrusive measures such as recycling, switching off lights, or cutting food waste and energy usage. This is nowhere near the needed scale. Everything we do will need to change – how we travel, what we eat and what we consume. According to surveys, willingness to pay to mitigate climate change goes up with income, and high earners are willing to go to greater lengths to protect the environment.[44] However, this does not detract from the fact that carbon emissions increase with income. What gives?

Little interest in participating

The high earners we spoke with, like much of the electorate, are disillusioned with the state of democracy and uneasy about an increasingly divisive and populist political culture. Many speak nostalgically about a missing 'centre ground'. Respondents such as Roy, a finance director with a top 3% income, remarked that change was unlikely with the political system we have "because of the structure of the parties. And you have to have a significant number of people in the marginals to change things."

Nevertheless, only a few of our respondents articulated the need for political reform. This is unsurprising, given that the system of representative democracy that we have has a tendency to favour the economic elite. Those who do argue for reform, therefore, are not seeking to improve on the representative model but are focused on 'the democratisation of democracy' through building in mechanisms such as citizens' assemblies into the formal political system.[45]

Despite a lack of public conversation about the country's political structure, British people do now want to see reforms. For the first time since records began, most of the public wants to scrap the first-past-the-post electoral system. According to a YouGov poll, 51% are in favour of switching to a form of proportional representation, while 44% prefer the status quo.[46] This reflects the policy of many parties and an increasing number of trade unions. Some respondents hinted that their voting would become more tactical, and this is consistent with wider trends. In the 2019 general election, almost a third of voters said they had voted tactically. Nobody we spoke with reflected on what would be required for the structural changes discussed in this book: namely, the liberal centre finding common ground with more progressive groups through an alliance, formal or otherwise. The prospect of a different kind of politics gathering momentum among the general public looks uncertain with an Electoral Calculus poll predicting a Labour landslide majority of 112 seats in the next general election.[47]

Nobody we spoke with currently participated actively in politics beyond voting or seemed to want to. The dwindling prospects for economic transformation coming from Westminster risk fostering further apathy. However, here again, we ask readers to consider the possibility of taking a less passive stance. The community wealth-building movements in the north are evidence of what can be achieved when local political parties, businesses and community groups work together.[48]

Expect more from the state

In the past few years, high earners have had their views of the state challenged by the pandemic, witnessing an unprecedented amount of peacetime state intervention. While Covid made huge demands on monetary, fiscal and welfare policy – particularly relating to state pensions, healthcare and net zero – the parameters for acceptable state spending have changed dramatically, with the fiscal line dividing political parties blurred.[49]

Recent events should have made clear that it's now 'everybody's business' for the state to work in the public interest, stepping up and confronting long-standing deficits in public infrastructure and in the quality and accessibility of public services. Those consulting progressive governments globally, such as economist Mariana Mazzucato, are clear that they must offer a new narrative on value creation, moving beyond the 'old, entrenched narratives' where the private sector plays the leading role and the state fixes market failures along the way, instead delivering:

> both a well-resourced welfare state and a dynamic innovation state, because the two go hand in hand. Without social services, too many people will remain vulnerable and unable to gain access to the basic ingredients of wellbeing and economic participation, including education, job security and health. And without innovation, economic growth and solutions to pressing societal problems – whether a pandemic, climate change or the digital divide – will remain out of reach.[50]

However, rather than a government with moral resolve and a bold, visionary plan for our future, the pandemic has exposed the moral bankruptcy of the corporate governance we currently have. It has allowed billions in public bailout money to be funnelled to shareholders while jobs are cut and massive companies are allowed to profiteer in crucial sectors of the economy.

Although we understand the circumstances of the emergence of the British modern welfare state were not the same as today's, we cannot continue to delay action on structural challenges such as net zero. If we do, we will disadvantage the country in the long run, producing higher costs, missed opportunities and prolonging the crises we already face.[51] The current juncture is an opportunity to present an honest but ambitious plan for the transition to net zero that includes a vision for local investment, bringing improvement to wellbeing, health, prosperity and inequality.[52] Showing at least a level of commitment to meet these challenges, our respondents repeatedly told us that they would welcome a stronger welfare state, provided it was efficient, transparent and didn't disincentivise work. We have to make the case that such a welfare state can exist and that it would empower not demotivate people on lower incomes. Work is becoming less effective at warding off poverty, with the percentage of working-age adults in poverty in work at its highest since records began.[53]

The government can take more risk than anyone else, certainly more than any individual or private company bound by short-term shareholders' interests. All the high earners we spoke to, even the most hard-nosed Merchants, said that the government has a responsibility to ensure its citizens' economic circumstances do not fall so low they cannot participate in society. They variously described this point as 'below the poverty line', 'a basic standard of living', 'enough to live on' and 'a duty to make sure people get a fair wage for a good day's work that will keep them at a level where they can eat, pay their bills and keep them safe and warm'.[54]

Whichever definition we want to use, it is difficult to argue that the state is adequately fulfilling that responsibility. In 2021–22, the food bank charity Trussell Trust distributed over 2.1 million food parcels. The trust calls for the government at all levels and across the UK to use its powers and take urgent action.[55] In September 2022, Disability Rights UK called for the government to put in place emergency uprating of benefits to at least match the latest Bank of England predicted inflation rates.[56] In the autumn statement, the government committed to raising working-age benefits and the state pension by 10.1% from April 2023, in line with September's inflation figure.[57]

In 2023, real household disposable incomes are expected to fall to their lowest levels since 2013/14.[58] In January 2023, 11.7 million households will be spending at least 25% of their income on fuel. Without an energy price freeze, combined bills for food and fuel would take up 80% of the budget of households on universal credit or the minimum wage.[59] Speaking of the extent to which charities have stepped up in the past years of crisis, Gordon Brown, former UK prime minister, wrote: 'With these last lines of defence now breached and charities about to hit a breaking point, only the government has the resources to end the unspeakable suffering caused by unpayable bills and unmet needs.'[60]

The pandemic has also highlighted our interdependence. A bolder government would respond to that by reassessing what activity is given recognition and promoting what are currently low-paid and low-status jobs such as those in the care sector. It would reassess the status of domestic work as well, which has an estimated value of between 10% and 39% of GDP and can surpass that of manufacturing, commerce, transportation and other key sectors.[61] Unpaid care and domestic work support the economy and often make up for the lack of public expenditure on social services and infrastructure. In effect, they represent a transfer of resources from women to others in the economy. In the 21st century, women still carry out at least two and half times more unpaid household work than men and are less than a third of the top 10%.[62]

As Grace Blakeley reminds us, 'States construct markets – they enforce contracts, provide basic services and uphold a monetary system needed for any kind of economic activity to take place – and they do so in a way that favours certain interests over others.'[63] A visionary future government would support and promote a wider range of sectors, particularly in net zero and creative industries, as well as the whole of our world-leading service sector (not just finance). It would also start weaning us off our reliance on GDP as an index of success.[64] Many of the activities included in GDP work against our environmental goals while neglecting areas that are essential to social reproduction such as domestic, family, political and charitable work.[65] GDP should be abandoned as the sole target and alternative targets should be considered, including indexes of quality of life, social health and carbon footprint.[66]

Getting serious about net zero

The government needs to lead on large-scale investment, taking more risks and moving faster, mobilising the workforce, and upskilling with technological skills that are currently in short supply. It needs to lead on "inspired regulation of the [energy] grid",[67] building trust among different actors, who, individually, would not take the risk on their own,[68] and promoting the growth of a UK green supply chain of net zero products such as heat pumps: "[making] net zero things in net zero ways".[69]

The fair financing of the net zero transition will be crucial for its progress and continued public support. However, the

UK government seems to be 'missing in action'.[70] The state's top priority should be to protect low-income households from the upfront costs.[71] It should lead the way by, for example, reinstating grants for home insulation that would give thousands the chance to improve the energy efficiency of their homes. Any tax reform therefore will be part of a broader package that includes investment in a Green New Deal, direct job creation, strengthening the social safety net and redistribution. Chancel warns us that 'there can be no deep decarbonization without profound redistribution of income and wealth'.[72]

Still, globally, decade by decade, countries have become more unequal in most regions of the world. In many places, the 10% richest take over 50% of national incomes. Earth4All, a group of leading economic thinkers, scientists and advocates warns that this is a recipe for deeply dysfunctional, polarised societies. They propose all governments:

> increase taxes on the 10% richest in societies until they take less than 40% of national incomes by 2030 (and the share of wealth controlled by the top 10% should continue to decline this century). Stronger progressive taxation and closure of international loopholes are essential to deal with destabilising inequality and luxury carbon and biosphere consumption.[73]

A modest welfare tax on multi-millionaires with a pollution top-up could generate 1.7% of global income to fund the bulk of extra investment needed to mitigate climate change. It would make access to capital more expensive for fossil fuel industries and generate large revenues. It goes without saying that such a proposal would face fierce opposition not only from the fossil fuel industry directly, but also indirectly from its lobbyists in finance, government and other sectors populated by the top 10%.

Take back control of energy and transport

Currently, there is mounting pressure for the government to do more to bring down energy prices for consumers, including removing VAT (value added tax) on energy bills, legislating to compel energy companies to remove high-standing charges on domestic gas and electricity, and implementing a much bolder and comprehensive windfall tax. On the last point, the government's current windfall tax rate of 25% hasn't gone anywhere near far enough, especially as it includes opt-out clauses that reduce it from £15 billion to £5 billion.[74]

With the ongoing energy crisis, there is growing support for taking public services back into public ownership, including energy and water.[75] UK energy firms could make excess profits totalling £170 billion between 2022–24, according to Treasury estimates.[76] Meanwhile, millions of households struggle amid the cost of living crisis – or income crisis, as Green Party deputy leader Zack Polanski has asked everyone to rename it.[77] Taking companies that generate, distribute or supply energy into public ownership and democratically run them would lower energy bills but also speed up home efficiency improvements, cutting carbon emissions. Publicly owned utility companies would have more incentives to introduce these improvements and set energy prices, prioritising affordability to customers rather than maximising the profits in dividends delivered to shareholders. The energy price cap would also be reinstated. The same principles can be extended to food, with basic necessities distributed through a public and democratic national food service with 'a right to food' enshrined in law.[78] What's needed from the perspective of high earners in this respect is a destigmatisation of those whom they believe would benefit from such policies – because, actually, the whole of society (including the top 10%) would.

Get better at tax

Tax is good. It has unbounded potential when compared to individual consumption or charity.[79] The impulse to buy often comes from a universal desire to bond with others, but as many psychologists have noted, the satisfaction is fleeting and often followed by post-purchase dissonance: the disappointment we feel on realising that our latest purchase won't fulfil what it promised.[80] However, when something is created collectively – such as the NHS – there is the 'exhilarating vastness of what we might do next', the sense it bestows of our own power. In the words of Zoe Williams, 'it turns us all into adventurers. It is beautiful in itself.'[81]

By contrast, to quote Mick Lynch, Secretary-General of the National Union of Rail, Maritime and Transport Workers, there are "those of us that are on PAYE, [who] cannot avoid tax, we pay it out of our wages every week [but] there are many, many people in this country avoiding tax like it is some kind of disease".[82] While there is frequent reference to the record high tax take, this is largely due to the income made from regressive taxes such as VAT and national insurance that hit middle- and low-income earners the most. Responsible economic and social policy requires more than just marginal tax rates on incomes, even on the highest. Our tax system already focuses disproportionately on income rather than assets, where true wealth is concentrated. Perhaps Rob Barber, the BBC *Question Time* audience member with whom we started this book, was on the mark when he complained that as he pays his taxes through PAYE he's at a disadvantage compared with the truly wealthy.

Since the 1980s, the amount of wealth held by private households has risen from three to nearly seven times the national GDP, but there has been no increase in the related tax taken as a proportion of GDP.[83] Significant tax breaks for savings, private pensions and allowances are heavily concentrated among the wealthy. Some have argued for an annual wealth tax or reform of the inheritance tax, which is riddled with loopholes. Inheritance taxes are always a touchy subject: though their use should be consistent with a meritocratic discourse, they are often fervently opposed as being unfair towards those who have worked hard all their lives. Still, even high earners and Conservative voters have acknowledged that the time to tax wealth properly has arrived.[84] As Martin Sandbu puts it: 'The importance of wealth in our economies and the inequality of that wealth have been going up for decades but the revenue raised from that wealth has not followed suit. So, I think politicians, facing pressure on their public finances, are missing a trick.'[85]

Advani and Summers make the same point:

> In the coming years, the pressure to rebuild public finances and to place crucial public services on a

sustainable footing will inevitably require politicians to make tough choices about who should bear the burden of additional taxes. It is important that these debates are not framed exclusively through the prism of headline rates. What matters – both for revenue and the fairness of the tax system – is effective rates. Instead of asking 'can the rich pay more?', a better question may therefore be 'who amongst the rich is not paying enough?'[86]

In the year 2015–16, the average rate of tax paid by people who received one million pounds in taxable income and gains was just 35%, the same as someone earning £100,000. But one in four of those people paid 45% – close to the top rate – while another quarter paid less than 30% overall. One in ten paid just 11%, the same as someone earning £15,000.[87] As Summers and Advani conclude, 'the rich are not all in it together'. Crucially, they also point out that those low tax rates are not due to complex tax avoidance schemes; they're a feature of how our system is designed.[88]

As we finish this book, the current government's plans for corporate tax are uncertain. Corporate tax rates had been going to be brought in line with the OECD average from 2023, which would increase tax revenue. That was after a decade-long experiment of seeing if lowering corporation tax increased productivity in the UK. The evidence by now should be clear: it didn't. However even if or when the tax rate is increased to 25%, this will still be lower than its lowest rate under Margaret Thatcher (34%).[89]

In addition, removing loopholes for rich individuals and large corporations would alleviate some of the current rigging of the tax system against average income earners. It would also make it easier to ask the top 10% to gradually increase their contributions. They would be willing to pay more, as interviews and polls suggest, in return for what they perceive to be a well-functioning state. The system of taxing multinational companies, as economist Jo Michell has written, is a hundred years out of date, designed when physical goods were moved around. It allows firms such as Amazon to pay offensively low tax rates.[90] Reform through the creation of unitary taxation, combined with an effective corporate tax rate, would allow governments to tax the profits of such large multinationals based on where they employ people, own assets and make sales. Furthermore, a progressive global tax on capital is perhaps the best-suited instrument to face the inequalities of the 21st century, as Piketty suggested.[91] For the very wealthiest and for the top 10%, mobility shouldn't be a way of evading contribution to the societies that make their affluence possible in the first place.

The way our property is taxed is also in urgent need of reform. Council tax is out of date and deeply regressive. Replacing it with a progressive property tax, as outlined in current Labour Party proposals, which would be set nationally and paid by property owners rather than tenants, would reduce the tax paid by a majority of households and discourage the use of homes as financial assets.[92]

High earners also want action on tax avoidance and evasion. We know that avoidance costs governments 4–10% of global corporate tax revenues, money that could be spent on health, education or infrastructure for the energy transition. Even though tax fraud costs the economy 9 times more than benefits fraud (£20 billion versus £2.2 billion), you are 23 times more likely to be prosecuted for the latter.[93] Tackling tax avoidance and evasion through fixing structural problems in the system, enforcing rules and regulations, would not only raise revenue but also restore public faith in the tax system.

Realism is defined by those in power

Some of the policies described in this chapter would be difficult to implement and require extraordinary political will. They would need what Gary Younge has called 'sufficient collective imagination for a shared sense of possibility and a set of principles that could apply to a common future; the idea that Britain stands for something more than posterity and itself'.[94]

Britain's political culture doesn't currently seem to have that, though that may change. The ideas in this chapter also challenge the meritocratic, pro-austerity and pro-insulation 'common sense' we have described throughout the book and would be staunchly opposed by those with too many assets to lose. Making them a reality would need a level of public trust and confidence in our political system, which is currently at an all-time low.

We argue, however, that the vast majority of the top 10% won't lose out. The 'common sense' and attitudes that have served them well up to now in reaching a comfortably-off position may not help them remain there. We hope to convince people like Rob Barber that marginal income tax rises over £80,000 would not only sustain the quality of life that they have come to expect but would even improve their lives, their children's and those of the majority in the communities in which they live. There's a reason, after all, why the famous Occupy movement slogan makes reference to 'the 99%', not 'the 90%'.

Conclusion:
Accepted truths, social
distance and discomfort

To start with, high-income earners don't know that their incomes are high. They don't think they are rich and have little idea of where they fit on the income distribution. Although they feel relatively comfortable and privileged, they worry about downward mobility, especially for their children. The near inevitability of their family falling down the ranks at some point means that they are right to worry. All in all, the UK's top 10% is a fragile group. Most people aren't in it for the majority of their lives. They are generally high earners only in middle age when they are compelled to cement their position by acquiring assets and contributing towards their children's education which, in turn, will allow them to differentiate themselves from the rest.

Despite believing in meritocracy, high-income earners know that the higher they go, the bigger the step beneath them.[1] This 'fear of falling' is one of the reasons why they feel so politically isolated. They support redistribution more than they used to but want higher taxes targeted on those earning more than they do. The truly rich are always above them, and they don't have to work. As such, the top 10% are yet to be convinced that their take is disproportionate, that it has negative consequences for others or that the way they seek to secure it affects their own wellbeing.

It could be argued that a crucial effect of their relative isolation and effort to distance themselves from the rest is the belief that their decisions affect only them. From that point of view, private education and healthcare are the business only of those who pay for them. We know this is not the case. The main flaw of the small 'l' liberal mindset is the belief that the causes and consequences of one's actions are much more independent from the rest of the world than they actually are. In spite of raised awareness about the extent of inequality and the need for a new social contract after the pandemic, many in the top 10% remain unconvinced that they need and rely on public services and infrastructure, and that there's no shame in that. In the words of Danny Dorling:

> Without public higher education, their businesses could not function, their children would not be educated, their lives would be less enriched. This is the group who make by far the greatest use of public health services because they live the longest and are least likely to die a quick death at a younger age. Instead it is the best-off 10% who stagger on for the greatest time with the highest number of comorbidities. We at the top might wish for a more equitable future if those of us in this group thought a little more about [what] our final year of life might be like; often being cared for by people in the lowest 10% pay band in care homes (our successful children having migrated far away).[2]

If economic structures are not working for the most privileged in our society, then this is a sign that the wider system of reward is not working for anyone. As Mike Savage points out, inequality bothers those with privilege much more now because they cannot use wealth to guarantee their own security in a world they can no longer predict and control: 'The rules of the game, orientated toward a market-driven business logic (and that have shaped the world since the 1980s) can no longer be taken for granted.'[3]

What will these structural changes mean for them? As parents, they may be forced to accept that the economy and hiring demands are changing and that includes a hollowing out of middle-class jobs (not to mention current developments in artificial intelligence). If things continue as they are, their children might not be afforded the same opportunities or standard of living that they had. The legitimacy of new employment, consumption, and other lifestyle choices (which are different from those of previous generations) will be an expectable outcome of the diminishing value of meritocracy. This creates a dilemma for high earners and the current social settlement more broadly, with many asking themselves '[W]hy should young people support capitalism when they could never expect to own any capital?'[4]

High earners will increasingly see their children have different priorities and make different life choices. They might see them become more politically engaged than they were at the same age. They shouldn't blame them. Avocado on toast or shop-bought coffees are not at fault. The top 10% could choose to become a little less wary about the possibility of alternatives to the status quo or, conversely, they could entrench their position and reproduce the generational divides that we are seeing. Increasingly the only way to secure the future will be assets and other inherited advantages such as networks and status. This undermines the pretence that we live in a meritocratic society in the first place.

Will people who are relatively comfortable now realise that if they want to stay the same, things will have to change? And that this will mean paying attention to how power is exerted in Britain. Duncan Green, in his book *How Change Happens*, writes that '[p]ositive social change requires power, and therefore attention on the part of reformers to politics and the institutions within which power is exercised'.[5]

In his famous 1958 book *The Rise of the Meritocracy* – where the term was first coined – Michael Young predicts his fictional version of the year 2034. He concedes that there will be 'stir enough' but nothing:

> more serious than a few days' strike and a week's disturbance, which will be well within the capacity of the police (with their new weapons) to quell [...] The charter is too vague. The demands are, with one exception, not in any way a fundamental challenge to the government. This is no revolutionary movement but a caucus of disparate groups held together only by a few charismatic personalities and an atmosphere of crisis. There is no tradition of political organisation on which to draw.[6]

In 2001, four years into the last Labour government, Young reflected on what he had written in 1958, asking whether anything could be done about Britain's new meritocratic common sense. He wrote:

> It would help if Mr Blair would drop the word [meritocracy] from his public vocabulary, or at least admit to the downside. It would help still more if he and Mr Brown would mark their distance from the new meritocracy by increasing income taxes on the rich, and also by reviving more powerful local government as a way of involving local people and giving them a training for local politics.[7]

What Young said in 1958 and 2001 remains relevant today. However, structural political change seems at the moment unlikely, but this does not mean nothing can be done. As the Club of Rome warned the world decades ago, the way we live is not sustainable. The first step is for 'man [to] explore himself – his goals and values – as much as the world he seeks to change'.[8]

We have been taught to believe that the more we work, the more we are worth and the more we deserve. The rationale for being part of an elite is that high income is a reward for effort, whether in the form of work or qualifications. A key consequence of that assumed link between effort, reward, and status is believing that where we end up on the social ladder is a foregone conclusion in our own control. In this view, inequality is essential for remaining motivated, for keeping up with the Joneses. But it's also crucial for maintaining an economic settlement that has produced stagnation, global warming, pollution, reduced social mobility, and political instability, as well as apathy and anxiety. Crucially for Brahmins, this implies questioning whether they would value education and credentials so much if those things weren't so successful at distinguishing them from other people. Capital, even in the concept of 'cultural capital', is another word for assets, after all.

We hope this book prompts high earners to question accepted truths and to contest 'the process of self-delusion that has driven consensus about what is true'.[9] In other words, we ask readers to question long-held and powerful beliefs that affect how they see themselves as well as how they judge others. This needs to include looking beyond our own personal circumstances to observe wider societal trends, noticing how what we do every day affects everyone else.

Our research tells us that high-income earners think of social action in individual terms, carried out and mostly having effects on the individual concerned. But individual effort will only take us so far. What is needed is to open space for collective action and to stop using every waking hour in improving our CVs or our bottom line. If we don't make the collective investment, we will not have a resilient society and economy. In that sense, one of the things that members of the top 10% could do is less. That would allow the 90% to participate more fully in the decisions that concern us all by granting them a more prominent role in the institutions that shape the public conversation.

Our deadline for this book happened soon after Liz Truss became prime minister, in the chaotic days of October 2022, when the demand for urgent change of some sort was becoming harder to ignore. We hope by the time you read this that there's more political will to build the institutional infrastructure needed to address the problems we have covered. But change can't be expected to come only from the very top. This is because, as should now be clear, the stakes are too great for those already with the assets and with the financial, political, and media wealth and status. They have too much to lose. However, the growing gap between high earners and the top 1% provides an opportunity for change, a possible breaking point among the elites that govern key institutions. We have reached the point of diminishing returns not only from meritocracy but also from increased production: more is not always better.[10] A more equitable society could protect both ourselves in our old age, and our families long after we are gone. The children of the top 10% are likely to be more aware of the trends we have discussed than their parents and, as a result, may be forced to take different routes to those their parents took – or conversely, to rely mainly on their inheritance. Still, as things stand, the road has become too narrow to comfortably accommodate any more in the 'middle class'.

We hope to have convinced at least some high-earning readers that, however hard they work, they will remain 'uncomfortably off' if the economy and society continue to operate as usual.

Our social contract and democratic institutions need reviving, and that is true in spite of having been repeatedly told that a more collaborative and equitable society is impossible. The best alternative for the relatively well-off in a future world without such collective effort might be a post-apocalyptic bunker furnished with the latest Amazon gadgets, perhaps in Surrey or New Zealand.

Afterword:
'I spoke to a lady from Godalming...'

In March 2024, the British Chancellor of the Exchequer, Jeremy Hunt, said:

> I spoke to a lady from Godalming about eligibility for the government's childcare offer which is not available if one parent is earning over £100k. That is an issue I would really like to sort out after the next election as I am aware that it is not [a] huge salary in our area if you have a mortgage to pay.[1]

Jeremy Hunt is not a socially aware person. That can be ascertained from the majority of the comments he has made in public since becoming a politician. He may be unusually unaware. But this particular comment was especially telling because it came at a time when Britain was experiencing its longest pay squeeze since the one that began in 1798.[2] In fact, this comment was made on the day the British government released this country's worst-ever statistics on poverty. They recorded the sharpest-ever rise in poverty, especially among children.[3] Given how Hunt thinks, I doubt I have the teaching ability to explain to him why his observations were so very tone-deaf. At the same time, they reveal how many extremely well-off people in Britain think.

Lack of awareness among the elite is among our most urgent problems in Britain, and one which has only become more relevant since the hardback edition of this book was published last year. We live in a society where people in the top 1% of earners, like Hunt, mostly only ever meet people from the top 10%. When Hunt looks down, he sees someone on £100,000, treats them with pity and talks of how he can understand their plight. Those of us in the top 10% tend to look up more than we look down.

Jeremy Hunt was a student in my hometown when I was a schoolboy. I often came across his kind of people and so I got to see just how unaware they were when they were young; I also had pity for boys like him who had never been allowed to mix with other classes and who were afraid to walk the streets of Oxford because they might be set upon by the lower orders.

There are times when it appears that almost everything is changing. Now might well be one of those times, because there is little respect left in Britain today for 'our betters'.[4] Hunt's comments were greeted with derision. Even the Labour Party – who, in 2024, are desperately trying to be like the Tories – derided him. Labour has said there is not enough money for more than two children in any family to receive child benefits, ensuring many children would remain poor if they live with more than one sibling. Labour also promised to crack down on the 'workshy' and find a way to 'stop the boats'. Despite all this, it was still able to describe Hunt as '"desperately out of touch" with the lives of ordinary people.'[5] Nevertheless, Labour in 2024 remains wary, presenting itself as the party of the top 10% – that is, the political party of sensible managers of the lives of the poor, and friends of big business.

If you were to indicate that you were a single person living alone and typed '£41,000' into the Institute for Fiscal Studies (IFS) household income calculator, it would tell you that, 'With a household after tax income of £805 per week, you have a higher income than around 90% of the population – equivalent to about 59.8 million individuals.'[6] That data, in the 2024 IFS online calculator, relates to 2022. In 2022, the Chancellor of the Exchequer was paid £159,038 per year. For someone like Hunt, such a sum of money is peanuts, given his 'private interests' (don't ask – his businesses are none of your business).

No wonder Hunt said, 'I am aware that it is not [a] huge salary in our area...'. We are all aware only of what we have experienced, what we have been told, what we understand and what we have thought about. The concerns and desires of the best-off 10% of people is detailed in this book in a way that helps us understand their fears, hopes and wishes.

This book combines careful quantitative and qualitative evidence to show why the best-off are yet to be convinced that their take is disproportionate, or that their taking so much causes huge problems for others. As explained in great detail, the top 10% rely on public services as much, if not more, than everyone else. Without public/charity higher education, for example, their businesses could not function, their children would not be educated and their lives would be less enriched. They are also the group who make by far the greatest use of public health services because they live the longest and are least likely to die a quick death; they end up having the highest number of comorbidities. If those of us in the top group thought a little more about what our final year of life could be like, we might wish for a more equitable future. We are very likely to be cared for by people in the lowest 10% pay band in care homes (our successful children having migrated far away).

Since first publication, this book has received widespread media attention, with headlines such as 'Why are Brits on £180k so sad?'[7] and 'Why a six-figure salary no longer means you're rich'[8] showing us why we need to pay attention to the woes of high earners in the fight against inequality. However, publications like the *New Statesman* and *The Telegraph*, in which these headlines appear, almost never explain why living in a country that is so unequal makes the best-off among us so unhappy.

The groups that people like me sometimes label the 'hoping to be well-off' (university students who are better off than most other university students), the 'actually affluent' (young adults who think their salary is low), the 'slightly rich' (older adults who have much more wealth than most people their age) and the 'very greedy' (most of the 1%) are much more sympathetic to issues such as racial inequality and gender inequality than they are to income and wealth inequality. They have been taught to believe they are 'worth it'. These five groups include, when polled, the majority of British university students and their parents, who think they should be paid much more than others because of the hard work they put into their university degrees – or perhaps, in some cases, because they think they are more able and valuable than those on lower incomes. In the UK, many university students believe they should be in the top 10%. As of 2024, a majority of young people go to university in the UK.[9]

A final thought.[10] Could people who are actually in the top 10% think of their future grandchildren or great-grandchildren, or their great-nieces and nephews? And think of the one who has had the least luck in life, who is ill on the day of an exam, whose marriage falls apart, who starts a business the year before a recession? Rising up into the top 10% is as much a matter of luck as falling down out of it. And no one makes their own luck. Even if you do not give a damn for anyone you are not related to, a more equitable future society will protect both you in your old age and your family long after you are dead. The alternative is not just inequitable – it is ignorant.

Danny Dorling
University of Oxford
April 2024

Notes

Introduction

[1] Bell, 2019; see also Joyce et al, 2019

[2] Statista, 2022

[3] Goodwin and Heath, 2019

[4] Race, 2022

[5] Parsons, 2022

[6] Although, as we discuss later, this does not mean people in this income bracket would identify with those labels.

[7] Matthew Stewart, for instance, talks about the 9.9%. See Stewart, 2018, 2021. See also Reeves, 2017.

[8] TASC, 2020

[9] Piketty, 2014

[10] See HMRC, 2022. Other sources vary, but all are roughly in the £55,000–60,000 region. The relatively low median income in this data source compared to others may be because it includes all sources liable to income tax (including pensions and some state benefits).

[11] The threshold to be part of the top 10% of households for equivalised disposable income (that is, after taxes and benefits and accounting for household composition) is, according to the ONS, £62,682 for 2021. See ONS, 2022a.

[12] Atkinson, 2007; Bollinger et al, 2018; Advani et al, 2022; Edmiston, 2022

[13] Gilens, 2012; Page et al, 2013

[14] Atkinson and Flint, 2001

[15] Despite 14% of the working population being from a BME (Black and minority ethnic) background, many minority ethnic groups are concentrated in low-paying jobs. However, this is not uniform across ethnicities, some of which are underrepresented in the sample. See ONS, 2020a.

[16] Agrawal and Phillips, 2020

[17] ONS, 2022b

[18] All interviews were recorded, but any reference to individuals or organisations has been anonymised.

[19] UCU, 2019

[20] See Laurison, 2015

[21] OECD, 2015; TASC, 2020

[22] TASC, 2020

[23] World Inequality Database, 2021; see also Equality Trust, 2020

[24] Piketty, 2020

[25] Milanovic, 2019
[26] Milburn, 2019
[27] Stevenson, 2021
[28] Haidt, 2012
[29] Wilkinson and Pickett, 2010, 2019
[30] Markovits, 2020

Chapter 1

[1] Unless otherwise stated, the figures below and in the remainder of the text are based on the European Survey of Income and Living Conditions, mostly on an individual's total income (from all sources) before tax rather than the household's, as were used in the 2020 TASC report from which this book draws. Though the top 10% of individual income earners and the top 10% of households overlap to a great degree, they are not the same, because a family of five would tend to be under much more financial strain than a single person if they earned the same amount. The advantage of using the figure for individuals is that it makes it easier to find individuals who belong to the top 10% to be interviewed. A considerable disadvantage of using individual rather than household income is that it neglects those who are part of wealthy households but do not earn well themselves, such as the children of the top 10%. Also, we concentrate mostly on income rather than wealth, not because we think one is more important than the other, but because we want to see the degree to which high-income earners may be feeling the pinch, as Piketty's theory on the increasing primacy of capital and wealth in relation to wages from labour implies.

[2] Higgins et al, 2018
[3] Guyton et al, 2021
[4] Gallup, 2017
[5] https://stats.oecd.org/Index.aspx?QueryId=66597
[6] https://stats.oecd.org
[7] Davis et al, 2020, p. 9
[8] Davis et al, 2020, p. 11, emphasis in original
[9] TASC, 2020
[10] ONS, 2018
[11] Evans and Mellon, 2016
[12] Walker, 2019
[13] IFS, 2021
[14] Friedman and Laurison, 2019, pp. 33–5
[15] Hanley, 2019
[16] Adams-Prassl et al, 2020
[17] Eurofound, 2020, pp. 7–11
[18] TASC, 2020
[19] TASC, 2020, p. 39
[20] The Sutton Trust and Social Mobility Commission, 2019
[21] University of Cambridge, 2021; University of Oxford, 2021
[22] University of Cambridge, 2022; University of Oxford, 2022

23 ONS, 2021a
24 ONS, 2021a
25 See also Toft and Friedman, 2021
26 TASC, 2020, p. 41; see also Phipps, 2021
27 ONS, 2021b
28 ONS, 2021c. See also Guvenen et al, 2014
29 House of Commons Library, 2021
30 ONS, 2022c
31 Piketty and Saez, 2013; Cingano, 2014; *Financial Times*, 2014
32 Friedman and Laurison, 2019, pp. 12–13
33 Streib, 2020
34 TASC, 2020, pp. 30–1
35 World Inequality Database, 2021
36 TASC, 2020
37 TASC, 2020
38 www.ons.gov.uk/economy/inflationandpriceindices/bulletins/houseprice index/march2022
39 TASC, 2020
40 Berman and Milanovic, 2020; see also Milanovic, 2018
41 Bangham and Leslie, 2020
42 Please note that changes in any one respondent's income percentiles throughout the book are the result of either (1) adjustments (increases or decreases) in income between the first and follow-up interviews, or (2) income positioning in 2022 compared with when we interviewed them in 2019/20.
43 Dorling, 2014
44 Sherman, 2017
45 We thank Professor Danny Dorling for these estimates.
46 Törmälehto, 2017
47 Ehsan and Kingman, 2019

Chapter 2

1 This way of distinguishing between the middle and working class doesn't make sense everywhere, and how we interpret class is always tricky. In the US, for instance, most people think of themselves as middle class, except perhaps those who are forced to learn they are not.
2 Evans and Mellon, 2016; see also McCall, 2013
3 Pakulski and Waters, 1995
4 Durose, 2022, p. 30
5 Durose, 2022, p. 30, emphasis added
6 Bourdieu, 1984
7 Friedman and Laurison, 2019, pp. 124–44; see also Friedman et al, 2021
8 Piketty, 2018
9 Piketty, 2018
10 Gilens, 2012
11 House of Commons Library, 2022a

12   Lamont, 1992
13   Sherman, 2017
14   Graeber, 2018, p. 258
15   https://openknowledge.worldbank.org/bitstream/handle/10986/30418/9781464813306.pdf
16   Frank, 2017; see also Sauder, 2020
17   Coenen et al, 2018
18   Edmiston, 2018a, 2018b; see also Rowlingson and McKay, 2012
19   Edmiston, 2018b, p. 986
20   Paugam et al, 2017; see also Krozer, 2018
21   Chancel et al, 2022

Chapter 3

1   Whyte, 1943, p. 60
2   Sen, 1975
3   Tilly and Tilly, 1998, p. 22
4   Dhar, 2020
5   Rivera, 2016
6   Friedman and Laurison, 2019
7   Social Mobility Commission, 2019, p. 16
8   For an explanation of the Social Grade classification system based on occupation, see www.nrs.co.uk/nrs-print/lifestyle-and-classification-data/social-grade.
9   Kirk, 2022
10   Kirk, 2022, p. 8
11   Major and Machin, 2019
12   Social Mobility Commission, 2020
13   See Reis and Moore, 2005
14   Dorling, 2014, p. 35; The Sutton Trust and Social Mobility Commission, 2019
15   https://assets.publishing.service.gov.uk/government/uploads/system/uploads/attachment_data/file/347915/Elitist_Britain_-_Final.pdf
16   See, for example https://assets.publishing.service.gov.uk/government/uploads/system/uploads/attachment_data/file/347915/Elitist_Britain_-_Final.pdf
17   Social Mobility and Child Poverty Commission, 2015, p. 4.
18   Major and Machin, 2019
19   Siddique, 2022
20   Hecht, 2017
21   Coote et al, 2010
22   Xue and McMunn, 2021
23   Beck, 1992; Giddens, 2000
24   Graeber, 2018
25   The 'Big Four' refer to the four largest global accounting and professional services accounting firms. On the topic, we recommend Brooks, 2018.
26   Standing, 2019, p. 16; see also Mijs and Savage, 2020

27 Chun et al, 2018
28 Wilkie, 2015
29 Blackman et al, 2015, p. 79
30 With thanks to Irina Predescu for her reflections and references on this issue.
31 Forrest, 2022a
32 Roper, 2020
33 Alamillo-Martinez, 2014; see also Salverda and Grassiani, 2014
34 Shackle, 2019
35 *The New York Times*, 2022
36 Soper, 2020; see also Jaffe, 2021
37 Graeber, 2018, p. 220

Chapter 4

1 TASC, 2020. See also Armingeon and Schädel, 2015
2 Enns and Wlezien, 2011; Gilens, 2012; Lindh and McCall, 2020
3 ONS, 2020b; see also Afonso, 2015
4 Surridge, 2021
5 Dorling, 2016; IPPR, 2019; Joyce and Xu, 2019
6 Kalinina and Shand, 2018; Joyce and Xu, 2019
7 Lucchino and Morelli, 2012; Joyce and Xu, 2019
8 Standing, 2019, p. 13
9 Joyce and Xu, 2019
10 Davis et al, 2020
11 Quantitative Easing, or QE, is a monetary policy tool whereby a central bank (in this case the Bank of England) purchases government bonds and other securities to increase the money supply and incentivise loans and economic activity.
12 See Goldman Sachs, 2022
13 Wren-Lewis, 2018
14 See Gov.uk, 2015
15 Carpenter, 2018
16 Brown and Jones, 2021, p. 5
17 Martin et al, 2021
18 Lee, 2015
19 Blakeley, 2018
20 Moore, 2016
21 What UK Thinks, 2022
22 Eliasoph, 1998, 2012; Putnam, 2000
23 University of Southampton, 2016
24 University of Southampton, 2016
25 Foa et al, 2020
26 Labour for a New Democracy, 2022
27 Clery et al, 2021; see also University of Southampton, 2016
28 Brown and Jones, 2021
29 Perryman, 2019
30 Berry and Guinan, 2019

[31] Nixon, 2015, p. 252
[32] Nixon, 2015; Mitchell, 2020
[33] Keen and Audickas, 2016
[34] Bale, 2021
[35] Game, 2019
[36] Barnett et al, 2021
[37] Shames, 2017; Patel and Quilter-Pinner, 2022
[38] Toynbee and Walker, 2008
[39] Handscomb et al, 2021
[40] Jackson, 2021, p. 41; see also Driscoll, 2022
[41] Williams, 2015, p. 326
[42] González Hernando, 2019
[43] Wren-Lewis, 2018
[44] Davies, 2021
[45] Lister, 2004, p. 166
[46] *The Spectator*, 2016
[47] Goodhart, 2017, 2020
[48] Manza and Crowley, 2018
[49] Proctor, 2019

Chapter 5

[1] Gilens, 2012; Schlozman et al, 2012; Rigby and Wright, 2013
[2] Lutz et al, 2015
[3] Dorling, 2016
[4] https://blogs.lse.ac.uk/politicsandpolicy/brexit-inequality-and-the-demographic-divide
[5] Skinner, 2021
[6] *The New York Times*, 2017
[7] Wright, 2021
[8] Dunn et al, 2020
[9] Dunn et al, 2020
[10] Booth, 2022
[11] UK Parliament Public Accounts Committee, 2021
[12] Local Government Association, 2018
[13] Jooshandeh, 2021; see also Reeves and Rothwell, 2020
[14] Edmiston et al, 2020
[15] Adams-Prassl et al, 2020
[16] Elliott, 2022
[17] Bartrum, 2022
[18] Johnson, 2022a
[19] Brown, 2022a; Johnson, 2022b; Partington, 2022
[20] Toynbee, 2022
[21] Resolution Foundation and Centre for Economic Performance, 2022
[22] Sillars, 2022
[23] Sridhar, 2022; Walker, 2022
[24] Allegretti, 2022a; Carson and Finnerty, 2022; Forbes, 2022

[25] Cotton, 2022

[26] Baines et al, 2022; *Financial Times*, 2022a

[27] Neame, 2022

[28] Mallet and Aloisi, 2022

[29] Allen et al, 2021

[30] Jackson and Cooney, 2022

[31] UK Parliament, 2022

[32] Davies, 2022

[33] CICTAR, 2021

[34] Mitchell, 2022

[35] An Association of Directors of Adult Social Services survey found that, between May and July 2021, social services departments were unable to meet 355,554 needed hours of home care due to lack of capacity. See ADASS, 2021

[36] Pembroke, 2019

[37] Mok and Zinkula, 2023

[38] Handscomb et al, 2021, p. 7

[39] TASC, 2020

[40] Spencer, 2022

[41] Shrubsole, 2019, p. 5

[42] Advani and Tarrant, 2022

[43] Mulheirn, 2019; Standing, 2019, p. 58

[44] *Financial Times*, 2020

[45] Corlett and Odamtten, 2021

[46] Allen et al, 2021

[47] Davis et al, 2020; Hills, 2014; Standing, 2019

[48] Alstadsæter et al, 2018

[49] Alvaredo et al, 2018

[50] Broome and Leslie, 2022

[51] Lansley, 2022, p. 240

[52] Stevenson, 2021

[53] Savage, 2021, p. 161

[54] Piketty, 2014, p. 746

[55] Davies, 2022

[56] Bullough, 2022, p. 14

[57] Bullough, 2022, p. 14

[58] Akenji et al, 2021

[59] Whitmarsh, 2022

[60] Lansley, 2022, p. 241

[61] Committee on Climate Change, 2019

[62] Chancel et al, 2022; see also Jorgenson et al, 2016

[63] Chancel, 2021a

[64] Marmot et al, 2020

[65] Raleigh, 2021

[66] Marmot et al, 2020, p. 37

[67] *Financial Times*, 2022b

68   Marmot, 2015
69   Woodward and Kawachi, 2000
70   Wilson and Daly, 1997
71   Woodward and Kawachi, 2000, p. 928
72   Hastings et al, 2015
73   Marmot et al, 2020, p. 5
74   Corlett and Odamtten, 2021
75   Belfield et al, 2017
76   Intergenerational Commission, 2018, p. 11
77   Chakelian et al, 2022
78   Chakelian et al, 2022
79   Mahmood, 2022; see also Department for Education, 2012; Iniesta-Martinez and Evans, 2012
80   Jones, 2014; Friedman and Laurison, 2019
81   Rivera, 2016
82   Davies, 2021
83   Webber et al, 2022
84   *Financial Times*, 2021
85   Winter, 2019, p. 8
86   www.makevotesmatter.org.uk/first-past-the-post
87   www.bhcompass.org.uk/a/44852767-45609270
88   Thomas, 2020
89   Thomas, 2019
90   Gethins, 2022
91   Wilkinson and Pickett, 2019, p. 217; see also Stiglitz, 2016
92   Coglianese, 2020

Chapter 6

1   On sociological work on modernity and flexibility, see Giddens, 2000; Bauman, 2005; Boltanski and Chiapello, 2018. On capital flight, see Harrington, 2016; Young, 2017
2   Adams-Prassl et al, 2020
3   Uni Global Union, 2020; EMG Transmission Group, 2021
4   Leslie and Shah, 2021
5   Klein, 2020
6   Rosa, 2015
7   Duffy and Thain, 2022
8   Graeber, 2018, p. 247
9   Putnam, 2000, p. 107
10   Klinenberg, 2018
11   Paugam et al, 2017
12   Reeves and Venator, 2014
13   Wilkinson and Pickett, 2010
14   Wilkinson and Pickett, 2019, p. 228
15   Garrett, 2021
16   Coyle, 2011, p. 10

[17] Sklair and Glucksberg, 2021

[18] Cited in Ambler et al, 2022, p. xv

[19] Jones, 2012, p. 250

[20] For further discussion of what Paul is describing, see for example, Madden, 2020.

[21] Williams, 2015, p. 128; Soper, 2020, p. 108

[22] When we conducted a follow-up interview with Michael, just after the pandemic, a pay rise had moved him into the top 6% income band.

[23] Wilkinson and Pickett, 2019

[24] Chancel, 2021a, p. 20

[25] Raworth, 2021

[26] OECD, 2018

[27] Social Mobility Commission, 2019

[28] Estimated figures provided by Danny Dorling.

[29] Social Mobility Commission, 2019, p. 180

[30] Wilkinson and Pickett, 2010

[31] Edmiston, quoted in Chakelian et al, 2022

[32] Ofsted is the Office for Standards in Education, Children's Services and Skills. It inspects services providing education and skills for learners of all ages. It also inspects and regulates services that care for children and young people. www.gov.uk/government/organisations/ofsted/about

[33] OBR, 2021

[34] House of Commons Library, 2022b

[35] ONS, 2018

[36] Ward and Chijoko, 2018

[37] Ward and Chijoko, 2018

[38] Ward and Chijoko, 2018

[39] Wilkinson and Pickett, 2019, p. 217

[40] Harrop, 2022

[41] Blakeley, 2020a, p. 8

[42] A £137 billion package (Full Fact, 2019).

[43] See Van Lerven and Jackson (2018) on why such interpretations are a fallacy.

[44] This occurs when a company buys shares of its own stock from its shareholders. This repurchase reduces the number of shares outstanding, thereby inflating (positive) earnings per share and, often, the value of the stock (Ghosh, 2022a).

[45] Soper, 2020, p. 69

[46] Sandel, 2013

[47] Reich, 2020

[48] Savage, 2022a

[49] Dunne and Gabbatiss, 2022

[50] Evans, 2022

[51] Monbiot, 2022

[52] Cited in Fisher and Gilbert, 2013, p. 90

[53] Stronge and Lewis, 2021, p. 95

[54] Davies, 2022

55 Mason, 2022
56 Ghosh, 2022b
57 A non-fungible token is a unique digital identifier in a blockchain (a decentralised log shared across a network) that cannot be copied, merged or subdivided. Its purpose is to certify the authenticity or ownership of a digital object, turned into a commodity.
58 Pymnts, 2022
59 European Central Bank, 2022
60 Olson, 2022
61 Blundell et al, 2020
62 Coyle, 2011, p. 11

Chapter 7

1 Wilkinson and Pickett, 2019
2 See Markovits, 2020
3 Dorling, 2014, p. 46
4 Dorling, 2014, p. 46
5 Dorling, 2014, p. 46
6 Dorling, 2014, p. 40
7 Mandler, 2022, pp. 44–5
8 Jones, 2012, p. 258
9 Lister, 2004
10 Tilly and Tilly, 1998, p. 22; Dhar, 2020
11 'No man is an island, entire of itself; every man is a piece of the continent, a part of the main.' John Donne (1572–1631), *Meditation XVII*.
12 Sandel, 2020, p. 20
13 Reed and Lansley, 2016
14 Lister, 2020
15 Ehrenreich, 1989
16 Partington, 2019
17 With acknowledgements to Neal Lawson, 2009.
18 Khan, 2016
19 Khan, 2016
20 Khan, 2012
21 Lawson, 2009
22 ONS, 2021a
23 Dorling, 2014
24 Hecht, 2017
25 Mijs, 2021
26 Mijs, 2021
27 Dorling, quoted in Wilkinson and Pickett, 2019, p. 180
28 Mijs, quoted in Liscomb, 2022
29 Putnam, 1995
30 Putnam, 1995, p. 85
31 Putnam, 1995, p. 86
32 Arlie Russell Hochschild, quoted in Putnam, 1995, p. 86

[33] Graeber, 2018, p. 118
[34] Putnam, 1995, p. 91
[35] Putnam, 1995, p. 92
[36] Bellah et al, 1985, p. 251
[37] Bellah et al, 1985, p. 194

Chapter 8

[1] We chose this apocryphal quote, attributed to several historical public figures, including Winston Churchill and John Maynard Keynes, as it reminds us that economics is 'the science which studies human behaviour as a relationship between ends and scarce means which have alternative uses' (Lionel Robbins quoted in Kishtainy, 2012, p. 13). In other words, unlike other sciences, the systems it examines are fluid and, as with the 'soft sciences' of psychology, sociology and politics, there is modelling, describing and storytelling involved.

[2] On this topic, we recommend the work of Green and Kynaston, 2019.

[3] Jackson and Cooney, 2022

[4] Wilkinson and Pickett, 2019

[5] Resolution Foundation and Centre for Economic Performance, 2022, pp. 19–20

[6] Raworth, 2017, p. 64

[7] Soper, 2020, p. 74

[8] Coyle, 2011, p. 14; Williams, 2015, p. 4

[9] Corlett et al, 2022

[10] Bastani, 2022

[11] Byline TV, 2022

[12] See Hunt (2021) for a discussion of unions' renewed sense of purpose and increased membership since 2020.

[13] TASC, 2020, p. 62

[14] Titmuss's 1967 lecture on 'Welfare and wellbeing' to the British National Conference on Social Welfare, quoted in Glennerster, 2014.

[15] Blakemore, 2003

[16] Blakemore, 2003

[17] Newman and Dehaghani, 2022

[18] Hills, 2014, p. 267

[19] Hills, 2014, p. 268

[20] Ramsay, 2022

[21] Ramsay, 2022

[22] Federal Government, 2022

[23] Ramsay, 2022

[24] Osborne, 2022. In 2009, for example, the UK was the world's most indebted country, with household, finance and business debt at 420% of GDP.

[25] Grace Blakeley speaking on Byline TV, 2022

[26] Holland and Portes, 2012

[27] Hirsch, 2021

[28] OBR, 2021

29 IFS TaxLab, 2021
30 Brien and Keep, 2022
31 ONS, 2018
32 Elgot and Stewart, 2022
33 Adams, 2019
34 Blakemore, 2003
35 TASC, 2020, p. 68
36 Michell, 2021, p. 228
37 See Riso, 2021
38 Murray, 2020, p. 31
39 Coote et al, 2020, p. 3
40 Duff, 2020
41 Stronge and Lewis, 2021
42 Chancel, 2021b
43 CAST, 2021
44 Graham et al, 2019; Streimikiene et al, 2019
45 White, 2022
46 Pack, 2022; YouGov Poll, 2022
47 Davies, 2021; Electoral Calculus, 2022
48 Brown and Jones, 2021, p. 128
49 Mishra and Rath, 2020
50 Mazzucato, 2022
51 Meyer and Newport, 2022, p. 3
52 See, for example, Intergovernmental Panel on Climate Change, 2021.
53 Joseph Rowntree Foundation, 2022
54 David Willetts, in Resolution Foundation, 2022
55 The Trussell Trust, 2022
56 Disability Rights UK, 2022
57 Employers for Childcare, 2022
58 Employers for Childcare, 2022
59 Allegretti, 2022b
60 Brown, 2022b
61 United Nations Economic and Social Council, 2017
62 International Labour Organization, 2016
63 Blakeley, 2020b
64 Dutkiewicz and Sakwa, 2013
65 Meda, 2022
66 Hickel, 2020
67 Julia King, in Resolution Foundation, 2022
68 Mike Biddle, in Resolution Foundation, 2022
69 Mike Biddle, in Resolution Foundation, 2022
70 Jo Michell, in Resolution Foundation, 2022
71 Resolution Foundation and Centre for Economic Performance, 2022, p. 133
72 Chancel, 2021b
73 Earth4All, 2022
74 Stewart, 2022

Notes

75 Shoben, 2022
76 Forrest, 2022b
77 Polanski, 2022
78 Byrne, 2022; Neame, 2022
79 Giridharadas, 2019; Glucksberg and Russell-Prywata, 2020
80 Jackson, 2021, p. 226
81 Williams, 2015, p. 129; see also Murphy, 2016, 2020
82 Novara Media, 2022
83 Leslie and Shah, 2021, p. 130
84 Chappell, 2022
85 Sandbu, 2022
86 Advani and Summers, 2020
87 Summers and Advani, 2021
88 Summers and Advani, 2021
89 Browning, 2017
90 Michell, 2021
91 Piketty, 2014
92 Monbiot et al, 2019
93 Chakelian, 2021
94 Younge, 2022

Conclusion

1   Phillips, 2020, p. 66
2   Dorling in TASC, 2020, p. 10
3   Savage, 2022b, p. 44
4   Blakeley, 2020a, p. 17
5   Green, 2016, p. 250
6   Young, 1958, p. 189
7   Young, 2001
8   Meadows et al, 1972, p. 197
9   Lothian-McLean, 2022
10 Jackson, 2021, p. 42

Afterword

1   Baker, T. (2024) £100,000 a year 'not a huge salary', Chancellor Jeremy
    Hunt claims, *Sky News*, 22 March, https://news.sky.com/story/100-000-a-
    year-not-a-huge-salary-chancellor-jeremy-hunt-claims-13099962
2   https://www.tuc.org.uk/blogs/17-year-wage-squeeze-worst-two-hundred-
    years#:~:text=We%20found%20that%20the%20only,Napoleonic%20
    Wars%20and%20their%20aftermath
3   Borrett, A. (2024) Fastest rise in UK child poverty for 30 years, *Financial
    Times*, 21 March, https://www.ft.com/content/dd180705-6331-4187-
    acd5-fc07ca6da3ac. See also https://www.gov.uk/government/statistics/
    households-below-average-income-for-financial-years-ending-1995-
    to-2023/households-below-average-income-an-analysis-of-the-uk-income-
    distribution-fye-1995-to-fye-2023

[4] Aziz, S. (2024) Anti-Muslim bias in British politics: in conversation with Rabi Mehmood, New Wave Global Productions, 4 April, https://www.youtube.com/watch?v=FvmDQA8vT_I

[5] Heren, K. (2024) Labour calls Jeremy Hunt 'desperately out of touch' after Chancellor says £100,000 is 'not a huge salary' LBC, 23 March, https://www.lbc.co.uk/news/labour-jeremy-hunt-out-of-touch-100-000-not-a-huge-salary/

[6] IFS (2022) calculator, Institute for Fiscal Studies, 22 August, https://ifs.org.uk/tools_and_resources/where_do_you_fit_in?income=41000&form%5Bperiod%5D=yearly#tool-results-section

[7] Chakelian, A. (2023) Why are Brits on £180k so sad? New Statesman, 7 July, https://www.newstatesman.com/politics/economy/2023/07/rich-people-britain-sad

[8] Binns, K. and Hallal, M. (2024) Why a six-figure salary no longer means you're rich, The Telegraph, 11 January, https://www.telegraph.co.uk/money/consumer-affairs/why-earning-six-figure-salary-not-mean-you-are-rich/

[9] 'As of 2022, there were over 2.86 million students at UK universities. Among people aged between 30 and 34 in the United Kingdom, half were educated to a tertiary level, one of the highest shares in Europe. Additionally, there were around 767,000 applications to study at university in 2022, an increase of around 345,000 when compared with 1994, when there were 405,000 applications.' Clark, D. (2023) Higher education in the UK – Statistics & Facts, Statistica, 20 December, https://www.statista.com/topics/6938/higher-education-in-the-uk/#topicOverview

[10] An argument I first tried to make in the preface to the precursor of this book: Dorling, D. (2020) Preface in Cohen, S., González Hernando, M., Mitchell, G., Pelling, L., Ruiz-Huerta Carbonell, J., San Vicente Feduchi, J., Velasco Monasterio, G., Inequality and the Top 10% in Europe, Brussels: FEPS (Foundation for European Progressive Studies), p. 10, https://www.tasc.ie/assets/files/pdf/top_10-report-final-oct20v.pdf

References

Adams, R. (2019) One in five teachers using own money for school supplies – report. 19 April. *The Guardian*. www.theguardian.com/education/2019/apr/19/one-in-five-teachers-using-own-money-for-school-supplies-report

Adams-Prassl, A., Boneva, T., Golin, M. and Rauh, C. (2020) Work that can be done from home: Evidence on variation within and across occupations and industries. *IZA Discussion Paper, n.13374*. Bonn: IZA Institute of Labor Economics.

ADASS (2021) *ADASS home care and workforce snap survey, September 2021*. London: ADASS. www.adass.org.uk/media/8863/final-rapid-survey-report-070921-publication.pdf

Advani, A. and Summers, A. (2020) Raising money from 'the rich' doesn't require increasing tax rates. LSE blog. https://blogs.lse.ac.uk/businessreview/2020/06/15/raising-money-from-the-rich-doesnt-require-increasing-tax-rates

Advani, A. and Tarrant, H. (2022) Official statistics underestimate wealth inequality in Britain. *LSE British Politics and Policy*. 7 January. https://blogs.lse.ac.uk/politicsandpolicy/official-statistics-underestimate-wealth-inequality

Advani, A., Ooms, T. and Summers, A. (2022) Missing incomes in the UK: Evidence and policy implications. *Journal of Social Policy* [onlinefirst], 1–21. www.cambridge.org/core/journals/journal-of-social-policy/article/missing-incomes-in-the-uk-evidence-and-policy-implications/6F454FD9D74613B182631F9453EDB671

Afonso, A. (2015) To explain voting intentions, income is more important for the Conservatives than for Labour. https://blogs.lse.ac.uk/politicsandpolicy/to-explain-voting-intentions-income-is-more-important-for-the-conservatives-than-for-labour

Agrawal, S. and Phillips, D. (2020) *Catching up or falling behind? Geographical inequalities in the UK and how they have changed in recent years.* London: Institute for Fiscal Studies.

Akenji, L., Bengtsson, M., Toivio, V. and Lettenmeier, M. (2021) *1.5-Degree lifestyles: Towards a fair consumption space for all. Summary for policy makers.* Berlin: Hot or Cool Institute.

Alamillo-Martinez, L. (2014) Never good enough. *Comparative Sociology*, 13:1, 12–29.

Allegretti, A. (2022a) Ministers warn of scammers posing as energy bill support scheme. *The Guardian*. 1 October. www.theguardian.com/money/2022/oct/01/energy-bill-support-scheme-scam-alert

Allegretti, A. (2022b) Gordon Brown urges Liz Truss to 'show up' for workers struggling with bills. *The Guardian*, 7 September. www.theguardian.com/politics/2022/sep/07/gordon-brown-urges-liz-truss-to-show-up-for-workers-struggling-with-bills

Allen, P., Konzelmann, S.J. and Toporowski, J. (2021) *The return of the state: Restructuring Britain for the common good.* Newcastle: Agenda Publishing.

Alstadsæter, A., Johannesen, N. and Zucman, G. (2018) Who owns the wealth in tax havens? Macro evidence and implications for global inequality. *Journal of Public Economics*, 162, 89–100.

Alvaredo, F., Chancel, L., Piketty, T., Saez, E. and Zucman, G. (2018) *World Inequality Report 2018.* Paris: World Inequality Lab.

Ambler, L., Earle, J., and Scott, N. (2022) *Reclaiming economics for future generations.* Manchester: Manchester University Press.

Armingeon, K. and Schädel, L. (2015) Social inequality in political participation: The dark sides of individualisation. *West European Politics*, 38:1, 1–27.

Atkinson, A. (2007) Measuring top incomes: methodological issues. In: A. Atkinson and T. Piketty (eds) *Incomes over the twentieth century: A contrast between continental European and English-speaking countries.* Oxford: Oxford University Press, pp. 18–42.

Atkinson, R. and Flint, J. (2001) Accessing hidden and hard-to-reach populations: Snowball research strategies. University of Surrey *Social Research Update*, 33.

Baines, J., Hager, S. and Peggs, A. (2022) The sector secretly profiting from the cost of living crisis. *Open Democracy*. 5 May. www.opendemocracy.net/en/oureconomy/uk-energy-distribution-networks-nationalise-profit-cost-living

Bale, T. (2021) Ploughed under? Labour's grassroots post-Corbyn. *The Political Quarterly*. 92:2, 220–8. https://onlinelibrary.wiley.com/doi/full/10.1111/1467-923X.12987

Bangham, G. and Leslie, J. (2020) *Rainy days: An audit of household wealth and the initial effects of the coronavirus crisis on saving and spending in Great Britain*. London: Resolution Foundation. www.resolutionfoundation.org/app/uploads/2020/06/Rainy-Days.pdf

Barnett, N., Giovannini, A. and Griggs, S. (2021) Local Government in England: Forty years of decline. Unlock Democracy. https://unlockdemocracy.org.uk/resources-research/2021/6/17/local-government-in-england-40-years-of-decline

Bartrum, O. (2022) Russia–Ukraine war: How could it affect the UK economy? Institute for Government, 3 March www.instituteforgovernment.org.uk/explainers/ukraine-war-uk-economy

Bastani, A. (2022) The coming recession will be worse than 2008: Expect living standards to collapse as five years of zero-growth meets a 15-year downturn. London: Novara Media. https://novaramedia.com/2022/08/10/the-coming-recession-will-be-worse-than-2008

Bauman, Z. (2005) *Liquid life*. Cambridge: Polity.

Beck, U. (1992) *Risk society: Towards a new modernity*. London: Sage.

Belfield, C., Crawford, C. and Sibieta, L. (2017) *Long-run comparisons of spending per pupil across different stages of education*. London: Institute for Fiscal Studies.

Bell, T. (2019) Question Time's £80K man was wrong about the top 5%. But the super-rich are on another planet. *The Guardian*, 22 November. www.theguardian.com/commentisfree/2019/nov/22/question-time-80000-super-rich-earning-workers

Bellah, R., Madsen, R., Sullivan, W., Swidler, A. and Tipton, S. (1985) *Habits of the heart: Individualism and commitment in American life*. Berkeley, CA: University of California Press.

Berman, Y. and Milanovic, B. (2020) Homoploutia: Top labor and capital incomes in the United States, 1950–2020. *World Inequality Lab Working Paper*, 2020/27, 1–29.

Berry, C. and Guinan, J. (2019) *People get ready: Preparing for a Corbyn government*. New York: Or Books.

Blackman, D., West D., O'Flynn, J., Buick, F. and O'Donnell, M. (2015) Performance management: creating high performance not high anxiety. In J. Wanna, H-A. Lee and S. Yates (eds) *Managing under austerity, delivering under pressure: Performance and productivity in public service*. Sydney: ANU Press, pp. 79–102.

Blakeley, G. (2018) *On borrowed time: Finance and the UK's current account deficit*. London: IPPR.

Blakeley, G. (2020a) *The corona crash*. London: Verso.

Blakeley, G. (2020b) The era of state-monopoly capitalism. *Tribune*. 7 June. https://tribunemag.co.uk/2020/06/the-era-of-state-monopoly-capitalism

Blakemore, K. (2003) *Social policy: An introduction*. Buckingham: Open University Press.

Blundell, R., Costa Dias, M., Joyce, R. and Xu, X. (2020) *COVID-19 and inequalities*. London: Institute for Fiscal Studies.

Bollinger, C.R., Hirsch, B., Hokayem, C. and Ziliak, J. (2018) Trouble in the tails? What we know about earnings nonresponse thirty years after Lillard, Smith, and Welch. *Andrew Young School of Policy Studies Research Paper Series*, No. 18–08. https://ssrn.com/abstract=3296464

Boltanski, L. and Chiapello, E. (2018) *The new spirit of capitalism*. London: Verso.

Booth, R. (2022) Covid care home discharge policy was unlawful, says court. *The Guardian*, 27 April. www.theguardian.com/world/2022/apr/27/covid-discharging-untested-patients-into-care-homes-was-unlawful-says-court

Bourdieu, P. (1984) *Distinction: A social critique of the judgement of taste*. Cambridge, MA: Harvard University Press.

Brien, P. and Keep, M. (2022) *Public spending during the Covid-19 pandemic*. House of Commons Library. Research Briefing No. 09309. UK: Parliament. https://researchbriefings.files.parliament.uk/documents/CBP-9309/CBP-9309.pdf

Brooks, R. (2018) *Bean counters: The triumph of the accountants and how they broke capitalism*. London: Atlantic.

Broome, M. and Leslie, J. (2022) *Arrears fears. The distribution of UK household wealth and the impact on families.* London: The Resolution Foundation.

Brown, G. (2022a) Kwasi Kwarteng may have U-turned, but huge spending cuts are still coming. *The Guardian.* 4 October. www.theguardian.com/commentisfree/2022/oct/04/liz-truss-kwasi-kwarteng-chancellor-u-turn-tax-cuts-public-services-benefits

Brown, G. (2022b) Britain's charities have done all they can to help desperate people. What will Truss do? *The Guardian.* 7 September. www.theguardian.com/commentisfree/2022/sep/07/britain-charity-help-liz-truss-government-cost-of-living

Brown, M. and Jones, R.E. (2021) *Paint your town red: How Preston took back control and your town can too.* London: Repeater Books.

Browning, C. (2017) Corporation tax: could we have raised more? Full Fact. 2 June. https://fullfact.org/economy/corporation-tax-rates-and-revenues

Bullough, O. (2022) *Butler to the world: How Britain helps the world's worst people launder money, commit crimes, and get away with anything.* New York: St. Martin's Press.

Byline TV (2022) How to solve the cost of living crisis. 4 September. https://byline.tv/title/consensus-cabinet-how-to-solve-the-cost-of-living-crisis

Byrne, I. (2022) It's time to enshrine the right to food. *Tribune.* 9 February. https://tribunemag.co.uk/2022/02/right-to-food-hunger-cost-of-living-crisis

Carpenter, N. (2018) Austerity's victims: Living with a learning disability under Cameron and May. Great Britain: Amazon (CreateSpace Independent Publishing Platform).

Carson, R. and Finnerty, D. (2022) Pound hedges become most expensive since Brexit as fears grow. Bloomberg. 3 October. www.bloomberg.com/news/articles/2022-10-03/pound-hedges-become-most-expensive-since-brexit-as-fears-grow?leadSource=uverify%20wall

CAST (Centre for Climate Change and Social Transformations) (2021) UK public willing to take significant action to tackle climate change. 22 April. https://cast.ac.uk/ipsos-earthday21

Chakelian, A. (2021) New: You're 23 times more likely to be prosecuted for benefit fraud than tax fraud in the UK: Yet tax crimes cost the economy nine times more. *The New Statesman.* 19 February. www.newstatesman.com/politics/welfare/2021/02/new-you-re-23-times-more-likely-be-prosecuted-benefit-fraud-tax-fraud-uk

Chakelian, A., Goodier, M. and Swindells, K. (2022) Britain is falling harder for the myth of Molly-Mae meritocracy. *The New Statesman.* 7 April. www.newstatesman.com/society/2022/04/britain-is-falling-harder-for-the-myth-of-molly-mae-meritocracy

Chancel, L. (2021a) Climate change and the global inequality of carbon emissions, 1990–2020. World Inequality Lab, Paris School of Economics, Sciences Po.

Chancel, L. (2021b) The richest 10% produce about half of greenhouse gas emissions. They should pay to fix the climate. *The Guardian.* 7 December. www.theguardian.com/commentisfree/2021/dec/07/we-cant-address-the-climate-crisis-unless-we-also-take-on-global-inequality

Chancel, L., Piketty, T., Saez, E. and Zucman, G. (2022) *World Inequality Report 2022.* Paris: World Inequality Lab, Paris School of Economics, Sciences Po.

Chappell, E. (2022) Uxbridge and South Ruislip focus group: Labour has more to do to set out its stall. 22 July. *LabourList.* https://labourlist.org/2022/07/uxbridge-and-south-ruislip-focus-group-labour-has-more-to-do-to-set-out-its-stall

Chun, J., Brockner, J. and De Cremer, D. (2018) How temporal and social comparisons in performance evaluations affect fairness perceptions. *Organizational Behavior and Human Decision Processes.* 145, 1–15.

CICTAR (Centre for International Corporate Tax Accountability and Research) (2021) *Death, deception & dividends: Disturbing details of the UK's largest care home operator.* London: CICTAR. https://cictar.org/wp-content/uploads/2021/12/Death-Deception-Dividends-Dec-3.5.pdf

Cingano, F. (2014) Trends in income inequality and its impact on economic growth. *OECD Social, Employment and Migration Working Papers, n.163.* Paris: OECD Publishing.

Clery, E., Curtice, J., Frankenburg, S., Morgan, H. and Reid, S. (eds) (2021) *British Social Attitudes: The 38th report.* London: NatCen Social Research.

Coenen, P., Huysmans, M.A. and Holtermann, A. (2018) Do highly physically active workers die early? A systematic review with meta-analysis of data from 193 696 participants. *British Journal of Sports Medicine* 2018; 52:1320–6. https://bjsm.bmj.com/content/52/20/1320

Coglianese, C. (2020) Solving climate risk requires normative change. Blog. UPenn Risk Management and Decision Processes Center. https://riskcenter.wharton.upenn.edu/climate-risk-solutions-2/solving-climate-change-requires-normative-change-2

Committee on Climate Change (2019) *UK housing: Fit for the future?* February. London: Committee on Climate Change. www.theccc.org.uk/wp-content/uploads/2019/02/UK-housing-Fit-for-the-future-CCC-2019.pdf

Coote, A., Franklin, J. and Simms, A. (2010) *21 Hours: Why a shorter working week can help us all to flourish in the 21st century.* London: New Economics Foundation.

Coote, A., Harper, A. and Stirling, A. (2020) *The case for a four day week.* Cambridge: Polity.

Corlett, A. and Odamtten, F. (2021) *Hope to buy: The decline of youth home ownership.* London: Resolution Foundation. www.resolutionfoundation.org/publications/hope-to-buy

Corlett, A., Odamtten, F. and Try, L. (2022) *The Living Standards Audit 2022.* London: Resolution Foundation. www.resolutionfoundation.org/app/uploads/2022/07/Living-Standards-Audit-2022.pdf

Cotton, J. (2022) We are planning 'warm banks' in Birmingham to try to save people abandoned by government. *The Guardian.* 7 September. www.theguardian.com/commentisfree/2022/sep/07/birmingham-warm-banks-government-council-fuel-poverty-national

Coyle, D. (2011) *The economics of enough: How to run the economy as if the future matters.* Princeton, NJ: Princeton University Press.

Davies, R. (2022) Thousands of UK pubs 'face closure' without energy bills support. *The Guardian*. 30 August. www.theguardian. com/business/2022/aug/30/thousands-of-uk-pubs-face-closure-without-energy-bills-support

Davies, W. (2021) *This is not normal: The collapse of liberal Britain*. London: Verso.

Davies, W. (2022) Destination Unknown. *London Review of Books*, 44:11, 9 June. www.lrb.co.uk/the-paper/v44/n11/william-davies/destination-unknown

Davis, A., Hecht, K., Burchardt, T., Gough, I., Hirsch, D., Rowlingson, K. and Summers, K. (2020) *Living on different incomes in London: Can public consensus identify a 'riches line'?* London: Trust for London.

Department for Education (2012) *Pupils not claiming free school meals*. https://assets.publishing.service.gov.uk/government/ uploads/system/uploads/attachment_data/file/183380/DFE-RR235.pdf

Dhar, D. (2020) Women's unpaid care work has been unmeasured and undervalued for too long. www.kcl.ac.uk/news/womens-unpaid-care-work-has-been-unmeasured-and-undervalued-for-too-long

Disability Rights UK (2022) *DR UK says £150 September cost of living payment to disabled people 'nowhere near enough'*. www. disabilityrightsuk.org/news/2022/august/dr-uk-says-£150-september-cost-living-payment-disabled-people-"nowhere-near-enough"

Dorling, D. (2014) *Inequality and the 1%*. London: Verso.

Dorling, D. (2016) Middle classes (not working class) voted for Brexit, argues Danny Dorling on BBC Newsnight. 29 September. www.youtube.com/watch?v=eOMiUONDLno

Driscoll, J. (2022) Our political consensus is built on lies and fear. Letters. *The Guardian*. 1 April. www.theguardian.com/ politics/2022/apr/01/our-political-consensus-is-built-on-lies-and-fear

Duff, C. (2020) Why you should try a 4-day workweek (+ how to pitch it). 15 June. Owl Labs. https://resources.owllabs.com/ blog/four-day-work-week

Duffy, B. and Thain, M. (2022) Do we have your attention? How people focus and live in the modern information environment. The Policy Institute. The Centre for Attention Studies. King's College London. www.kcl.ac.uk/policy-institute/assets/how-people-focus-and-live-in-the-modern-information-environment.pdf

Dunn, P., Allen, L., Cameron, G., Malhotra, A. and Alderwick, H. (2020) COVID-19 policy tracker: A timeline of national policy and health system responses to COVID-19 in England. www.health.org.uk/news-and-comment/charts-and-infographics/covid-19-policy-tracker

Dunne, D. and Gabbatiss, J. (2022) Factcheck: Why fracking is not the answer to the UK's energy crisis. 9 September. www.carbonbrief.org/factcheck-why-fracking-is-not-the-answer-to-the-uks-energy-crisis

Durose, O. (2022) *Suburban socialism (or barbarism)*. London: Repeater Books.

Dutkiewicz, P. and Sakwa, R. (eds) (2013) *22 Ideas to fix the world: Conversations with the world's foremost thinkers*. New York: New York University Press.

Earth4All (2022) Earth for all: A survival guide for humanity: Executive summary. www.earth4all.life/publications

Edmiston, D. (2018a) *Welfare, inequality and social citizenship: Deprivation and affluence in austerity Britain*. Bristol: Policy Press.

Edmiston, D. (2018b) The poor 'sociological imagination' of the rich: Explaining attitudinal divergence towards welfare, inequality, and redistribution. *Social Policy and Administration*, 52:5, 983–97.

Edmiston, D. (2022) Plumbing the depths: The changing (socio-demographic) profile of UK poverty. *Journal of Social Policy*, 51:2, 385–411. doi:10.1017/S0047279421000180

Edmiston, D., Geiger, B.G., de Vries, R., Scullion, L., Summers, K., Ingold, J., Robertshaw, D., Gibbons, A. and Karagiannaki, E. (2020) *Who are the new COVID-19 cohort of benefit claimants?* Rapid Report #2. The Welfare at a (Social) Distance project. September. https://hub.salford.ac.uk/welfare-at-a-social-distance/wp-content/uploads/sites/120/2020/09/WaSD-Rapid-Report-2-New-COVID-19-claimants.pdf

Ehrenreich, B. (1989) *Fear of falling: The inner life of the middle class*. New York: Twelve.

Ehsan, M.R. and Kingman, D. (2019) *Escape of the wealthy: The unfairness of the English student finance system*. London: Intergenerational Foundation. www.if.org.uk/wp-content/uploads/2019/01/Escape-of-the-Wealthy_Jan_2019_final-1.pdf

Electoral Calculus (2022) Regression Poll September 2022. www.electoralcalculus.co.uk/blogs/ec_mrppoll_20220928.html

Elgot, J. and Stewart, H. (2022) Liz Truss U-turns on plan to cut public sector pay outside London. *The Guardian*. 2 August. www.theguardian.com/politics/2022/aug/02/liz-truss-u-turns-plan-cut-public-sector-pay-outside-london-tory-leadership

Eliasoph, N. (1998) *Avoiding politics: How Americans produce apathy in everyday life*. Cambridge: Polity.

Eliasoph, N. (2012) *The politics of volunteering*. Cambridge: Polity.

Elliott, L. (2022) UK to be major economy worst hit by Ukraine war, says OECD. *The Guardian*. 8 June. www.theguardian.com/business/2022/jun/08/uk-to-be-major-economy-worst-hit-by-ukraine-war-says-oecd

EMG Transmission Group (2021) COVID-19 risk by occupation and workplace, 11 February. https://assets.publishing.service.gov.uk/government/uploads/system/uploads/attachment_data/file/965094/s1100-covid-19-risk-by-occupation-workplace.pdf

Employers for Childcare (2022) *What does the Chancellor's autumn statement mean for families?* www.employersforchildcare.org/news-item/what-does-the-chancellors-autumn-statement-mean-for-families

Enns, P. and Wlezien, C. (eds) (2011) *Who gets represented?* New York: Russell Sage Foundation.

Equality Trust (2020) *The scale of economic inequality in the UK*. www.equalitytrust.org.uk/scale-economic-inequality-uk

ESS (2022) European Social Survey data portal. https://ess-search.nsd.no

Eurofound (2020) *Labour market change: Trends and policy approaches towards flexibilisation*. Luxembourg: Publications Office of the European Union.

European Central Bank (2022) Mining the environment: Is climate risk priced into crypto-assets? www.ecb.europa.eu/pub/financial-stability/macroprudential-bulletin/html/ecb.mpbu202207_3~d9614ea8e6.en.html

Eurostat (2018) *The European Union Statistics on Income and Living Conditions (EU-SILC), 2016.* Luxembourg: Eurostat.

Evans, G. and Mellon, J. (2016) Social class. Identity, awareness and political attitudes: Why are we still working class? In: J. Curtice, M. Phillips and E. Clery (eds) *British Social Attitudes: The 33rd Report,* London: NatCen Social Research. www.bsa.natcen.ac.uk

Evans, S. (2022) Analysis: Record-low price for UK offshore wind is nine times cheaper than gas. 8 July. www.carbonbrief.org/analysis-record-low-price-for-uk-offshore-wind-is-four-times-cheaper-than-gas

Federal Government (Bundesregierung) (2022) Investing in the future and securing stability. Federal budget 2022. 16 March. www.bundesregierung.de/breg-en/news/cabinet-federal-budget-2022-2016888

Financial Times (2014) Middle class 'cling-ons' squeezed out of London property market. www.ft.com/content/0664615a-90dc-11e3-a2bd-00144feab7de

Financial Times (2020) UK house prices show strongest start of year since 2005. www.ft.com/content/0d022c74-f506-4599-9acf-925761a43efe

Financial Times (2021) Johnson to strip electoral watchdog of prosecution powers www.ft.com/content/aff47fb4-34ec-49c7-8aca-ebd462f4142b

Financial Times (2022a) Gas and electricity networks top UK profit margin ratings. www.ft.com/content/aff47fb4-34ec-49c7-8aca-ebd462f4142b

Financial Times (2022b) UK healthcare is already being privatised, but not in the way you think. www.ft.com/content/dbf166ce-1ebb-4a67-980e-9860fd170ba2

Fisher, M. and Gilbert, J. (2013) Capitalist realism and neoliberal hegemony: A dialogue. *New Formations,* 80/81.

Foa, R.S., Klassen, A., Slade, M., Rand, A. and Collins, R. (2020) *Global satisfaction with democracy 2020.* Cambridge: Centre for the Future of Democracy.

Forbes (2022) What now for UK mortgage rates? Forbes Advisor www.forbes.com/uk/advisor/mortgages/mortgage-rates-10-07-22

Forrest, A. (2022a) Government vows to clamp down on 'fire and rehire' after P&O sackings. *The Independent.* 29 March. www.independent.co.uk/news/uk/politics/p-o-ferries-fire-rehire-b2046586.html

Forrest, A. (2022b) Leak reveals staggering profits ahead for energy companies. *The Independent.* 31 August. www.independent. co.uk/independentpremium/uk-news/gas-electricity-bills-energy-profits-b2157700.html

Frank, R.H. (2017) *Success and luck: Good fortune and the myth of meritocracy.* Princeton, NJ: Princeton University Press.

Friedman, S. and Laurison, D. (2019) *The class ceiling: Why it pays to be privileged.* Bristol: Policy Press.

Friedman, S., O'Brien, D. and McDonald, I. (2021) Deflecting privilege: Class identity and the intergenerational self. *Sociology,* 55(4): 716–33.

Full Fact (2019) £1 trillion was not spent on bailing out banks during the financial crisis. 4 July. https://fullfact.org/search/?q=137+billion#gsc.tab=0&gsc.q=137%20billion&gsc.page=1

Gallup (2017) What determines how Americans perceive their social class? https://news.gallup.com/opinion/polling-matters/204497/determines-americans-perceive-social-class.aspx

Game, C. (2019) Local elections 2019: gone missing – 500 councillors. www.democraticaudit.com/2019/05/02/local-elections-2019-gone-missing-500-councillors

Garrett, B. (2021) *Bunker: Building for the end times.* London: Penguin.

Gethins, S. (2022) While 'beergate' dominates headlines, UK politics quietly changes forever. Open Democracy. 10 May. www.opendemocracy.net/en/beergate-keir-starmer-sinn-fein-win-uk-politics-change-scottish-independence

Ghosh, J. (2022a) Let's count what really matters. Project Syndicate. 16 June. www.project-syndicate.org/commentary/gdp-limitations-four-alternative-economic-indicators-by-jayati-ghosh-2022-06

Ghosh, J. (2022b) Control the vampire companies. *Social Europe.* https://socialeurope.eu/control-the-vampire-companies

Giddens, A. (2000) *Runaway world.* London: Routledge.

Gilens, M. (2012) *Affluence and influence: Economic inequality and political power in America.* Princeton, NJ: Princeton University Press.

Giridharadas, A. (2019) *Winners take all: The elite charade of changing the world.* London: Allen Lane.

Glennerster, H. (2014) Richard Titmuss: Forty years on. CASE paper no. 180. London: Centre for Analysis of Social Exclusion. https://sticerd.lse.ac.uk/dps/case/cp/casepaper180.pdf

Glucksberg, L. and Russell-Prywata, L. (2020) Elites and inequality: A case study of plutocratic philanthropy in the UK. UNRISD Occasional Paper – Overcoming Inequalities in a Fractured World: Between Elite Power and Social Mobilization, No. 9. 978-92-9085-112-7, United Nations Research Institute for Social Development, Geneva.

Goldman Sachs (2022) UK social mobility – a tough climb. 24 February. www.gspublishing.com/content/research/en/reports/2022/02/24/c9116edf-3ff1-4ec3-a459-bf9889763b0b.html

González Hernando, M. (2019) *British think tanks after the 2008 global financial crisis.* London: Palgrave.

Goodhart, D. (2017) *The road to somewhere: The populist revolt and the future of politics.* London: C Hurst & Co.

Goodhart, D. (2020) *Head, hand, heart: Why intelligence is over-rewarded, manual workers matter, and caregivers deserve more respect.* New York: Free Press.

Goodwin, M. and Heath, O. (2019) *Briefing: Low-income voters in UK general elections, 1987–2017.* London: Joseph Rowntree Foundation. www.jrf.org.uk/report/low-income-voters-uk-general-elections-1987-2017

Gov.uk (2015) PM speech on opportunity. David Cameron discusses plans to help working families and extend opportunities to all. 22 June. www.gov.uk/government/speeches/pm-speech-on-opportunity

Graeber, D. (2018) *Bullshit jobs: A theory.* London: Simon & Schuster.

Graham, H., de Bell, S., Hanley, N., Jarvis, S. and White, P. (2019) Willingness to pay for policies to reduce future deaths from climate change: evidence from a British survey. *Public Health*, 174, 110–17.

Green, D. (2016) *How change happens*. Oxford: Oxford University Press.

Green, F. and Kynaston, D. (2019) *Engines of privilege: Britain's private school problem*. London: Bloomsbury Press.

Guvenen, F., Kaplan, G. and Song, J. (2014) The glass ceiling and the paper floor: Gender differences among top earners, 1981–2012. *NBER Working Papers*, 20560. www.nber.org/papers/w20560

Guyton, J., Langetieg, P., Reck, D., Risch, M. and Zucman, G. (2021) Tax evasion at the top of the income distribution: Theory and evidence. *NBER Working Papers*, 28542. www.nber.org/papers/w28542

Haidt, J. (2012) *The righteous mind: Why good people are divided by politics and religion*. London: Penguin.

Handscomb, K., Judge, L. and Slaughter, H. (2021) *Listen up: Individual experiences of work, consumption and society*. London: The Resolution Foundation.

Hanley, L. (2019) The Class Ceiling review – why it pays to be privileged. *The Guardian*, 30 January. www.theguardian.com/books/2019/jan/30/class-ceiling-sam-friedman-daniel-laurison-review-pays-to-be-privileged

Harrington, B. (2016) *Capital without borders*. Cambridge, MA: Harvard University Press.

Harrop, A. (2022) *Faced with Liz Truss, the left can have confidence it will win the battle of ideas*. LabourList. https://labourlist.org/2022/09/faced-with-liz-truss-the-left-can-have-confidence-it-will-win-the-battle-of-ideas

Hastings, A., Bailey, N., Bramley, G., Gannon, M. and Watkins, D. (2015) *The cost of the cuts: The impact on local government and poorer communities*. London: Joseph Rowntree Foundation.

Hecht, K. (2017) A relational analysis of top incomes and wealth: Economic evaluation, relative (dis)advantage and the service to capital. *LSE International Inequalities Institute Working Paper*, 11.

Hickel, J. (2020) *Less is more: How degrowth will save the world*. London: Penguin.

Higgins, S., Lustig, N. and Vigorito, A. (2018) The rich underreport their income: Assessing biases in inequality estimates and correction methods using linked survey and tax data. *CEQ Working Paper Series* n.70. http://repec.tulane.edu/RePEc/ceq/ceq70.pdf

Hills, J. (2014) *Good times, bad times: The welfare myth of them and us.* Bristol: Policy Press.

Hirsch, D. (2021) The cost of child poverty in 2021. Centre for Research in Social Policy, Loughborough University.

HMRC (2022) Dataset: *Percentile points from 1 to 99 for total income before and after tax.* Release 16 March. www.gov.uk/government/statistics/percentile-points-from-1-to-99-for-total-income-before-and-after-tax#full-publication-update-history

Holland, D. and Portes, J. (2012) Self-defeating austerity? *National Institute Economic Review,* 222:1, 4–10.

House of Commons Library (2021) Income inequality in the UK. Research Briefing 7484. 30 November. https://researchbriefings.files.parliament.uk/documents/CBP-7484/CBP-7484.pdf

House of Commons Library (2022a) Research Briefing: Social background of Members of Parliament 1979–2019. Research Briefing 7483. 15 February. https://commonslibrary.parliament.uk/research-briefings/cbp-7483

House of Commons Library (2022b) Public spending during the Covid-19 pandemic. Research Briefing 09309. 29 March. https://researchbriefings.files.parliament.uk/documents/CBP-9309/CBP-9309.pdf

Hunt, T. (2021) COVID-19 and the work of trade unions: new challenges and new responses. Unions21. https://unions21.org.uk/files/Unions-21-Report-COVID-19-and-the-work-of-unions.pdf

IFS (Institute for Fiscal Studies) (2021) Comparisons of school spending per pupil across the UK. https://ifs.org.uk/articles/comparisons-school-spending-pupil-across-uk

IFS TaxLab (2021) What does the government spend money on? https://ifs.org.uk/taxlab/taxlab-key-questions/what-does-government-spend-money

Iniesta-Martinez, S. and Evans, H. (2012) *Pupils not claiming free school meals*. Research Report DFE-RR235. London: Department for Education. https://assets.publishing.service.gov.uk/government/uploads/system/uploads/attachment_data/file/183380/DFE-RR235.pdf

Intergenerational Commission (2018) *A new generational contract: The final report of the Intergenerational Commission*. London: Intergenerational Commission.

Intergovernmental Panel on Climate Change (2021) *Climate change 2022: Mitigation of climate change*. Working Group III contribution to the Sixth Assessment Report. www.ipcc.ch/assessment-report/ar6

International Labour Organization (2016) *Women at work: Trends 2016*. Geneva: ILO.

IPPR (2019) *Prosperity and justice: A plan for the new economy*. London: IPPR.

Jackson, M. and Cooney, C. (2022) Energy bills: Middle-earners will need help with rising prices too, says chancellor. BBC News. 27 August. www.bbc.com/news/uk-politics-62695778

Jackson, T. (2021) *Post growth: Life after capitalism*. Cambridge: Polity.

Jaffe, S. (2021) *Work won't love you back: How devotion to our jobs keeps us exploited, exhausted, and alone*. New York: Bold Type Books.

Johnson, P. (2022a) The mini-Budget explained. IFS. 23 September. https://ifs.org.uk/articles/mini-budget-explained

Johnson, P. (2022b) IFS response to U-turn on plan to cut 45p income tax rate. IFS. Press release, 3 October. https://ifs.org.uk/news/ifs-response-u-turn-plan-cut-45p-income-tax-rate

Jones, O. (2012) *Chavs: The demonisation of the working class*. London: Verso.

Jones, O. (2014) *The establishment: And how they get away with it*. London: Penguin.

Jooshandeh, J. (2021) *Key workers in the pandemic: Security traps among Britain's essential workers*. London: Trust for London. www.trustforlondon.org.uk/publications/key-workers-in-the-pandemic

Jorgenson, A., Schor, J., Knight, L. and Huang, X. (2016) Domestic inequality and carbon emissions in comparative perspective. *Sociological Forum*, 31:S1, 770–86.

Joseph Rowntree Foundation (2022) *UK poverty 2022: The essential guide to understanding poverty in the UK*. London: Joseph Rowntree Foundation.

Joyce, R., Pope, T. and Roantree, B. (2019) *The characteristics and incomes of the top 1%*. London: IFS.

Joyce, R. and Xu, X. (2019) *Inequalities in the twenty-first century: Introducing the IFS Deaton Review*. London: IFS.

Kalinina, E. and Shand, L. (2018) Executive pay: review of FTSE 100 executive pay. London: Chartered Institute of Personnel Development in association with High Pay Centre.

Keen, R. and Audickas, L. (2016) Membership of UK political parties. Briefing paper. Number: SN05125, 5 August. House of Commons Library. UK Parliament.

Khan, S. (2012) *Privilege: The making of an adolescent elite at St. Paul's School*. Princeton, NJ: Princeton University Press.

Khan, S. (2016) The many futures of élites research: a comment on the symposium. *Sociologica*, 10:2, 1–11.

Kirk, I. (2022) How many Britons have asked for a pay rise – and how many have been successful? YouGov. 4 April. https://yougov.co.uk/topics/economy/articles-reports/2022/04/04/how-many-britons-have-asked-pay-rise-and-how-many-

Kishtainy, N. (ed) (2012) *The economics book*. London: Penguin.

Klein, E. (2020) *Why we're polarized*. New York: Simon & Schuster.

Klinenberg, E. (2018) *Palaces for the people: How to build a more equal and united society*. London: Penguin.

Krozer, A. (2018) *Seeing inequality? Relative affluence and elite perceptions in Mexico*. Geneva: UNRISD. www.unrisd.org/en/library/publications/seeing-inequality-relative-affluence-and-elite-perceptions-in-mexico

Labour for a New Democracy (2022) Everything but the Commons: Why proportional representation is essential if constitutional reform is to address Britain's crises of democracy, inequality and the union. August. www.labourfornewdemocracy.org.uk/news/everything-but-the-commons

Lamont, M. (1992) *Money, morals & manners: The culture of the French and American upper-middle class.* Chicago, IL: University of Chicago Press.

Lansley, S. (2022) *The richer, the poorer: How Britain enriched the few and failed the poor. A 200-year history.* Bristol: Policy Press.

Laurison D. (2015) The right to speak: Differences in political engagement among the British elite. *The Sociological Review*, 63:2, 349–72.

Lawson, N. (2009) *All consuming: How shopping got us into this mess and how we can find our way out.* London: Penguin.

Lee, S. (2015) How has the UK's coalition government performed? London: Political Studies Association. www.psa.ac.uk/psa/news/how-has-uks-coalition-government-performed

Leslie, J. and Shah, K. (2021) *(Wealth) gap year: The impact of the coronavirus crisis on UK household wealth.* London: Resolution Foundation. www.resolutionfoundation.org/app/uploads/2021/07/Wealth-gap-year.pdf

Lindh, A. and McCall, L. (2020) Class position and political opinion in rich democracies. *Annual Review of Sociology*, 46:1, 419–41.

Liscomb, M. (2022) This professor went viral for asking students how much they think the average person makes, and it's eye-opening. BuzzFeed. 21 January. www.buzzfeed.com/meganeliscomb/wharton-average-american-income-guess

Lister, R. (2004) *Poverty.* Cambridge: Polity.

Lister, R. (2020) *Towards a good society.* London: Compass.

Local Government Association (2018) Local government funding: moving the conversation on. June. London: LGA. www.local.gov.uk/sites/default/files/documents/Moving%20the%20conversation%20on.pdf

Lothian-McLean, M. (2022) How bad do things have to get in Britain before we start to see solidarity emerge? *The Guardian.* 25 April. www.theguardian.com/commentisfree/2022/apr/25/bad-britain-solidarity-anger-division

Lucchino, P. and Morelli, S. (2012) *Inequality, debt and growth.* London: Resolution Foundation.

Lutz, G., Kissau, K. and Rosset, J. (2015) Representation of political opinions: Is the structuring pattern of policy preferences the same for citizens and elites? In: M. Bühlmann and J. Fivaz (eds) *Political representation: New insights into old questions*. London: Routledge.

Madden, D. (2020) Housing and the crisis of social reproduction. E-flux Architecture. June. www.e-flux.com/architecture/housing/333718/housing-and-the-crisis-of-social-reproduction

Mahmood, B. (2022) Private schools aren't 'losing' places at Oxbridge, their unfair privileges are being tackled – that's all. Left Foot Forward. https://leftfootforward.org/2022/05/private-schools-arent-losing-places-at-oxbridge-their-unfair-privileges-are-being-tackled-thats-all

Major, L.E. and Machin, S. (2019) *Social mobility*. Paper EA045. Centre for Economic Performance. London: London School of Economics. https://cep.lse.ac.uk/pubs/download/ea045.pdf

Mallet, B. and Aloisi, S. (2022) EDF issues fourth profit warning as nuclear output drops. Reuters. 28 July. www.reuters.com/business/energy/edf-issues-new-profit-warning-due-lower-nuclear-output-2022-07-28

Mandler, P. (2022) This idea must die: Grammar schools are a tool in promoting social mobility. *Cambridge Alumni*, 95. https://magazine.alumni.cam.ac.uk/this-idea-must-die-grammar-schools-are-a-tool-in-promoting-social-mobility

Manza, J. and Crowley, N. (2018) Ethnonationalism and the rise of Donald Trump. *Contexts*, 17:1, 28–33. https://doi.org/10.1177/1536504218766548

Markovits, D. (2020) *The meritocracy trap: How America's foundational myth feeds inequality, dismantles the middle class, and devours the elite*. London: Penguin.

Marmot, M. (2015) Middle classes being robbed of eight years of active life. Planning for Care blog. 10 September. www.planningforcare.co.uk/middle-classes-being-robbed-of-eight-years-of-active-life

Marmot, M., Allen, J., Boyce, T., Goldblatt, P. and Morrison, J. (2020) *Health equity in England: The Marmot Review 10 years on*. London: Institute of Health Equity.

Martin, S., Longo, F., Lomas, J. and Claxton, K. (2021) Causal impact of social care, public health and healthcare expenditure on mortality in England: Cross-sectional evidence for 2013/2014, *BMJ Open*, 11:10. https://bmjopen.bmj.com/content/11/10/e046417

Mason, P. (2022) Fresh-start Truss faces a 'sudden stop'. *Social Europe*. 19 September. https://socialeurope.eu/fresh-start-truss-faces-a-sudden-stop?s=08

Mazzucato, M. (2022) Toward a progressive economic agenda. *Social Europe*. 10 October. https://socialeurope.eu/toward-a-progressive-economic-agenda

McCall, L. (2013) *The undeserving rich: American beliefs about inequality, opportunity, and redistribution.* Cambridge: Cambridge University Press.

Meadows, D.H., Meadows, D.L., Randers, J. and Behrens, W.W. III (1972) *The limits to growth: A report for the Club of Rome's project on the predicament of mankind.* New York: Universe Books.

Meda, D. (2022) The urgent need for a post-growth society. Social Europe. 15 June. www.socialeurope.eu/the-urgent-need-for-a-post-growth-society

Meyer, B. and Newport, D. (2022) *Temperatures rising? Avoiding division on net zero.* London: Tony Blair Institute for Global Change.

Michell, J. (2021) Progressive tax reform. In P. Allen, S. Konzelmann and J. Toporowski (eds) *The return of the state: Restructuring Britain for the common good.* Progressive Economy Forum. Newcastle: Agenda Publishing, pp. 223–32.

Mijs, J. (2021) The paradox of inequality: Income inequality and belief in meritocracy go hand in hand. *Socio-Economic Review*, 19:1, 7–35.

Mijs, J. and Savage, M. (2020) Meritocracy, elitism and inequality. *The Political Quarterly*, 91:2, 397–404.

Milanovic, B. (2018) *Global inequality: A new approach for the age of globalization.* Cambridge, MA: Belknap Press.

Milanovic, B. [@BrankoMilan] (2019) Homoploutia is a neologism I invented (after some consultation w/my Greek friends). It indicates that the same people (homo) are wealthy (ploutia) is the space of capital & labor; your neighborly CEO who is in the top 1% by labor income and also in the top 1% by shares he owns. Twitter, 11 April. https://twitter.com/BrankoMilan/status/1116340273074921473?s=20&t=p6Tsbla wN5OfuyrjDX0LqQ [accessed 17 July 2022]

Milburn, K. (2019) *Generation left*. Cambridge: Polity.

Mishra, C. and Rath, N. (2020) Social solidarity during a pandemic: Through and beyond Durkheimian lens. *Social Sciences and Humanities Open*, 2:1, 1–7.

Mitchell, G. (2022) The clapping might have stopped, but our need for care is not going away. *LabourList*. 12 July. https://labourlist.org/2022/07/the-clapping-might-have-stopped-but-our-need-for-care-is-not-going-away

Mok, A. and Zinkula, J. (2023) ChatGPT may be coming for our jobs. Here are the 10 roles that AI is most likely to replace. Business Insider. 2 February. www.businessinsider.com/chatgpt-jobs-at-risk-replacement-artificial-intelligence-ai-labor-trends-2023-02?r=US&IR=T

Monbiot, G. (2022) Putin exploits the lie machine but didn't invent it. British history is also full of untruths. *The Guardian*. 30 March. www.theguardian.com/commentisfree/2022/mar/30/putin-lie-machine-history-untruths

Monbiot, G. (ed.), Grey, R., Kenny, T., Macfarlane, L., Powell-Smith, A., Shrubsole, G. and Stratford, B. (2019) *Land for the many: Changing the way our fundamental asset is used, owned and governed*. London: The Labour Party.

Moore, P. (2016) How Britain voted at the EU referendum. YouGov. 27 June. https://yougov.co.uk/topics/politics/articles-reports/2016/06/27/how-britain-voted

Mulheirn, I. (2019) *Tackling the UK housing crisis: Is supply the answer?* London: UK Collaborative Centre for Housing Evidence. https://housingevidence.ac.uk/wp-content/uploads/2019/08/20190820b-CaCHE-Housing-Supply-FINAL.pdf

Murphy, R. (2016) *The joy of tax: How a fair tax system can create a better society*. London: Corgi.

Murphy, R. (2020) The role of tax after the pandemic. Progressive Economy Forum. 4 May. https://progressiveeconomyforum. com/blog/the-role-of-tax-after-the-pandemic

Murray, N. (2020) Burnout Britain: Overwork in an age of unemployment. 4 Day Week Campaign/Compass/Autonomy. October. www.compassonline.org.uk/publications/burnout-britain-overwork-in-an-age-of-unemployment/

Neame, K. (2022) Miliband accuses Tories of being 'asleep at the wheel' as energy profits soar. *LabourList*. https://labourlist. org/2022/07/miliband-accuses-tories-of-being-asleep-at-the-wheel-as-energy-profits-soar

Newman, D. and Dehaghani, R. (2022) Why are barristers striking? Transforming Society [blog]. 6 July. Bristol: Policy Press. www.transformingsociety.co.uk/2022/07/06/why-are-barristers-striking

The New York Times (2017) No one knows what Britain is anymore. 4 October. www.nytimes.com/2017/11/04/sunday-review/britain-identity-crisis.html

The New York Times (2022) College admissions scandal: Complete coverage of a brazen cheating scheme. [News Event] www. nytimes.com/news-event/college-admissions-scandal

Nixon, B. (2015) *The 21st century revolution: A call to greatness*. Milton Keynes: Acorn Independent Press.

Novara Media (2022) Mick Lynch gives the BBC a reality check. TyskySour@NovaraMedia. www.youtube.com/watch?v=nbmQQ13UrMw

OBR (Office for Budget Responsibility) (2021) Welfare spending: Pensioner benefits. https://obr.uk/forecasts-in-depth/tax-by-tax-spend-by-spend/welfare-spending-pensioner-benefits

OECD (Organisation for Economic Co-operation and Development) (2015) *In it together: Why less inequality benefits all*. Paris: OECD.

OECD (2018) *A broken social elevator? How to promote social mobility*. Paris: OECD.

OECD (2019) *Under pressure: The squeezed middle class*. Paris: OECD.

Olson, D. (2022) Line goes up: The problem with NFTs. YouTube. 21 January. www.youtube.com/watch?v=YQ_xWvX1n9g

ONS (Office for National Statistics) (2018) Social protection, European comparisons of expenditure: 2015. 19 June. www.ons. gov.uk/peoplepopulationandcommunity/wellbeing/articles/ socialprotectioneuropeancomparisonsofexpenditure/2015

ONS (2020a) Dataset: Ethnicity pay gap reference tables. Release: 12 October. www.ons.gov.uk/employmentandlabourmarket/ peopleinwork/earningsandworkinghours/datasets/ethnicity paygapreferencetables

ONS (2020b) Population by Index of Multiple Deprivation (IMD), England, 2001 to 2019. Release: 19 October. www.ons.gov.uk/ peoplepopulationandcommunity/populationandmigration/ populationestimates/adhocs/12386populationbyindexofmulti pledeprivationimdengland2001to2019

ONS (2021a) Visualisation: What are the regional differences in income and productivity? Release: 17 May. www.ons.gov.uk/ visualisations/dvc1370

ONS (2021b) Gender pay gap in the UK: 2021; Differences in pay between women and men by age, region, full-time and part-time, and occupation. Release: 21 October. www. ons.gov.uk/employmentandlabourmarket/peopleinwork/ earningsandworkinghours/bulletins/genderpaygapintheuk/2021

ONS (2021c) National statistics: Distribution of median and mean income and tax by age range and gender. Release: 16 March 2022. www.gov.uk/government/statistics/distribution-of-median-and-mean-income-and-tax-by-age-range-and-gender-2010-to-2011

ONS (2022a) Dataset: The effects of taxes and benefits on household income, disposable income estimate. Release: 28 March. www.ons.gov.uk/peoplepopulationandcommunity/ personalandhouseholdfinances/incomeandwealth/datasets/ householddisposableincomeandinequality

ONS (2022b) Distribution of individual total wealth by characteristic in Great Britain: April 2018 to March 2020. Release: 7 January. www.ons.gov.uk/peoplepopulationandcommunity/ personalandhouseholdfinances/incomeandwealth/bulletins/ distributionofindividualtotalwealthbycharacteristicingreat britain/april2018tomarch2020

ONS (2022c) Dataset: A09 Labour market status by ethnic group. Release: 17 May. www.ons.gov.uk/employmentandlabour market/peopleinwork/employmentandemployeetypes/datasets/labourmarketstatusbyethnicgroupa09

Osborne, H. (2022) Number of UK households with large debts rises by a third. *The Guardian.* 22 March. www.theguardian.com/money/2022/mar/22/uk-households-debts-energy-prices-benefits

Pack, M. (2022) Highest support for PR since British Social Attitudes survey started. 22 September. Mark Pack/Political. www.markpack.org.uk/169824/highest-support-for-pr-since-british-social-attitudes-survey-started

Page, B., Bartels, L. and Seawright, J. (2013) Democracy and the policy preferences of wealthy Americans. *Perspectives on Politics,* 11:1, 51–73.

Pakulski, J. and Waters, M. (1995) *The death of class,* London: Sage.

Parsons, T. [@TonyParsonsUK] (2022) If you think the men and women earning £150,000 year are the 'super rich', you need to get out a bit more. Twitter, 3 October. https://twitter.com/TonyParsonsUK/status/1576870782780657664?s=20&t=jLR7V0vimBej-zqMbfeGVw [accessed 10 October 2022]

Partington, R. (2019) UK households spend above their income for longest period since 1980s. *The Guardian.* 29 March. www.theguardian.com/business/2019/mar/29/uk-households-spend-above-their-income-for-longest-period-since-1980s

Partington, R. (2022) OBR forecasts likely to show £60bn-£70bn hole after Kwarteng's mini-budget. *The Guardian.* 7 October. www.theguardian.com/politics/2022/oct/07/obr-forecasts-likely-to-show-60bn-70bn-hole-after-kwartengs-mini-budget

Patel, P. and Quilter-Pinner, H. (2022) Road to renewal: Elections, parties and the case for democratic reform. IPPR. April. www.ippr.org/publications/road-to-renewal

Paugam, S., Cousin, B., Giorgetti, C. and Naudet, J. (2017) *Ce que les riches pensent des pauvres* [What the rich think of the poor]. Paris: Seuil.

Pembroke, S. (2019) *Precarious work, precarious lives: How policy can create more security.* Dublin: TASC. www.tasc.ie/assets/files/pdf/precarious_workersweb_version.pdf

Perryman, M. (ed.) (2019) *Corbynism from below*. London: Lawrence & Wishart.

Phillips, B. (2020) *How to fight inequality (and why that fight needs you)*. Cambridge: Polity.

Phipps, C. (2021) Why we should still be concerned about gender inequality in the UK. 15 November. https://blogs.lse.ac.uk/socialbusinesshub/2021/11/15/why-we-should-still-be-concerned-about-gender-inequality-in-the-uk

Piketty, T. (2014) *Capital in the twenty-first century*. Cambridge, MA: Belknap Press.

Piketty, T. (2018) Brahmin left vs Merchant right: Rising inequality and the changing structure of political conflict (Evidence from France, Britain and the US, 1948–2017). *WID. World Working Paper Series*, n.2018/7. http://piketty.pse.ens.fr/files/Piketty2018.pdf

Piketty, T. (2020) *Capital and ideology*. Cambridge, MA: Belknap Press.

Piketty, T. and Saez, E. (2013) Top incomes and the Great Recession: Recent evolutions and policy implications. *IMF Economic Review*, 61:3, 456–78.

Polanski, Z. (2022) Zack Polanski's maiden speech as Deputy Leader, Green Party of England and Wales. 1 October. www.facebook.com/thegreenparty/videos/549383200359989

Proctor, K. (2019) Labour will be 'spending less on public services than Germany and France'. *The Guardian*. 25 November. www.theguardian.com/politics/2019/nov/25/labour-will-bring-uk-into-line-with-france-and-germany-says-corbyn

Putnam, R. (1995) *Bowling alone: America's declining social capital*. New York: Simon & Schuster.

Putnam R. (2000) *Bowling alone: The collapse and revival of American community*. New York: Simon & Schuster.

Pymnts (2022) NFTs hit $17B in trading in 2021, up 21,000%. 10 March. www.pymnts.com/nfts/2022/nfts-hit-17b-in-trading-in-2021-up-21000

Race, M. (2022) Income tax to be cut by 1p from April. BBC News. 23 September. www.bbc.co.uk/news/business-63007219

Raleigh, V. (2021) *What is happening to life expectancy in England?* London: The King's Fund.

Ramsay, A. (2022) Brexit Britain is all alone in a senseless pursuit of disaster capitalism. Open Democracy. 4 October. www.opendemocracy.net/en/liz-truss-kwasi-kwarteng-disaster-capitalism-brexit-britain/?utm_source=tw?utm_source=tw

Raworth, K. (2017) *Doughnut economics: Seven ways to think like a 21st-century economist.* London: Penguin.

Raworth, K. [@KateRaworth] (2021) When the @DailyMailUK reports that humanity is tracking the projections of the 1972 Limits to Growth report – and notes that pursuing endless economic growth looks near impossible – then you know something is shifting in the world… dailymail.co.uk/sciencetech/ar… h/t @PlanB_earth https://twitter.com/kateraworth/status/14164 28555903328256?s=61&t=DFCQuYBOujiLA0V07aBKQA. Twitter, 17 July. [accessed 20 August 2022]

Reed, H. and Lansley, S. (2016) *Universal Basic Income: An idea whose time has come?* London: Compass. www.compassonline.org.uk/wp-content/uploads/2016/05/UniversalBasicIncome ByCompass-Spreads.pdf

Reeves, R. (2017) *Dream hoarders: How the American upper middle class is leaving everyone else in the dust, why that is a problem, and what to do about it.* Washington, DC: Brookings Institution.

Reeves, R. and Rothwell, J. (2020) Class and COVID: How the less affluent face double risks. Brookings Institution. 27 March. www.brookings.edu/blog/up-front/2020/03/27/class-and-covid-how-the-less-affluent-face-double-risks

Reeves, R. and Venator, J. (2014) Opposites don't attract: Assortative mating and social mobility. Brookings Institution. 10 February. www.brookings.edu/blog/social-mobility-memos/2014/02/10/opposites-dont-attract-assortative-mating-and-social-mobility

Reich, R. (2020) Billionaires' donations to fight Coronavirus are largely self-serving. *NewsWeek.* 13 April. www.newsweek.com/robert-reich-billionaires-donations-fight-coronavirus-are-largely-self-serving-opinion-1497617

Reis, E. and Moore, M. (eds) (2005) *Elite perceptions of poverty and inequality.* London: Zed Books.

Resolution Foundation (2022) Event: Green growth: miracle or mirage? Webinar. 23 May. www.resolutionfoundation.org/events/green-growth-miracle-or-mirage

Resolution Foundation and Centre for Economic Performance (2022) *Stagnation nation: Navigating a route to a fairer and more prosperous Britain. The interim report of The Economy 2030 Inquiry.* 13 July. https://economy2030.resolutionfoundation.org/reports/stagnation-nation

Rigby, E. and Wright, G. (2013) Political parties and representation of the poor in the American states. *American Journal of Political Science*, 57:3, 552–65.

Riso, S. (2021) Monitoring and surveillance of workers in the digital age. Research Digest. Eurofound. 15 December. www.eurofound.europa.eu/data/digitalisation/research-digests/monitoring-and-surveillance-of-workers-in-the-digital-age

Rivera, L. (2016) *Pedigree: How elite students get elite jobs.* Princeton, NJ: Princeton University Press.

Roper, C. (2020) Union membership rises for third year running to 6.4 million. TUC blog. 27 May. www.tuc.org.uk/blogs/union-membership-rises-third-year-running-64-million

Rosa, H. (2015) *Social acceleration: A new theory of modernity.* New York: Columbia University Press.

Rowlingson, K. and McKay, S. (2012) *Wealth and the wealthy: exploring and tackling inequalities between rich and poor.* Bristol: Policy Press.

Salverda, T. and Grassiani, E. (2014) Introduction: Anxiety at the top. *Comparative Sociology,* 13:1, 1–11.

Sandbu, M. (2022) Why we need a wealth tax. *Financial Times.* 6 September. www.ft.com/video/6f73c51e-a1d8-48db-a8da-892dbd53c08d

Sandel, M. (2013) Why we shouldn't trust markets with our civic life. TED talk. 7 October. www.ted.com/talks/michael_sandel_why_we_shouldn_t_trust_markets_with_our_civic_life/transcript?language=en

Sandel, M. (2020) *The tyranny of merit: What's become of the common good?* London: Allen Lane.

Sauder M. (2020) A sociology of luck. *Sociological Theory,* 38:3, 193–216.

Savage, M. (2021) *The return of inequality: Social change and the weight of the past.* Cambridge, MA: Harvard University Press.

Savage, M. (2022a) Cameron's decision to cut 'green crap' now costs each household in England £150 a year. *The Guardian.* 19 March. www.theguardian.com/money/2022/mar/19/david-cameron-green-crap-energy-prices

Savage, M. (2022b) Millions of households will be spending nearly third of income on fuel by spring. *The Guardian.* 27 November. www.theguardian.com/society/2022/nov/27/millions-of-households-will-be-spending-nearly-third-of-income-on-fuel-by-spring

Schlozman, K., Verba, S. and Brady, H. (2012) *The unheavenly chorus: Unequal political voice and the broken promise of American democracy.* Princeton, NJ: Princeton University Press.

Sen, A. (1975) Minimal conditions for the monotonicity of capital value. *Journal of Economic Theory*, 11:3, 340–55.

Shackle, S. (2019) 'The way universities are run is making us ill': inside the student mental health crisis. *The Guardian*, 27 September. www.theguardian.com/society/2019/sep/27/anxiety-mental-breakdowns-depression-uk-students

Shames, S. (2017) *Out of the Running: Why Millennials Reject Political Careers and Why It Matters.* New York: NYU Press.

Sherman, R. (2017) *Uneasy street: The anxieties of affluence.* Princeton, NJ: Princeton University Press.

Shoben, C. (2022) New poll: Public strongly backing public ownership of energy and key utilities. Survation. 15 August. www.survation.com/new-poll-public-strongly-backing-public-ownership-of-energy-and-key-utilities

Shrubsole, G. (2019) *Who owns England? How we lost our green and pleasant land and how to take it back.* London: William Collins.

Siddique, H. (2022) Criminal barristers prepare for indefinite strike over legal aid. *The Guardian.* 4 September. www.theguardian.com/law/2022/sep/04/criminal-barristers-england-wales-prepare-indefinite-strike-legal-aid

Sillars, J. (2022) Energy price guarantee could cost taxpayer £140bn in 'extreme' scenario, market expert warns. Sky News. 5 October. https://news.sky.com/story/energy-price-guarantee-could-cost-taxpayer-140bn-in-extreme-scenario-market-expert-warns-12712574

Skinner, G. (2021) Both Remainers and Leavers retain a strong Brexit identity 5 years on. Ipsos. 29 December. www.ipsos. com/en-uk/both-remainers-and-leavers-retain-strong-brexit-identity-5-years

Sklair, J. and Glucksberg, L. (2021) Philanthrocapitalism as wealth management strategy: Philanthropy, inheritance and succession planning among the global elite. *The Sociological Review*, 69:2, 314–29.

Social Mobility and Child Poverty Commission (2015) *State of the nation 2015: Social mobility and child poverty in Great Britain.* London: SMCP.

Social Mobility Commission (2019) *State of the nation 2018–19: Social mobility in Great Britain*, London: The Stationery Office.

Social Mobility Commission (2020) *Moving out to move on. Understanding the link between migration, disadvantage and social mobility.* Research report. London: The Stationery Office.

Soper, K. (2020) *Post-growth living for an alternative hedonism.* London: Verso.

The Spectator (2016) Full text: Theresa May's conference speech. 5 October. www.spectator.co.uk/article/full-text-theresa-may-s-conference-speech

Spencer, T. (2022) Fairer Share's response to the Levelling Up White Paper. London: Fairer Share. https://fairershare.org.uk/wp-content/uploads/2022/02/Report_Levelling-Up_v4.pdf

Sridhar, D. (2022) Who's paying for Britain's disastrous mini-budget? We are, with our health. *The Guardian.* 3 October. www.theguardian.com/commentisfree/2022/oct/03/britain-mini-budget-paying-with-our-health-stress-illness-food-poverty-cold-homes-financial-chaos

Standing, G. (2019) *Piloting basic income as common dividends.* London: Progressive Economic Forum.

Statista (2022) Number of people employed in the United Kingdom from July 1971 to July 2022 (in 1,000s). www.statista.com/statistics/281998/employment-figures-in-the-united-kingdom-uk

Stevenson, G. (2021) I made millions betting against trickle-down economics – now I'm tackling wealth inequality. Wellbeing Economy Alliance. https://weall.org/gary-stevenson

Stewart, H. (2022) Rishi Sunak announces £5bn windfall tax on energy firms. *The Guardian.* 26 May. www.theguardian. com/politics/2022/may/26/sunak-announces-windfall-tax-energy-firms

Stewart, M. (2018) The 9.9 percent is the new American aristocracy. *The Atlantic.* www.theatlantic.com/magazine/archive/2018/06/the-birth-of-a-new-american-aristocracy/559130

Stewart, M. (2021) *The 9.9 percent: The new aristocracy that is entrenching inequality and warping our culture.* New York: Simon & Schuster.

Stiglitz, J. (2016) *The price of inequality: How today's divided society endangers our future.* New York: W.W. Norton & Co.

Streib, J. (2020) *Privilege lost: Who leaves the upper middle class and how they fall.* Oxford: Oxford University Press.

Streimikiene, D., Balezentis, T., Alisauskaite-Seskiene, I., Stankuniene, G. and Simanaviciene, Z. (2019) A review of willingness to pay studies for climate change mitigation in the energy sector. *Energies,* 12:8, 1481–519.

Stronge, W. and Lewis, K. (2021) *Overtime.* London: Verso.

Summers, A. and Advani, A. (2021) How much tax do the rich really pay? LSE. 14 January. www.lse.ac.uk/research/research-for-the-world/economics/how-much-tax-do-the-rich-really-pay

Surridge, P. (2021) Values, volatility and voting: Understanding voters in England 2015–2019. University of Bristol and UK in a Changing Europe. https://ukandeu.ac.uk/wp-content/uploads/2021/07/Values-volatility-and-voting-working-paper.pdf

The Sutton Trust and Social Mobility Commission (2019) *Elitist Britain 2019: The educational backgrounds of Britain's leading people.* London: The Sutton Trust/Social Mobility Commission www.suttontrust.com/wp-content/uploads/2019/12/Elitist-Britain-2019.pdf

TASC (2020) *Inequality and the top 10% in Europe.* Dublin: TASC. www.tasc.ie/publications/inequality-and-the-top-10-in-europe-full-report

Thomas, M.E. (2019) *99%: Mass impoverishment and how we can end it.* London: Head of Zeus.

Thomas, M.E. (2020) Saving democracy. The 99% Organisation. 9 September. https://99-percent.org/saving-democracy

Tilly, C. and Tilly, C. (1998) *Work under capitalism*. Oxford: Westview Press.

Toft, M. and Friedman, S. (2021) Family wealth and the class ceiling: The propulsive power of the bank of mum and dad. *Sociology*, 55:1, 90–109.

Törmälehto, V.-M. (2017) High income and affluence: Evidence from the European Union statistics on income and living conditions (EU-SILC). *Eurostat Working Papers*. Luxembourg: Publications Office of the European Union.

Toynbee, P. (2022) These Tories are heading for oblivion, and no amount of U-turns can change that. *The Guardian*. 3 October. www.theguardian.com/commentisfree/2022/oct/03/tories-heading-for-oblivion-u-turns-kwarteng-truss-45p-tax-rate

Toynbee, P. and Walker, D. (2008) *Unjust rewards: Exposing greed and inequality in Britain today*. London: Granta.

The Trussell Trust (2022) End of year stats. www.trusselltrust.org/news-and-blog/latest-stats/end-year-stats

UCU (University and College Union) (2019) *Counting the costs of casualisation in higher education*. London: UCU.

UK Parliament Public Accounts Committee (2021) 'Unimaginable' cost of test & trace failed to deliver central promise of averting another lockdown. 10 March. https://committees.parliament.uk/committee/127/public-accounts-committee/news/150988/unimaginable-cost-of-test-trace-failed-to-deliver-central-promise-of-averting-another-lockdown

UK Parliament (2022) Energy pricing and the future of the energy market. *Third Committee Report*. 26 July. https://publications.parliament.uk/pa/cm5803/cmselect/cmbeis/236/report.html

Uni Global Union (2020) Amazon & the COVID-19 crisis: Essentially irresponsible. https://uniglobalunion.org/wp-content/uploads/amazoncovid_en.pdf

United Nations Economic and Social Council (2017) Women's economic empowerment in the changing work of work. Report of the Secretary-General. Commission on the Status of Women. 13–24 March 2017. www.unwomen.org/sites/default/files/Headquarters/Attachments/Sections/CSW/MSForumCSW61.pdf

University of Cambridge (2021) The University of Cambridge continues to attract record numbers of economically disadvantaged and underrepresented students. www.cam.ac.uk/news/the-university-of-cambridge-continues-to-attract-record-numbers-of-economically-disadvantaged-and

University of Cambridge (2022) Cambridge at a glance. Website. www.cam.ac.uk/about-the-university/cambridge-at-a-glance

University of Oxford (2021) Oxford shows continued progress on state school and ethnic minority student admissions. News & Events. 4 February. www.ox.ac.uk/news-and-events

University of Oxford (2022) Facts and figures: Full version. Website. www.ox.ac.uk/about/facts-and-figures/full-version-facts-and-figures

University of Southampton (2016) *The rise of anti-politics in Britain.* Southampton: University of Southampton.

Van Lerven, F. and Jackson, A. (2018) A government is not a household. Positive Money. https://positivemoney.org/2018/10/a-government-is-not-a-household

Walker, A. (2019) Two-thirds of Boris Johnson's cabinet went to private schools. *The Guardian.* 25 July. www.theguardian.com/education/2019/jul/25/two-thirds-of-boris-johnsons-cabinet-went-to-private-schools

Walker, A. (2022) Kwasi Kwarteng's mini-budget was a reckless gamble. Letters. *The Guardian.* 25 September. www.theguardian.com/politics/2022/sep/25/kwasi-kwarteng-mini-budget-was-a-reckless-gamble

Ward, D. and Chijoko, L. (2018) *Spending on and availability of health care resources: How does the UK compare to other countries?* London: The King's Fund. www.kingsfund.org.uk/publications/spending-and-availability-health-care-resources

Webber, E., Lanktree, G. and Casalicchio, E. (2022) Boris Johnson's ethics adviser caved to the inevitable. Politico. 17 June. www.politico.eu/article/boris-johnson-ethics-adviser-geidt-resignation

What UK Thinks (2022) Poll data: In hindsight, do you think Britain was right or wrong to vote to leave the EU? https://whatukthinks.org/eu/questions/in-highsight-do-you-think-britain-was-right-or-wrong-to-vote-to-leave-the-eu

White, S. (2022) *Labour, pluralism and creative constitutionalism.* London: Compass and Unlock Democracy. www.compassonline. org.uk/wp-content/uploads/2022/08/Labour-Pluralism-and-Creative-Constitutionalism-v3.pdf

Whitmarsh, L. (2022) Resolution Foundation event: Consuming carbon: What does the net zero transition mean for households? 1 March. www.resolutionfoundation.org/events/consuming-carbon

Whyte, W.F. (1943) *Street corner society: The social structure of an Italian slum.* Chicago, IL: The University of Chicago Press.

Wilkie, D. (2015) Is the annual performance review dead? SHRM. 19 August. www.shrm.org/resourcesandtools/hr-topics/employee-relations/pages/performance-reviews-are-dead.aspx

Wilkinson, R. and Pickett, K. (2010) *The spirit level: Why equality is better for everyone.* London: Penguin.

Wilkinson, R. and Pickett, K. (2019) *The inner level: How more equal societies reduce stress, restore sanity and improve everyone's wellbeing.* London: Penguin.

Williams, Z. (2015) *Get it together: Why we deserve better politics.* London: Hutchinson.

Wilson, M. and Daly, M. (1997) Life expectancy, economic inequality, homicide, and reproductive timing in Chicago neighbourhoods. *BMJ*, 314, doi: 10.1136/bmj.314.7089.1271

Winter, O. (2019) *The path to proportional representation.* Bristol: Make Votes Matter/Labour Campaign for Electoral Reform. https://static1.squarespace.com/static/563e2841e4b09a6ae020bd67/t/5d931f32fb48423f80f53ffb/1569922999502/peterloo_web.pdf

Woodward, A. and Kawachi, I. (2000) Why reduce health inequalities? *Journal of Epidemiology & Community Health*, 54:12, 923–9.

World Inequality Database (2021) United Kingdom. https://wid.world/country/united-kingdom

Wren-Lewis, S. (2018) *The lies we were told: Politics, economics, austerity and Brexit.* Bristol: Bristol University Press.

Wright, O. (2021) Coronavirus: How the UK dealt with its first Covid case. BBC News. 29 January. www.bbc.co.uk/news/uk-england-55622386

Xue, B. and McMunn, A. (2021) Gender differences in unpaid care work and psychological distress in the UK Covid-19 lockdown. *PLoS ONE*, 16:3, 1–15. doi.org/10.1371/journal.pone.0247959

YouGov Poll (2022) Should we change our current British voting system? YouGov. https://yougov.co.uk/topics/politics/trackers/should-we-change-our-current-british-voting-system

Young, C. (2017) *The myth of millionaire tax flight: How place still matters for the rich*. Stanford, CA: Stanford University Press.

Young, M. (1958) *The rise of the meritocracy*. London: Pelican.

Young, M. (2001) Down with meritocracy. *The Guardian*. 29 June. www.theguardian.com/politics/2001/jun/29/comment

Younge, G. (2022) What does it mean to be British? America has its Dream, France its Republic – but Britain suffers from a failure of imagination. *The New Statesman*. 23 March. www.newstatesman.com/politics/a-dream-of-britain/2022/03/what-does-it-mean-to-be-british

Index

References to figures appear in *italic* type.

A

abortion, top 10% attitudes towards 6, 16
academics/academia 5, 9–10, 54
  knowledge production and enabling of the wealthy 132–3
acceleration, of the pace of life 128–9
accountancy firms 67, 68, 108, 109, 126
accumulation 135–6
Advani, A. 179, 180
affluence 22, 144, 162, 180
  see also top 1%; top 10%; wealth
age profile of the top 10% 8
agency 49
Alamillo-Martinez, Laura 73
Amazon 180
Ambler, L. 132–3
anti-elitism 12, 46, 96
anxiety 72, 130, 150
  and status 135, 165
  see also mental health
'anywheres' 96
ascriptive identities 153
attitudes
  to cultural issues 42, 84
  to economic issues 6, 8, 11, 16, 18–19, 42, *42*, 77, 92–3, 161–4
  to political issues 8, 16–17, 42, 76–99
  to social issues 6, 8, 16, 18–19, 42, 65–71, 77, *92*, 92–3, 161–3, 164–6
austerity policies 10, 11, 13, 16, 76, 78–9, 105, 115–16, 169–70
automation 79, 158, 160

B

Bangladeshi ethnicity, in the top 10% 30
Bank of England 78, 105, 164, 175
'bank of mum and dad' 29, 111
Barber, Rob 1, 2, 4, 181
Barclay family 121
BBC 11

Beck, U. 64
Bell, Torsten 2, 6
Berman, Y. 34
Berry, C. 82
Bezos, Jeff 144
Biden, Joe 142
Big Four accountancy firms 67, 68
  see also accountancy firms
Bill of Rights 121
Bitcoin 143
Black African/British/Caribbean ethnicity, in the top 10% 30
Black Lives Matter 113
Black Report 1977 115
Blair, Tony 9, 84, 185
Blakeley, Grace 139, 176
Bolsonaro, Jair 96, 98
'boundary work' of elites 45
Bourdieu, Pierre 40
Brahmins 38, 41–2, 43, 44, 45, 46, 47, 50, 51, 59, 61, 68, 73, 74–5, 84, 96, 167, 185
'brain drain' 124
  see also mobility
Brexit 11, 16, 76, 80, 86–7, 97, 101–2, 125
Brown, Gordon 175
Bullough, Oliver 113–14
bunkers 130, 131, 144, 187
Burgon, Richard 1, 3, 6
business support schemes, COVID-19 pandemic 15, 104, 126–7, 140, 151

C

Cambridge University 28–9, 119
Cameron, David 84
capital, income from 33–4
capital flight 124
capital tax, global 180
car ownership 153
carbon emissions 54, 114–15, 135, 143, 145, 171, 172, 178
  see also climate change

care *see* social care
Centre for Economic Performance 163
Chancel, L. 176–7
charitable donations 70–1
charitable sector 132
child poverty 170
  see also poverty
children of the top 10% 27, 35–6, 100–1, 109, 111–12, 183–4, 186
  'bank of mum and dad' 29, 111
  childcare costs 135–6
  downward social mobility 31–2, 162
  social reproduction 135–7
  US 57
Chinese ethnicity, in the top 10% 30
class 39–40
  cultural signifiers of 39, 40–1
  'death of' 39
  and education 40–1, 46, 51, 58–9
  inherited nature of 148
  middle class 33, 39, 40, 133, 136, 148
  and social mobility 57–8
  terminology of 38–9
  upper class 38–9, 133
  upper-middle class 4, 16, 27, 31–2, 38–54, 39 (*see also* top 10%)
  working class 24, 39, 57, 101–2, 148
climate change 54, 100, 101, 114–15, 125, 135, 141, 171–2
  carbon emissions 54, 114–15, 135, 143, 145, 171, 172, 178
  need for collective action on 122–3
  net zero 174, 176–7
coalition government (Conservative/Liberal Democrat) 78
collective denial 139–42
common sense 11, 19, 74, 89, 90, 108, 126, 130, 147
community
  gender and community involvement 70
  top 10%'s lack of awareness of/involvement in 45–6, 49–50, 127–31, *131*, 150–1, 154–7, 164–6
'compensatory consumption' 129, 134
Conservative Party/Conservatives 3, 16, 53, 76–7, 84, 85, 88, 97, 99, 120, 179
  leadership election, 2022 39
  taxation policy 3, 53
  traditional supporters 44
consumption 152–4, 169, 171, 178

'compensatory consumption' 129, 134
  environmental impact of 135
  luxury consumption, and climate change 114–15
Corbyn, Jeremy 11, 16, 80, 84, 85, 87, 96, 97
corporate governance 174
corporate responsibility 70–1
corporate sector 46, 51, 59, 64, 65–6, 67–8, 71, 88–9, 108, 128, 153
corporation tax 105–6, 113, 180
cost of living crisis 14, 52, 76, 101, 104, 106, 127, 177–8
council tax 110, 180
COVID-19 pandemic 13, 15, 72–3, 103–4, 116, 126, 134, 142, 144, 151
  furlough and business support schemes 15, 104, 126–7, 128, 140, 151
  political impact of 87–8
Coyle, Diane 145
crises
  cost of living crisis 14, 52, 76, 101, 104, 106, 127, 177–8
  of democracy 119–21
  global financial crisis, 2008 31, 77–9, 126, 140
cryptocurrencies 143–4
cultural attitudes of the top 10% 42, 84
cultural capital 40, 41, 46, 51
cuts, in public services 78–9, 105, 117, 170

D
deindustrialisation 28
democracy
  crisis of 119–21
  erosion of 76, 81–2
demographic profile of the top 10% 8
depression 130, 150
  see also mental health
'deserving', the 23, 57, 74
  see also 'undeserving', the
disability
  and social mobility 58
  welfare benefits 78, 79, 175
Disability Rights UK 175
diversity and inclusion targets 57
domestic work *see* unpaid work
Dorling, Danny 35, 146–7, 156, 183
downward orientation 35, 46, 47
downward social mobility 14, 36, 73, 136, 152, 162, 182

children of the top 10% 31–2, 162
income and status insecurity 51–2
Dubai 133
Durose, Oly 39–40

E

Earth4All 177
economy
economic attitudes of the top 10%
6, 8, 11, 16, 18–19, 42, *42*, 77,
92–3, 161–4
economic common sense 89, 90
GDP, as indicator of success 176
Economy 2030 Enquiry 109
EDF 106
Edmiston, Daniel 49
education
and class 40–1, 46, 51, 58–9
inequalities 17, 100–1, 117–19, 136
Ofsted ratings and league tables 137
and political attitudes 41, 42
and social capital 60
and social mobility 58–60, 147–8
state education 36, 60, 119, 136,
137, 148, 170
see also higher education; private
education
Ehrenreich, Barbara 152
Elections Bill 2021 120
Electoral Calculus 173
Electoral Commission 120
electoral system reform 172–3
Eliasoph, Nina 81
elites 39, 44–5, 77
anti-elitism 12, 96
employment 151
blue-collar 28
good jobs 55–61
hard work 48, 50, 61–73, 162
impact on society of 65–71
inequalities 17, 100, 107–9
low-wage work 62, 127
precarity 61, 107–9
presenteeism 64
public sector 109
and purpose 66–7, 71, 75, 162
and self-respect 55–6
and status 55–7, 68, 74
structural labour market change
27–8, 158
top 10% 6, 16, 24, *25*, 26–8, 55–75
total British employed 2
white-collar 28
work-life balance 18, 171
workplace reform 71–2
see also unpaid work
energy costs 101, 104, 105–7, 175

energy industry
privatisation of 177–8
windfall taxes 177
environmental issues 54, 161
carbon emissions 54, 114–15, 135,
143, 145, 171, 172, 178
net zero 174, 176–7
equality of opportunity 57, 153
equality of outcome 57
ESS (European Social Survey) 89, 92
ethnicity *see* race and ethnic origin
Eton College 26, 119
EU-SILC (European Union Statistics
on Living Conditions) 24, 28,
29–30, 32, 33
Eurofound 27–8, 36–7
European Convention on Human
Rights 121
European Social Survey (ESS) 89, 92
European Union Statistics on Living
Conditions (EU-SILC) 24, 28,
29–30, 32, 33
experts, anti-elitist attitudes towards 12
Extinction Rebellion 84
'extraction capitalism' 112

F

Farage, Nigel 96
'fear of falling' 152, 182
see also downward social mobility
feminism 56
financial sector 51–2, 88–9
food
food banks 93, 175
'right to' 178
foreign policy, top 10% attitudes towards
6, 42
formal work *see* employment
'fortification mentality' 134–5
Frank, Robert H. 48
Friedman, Sam 27, 29, 31, 40, 57
furlough scheme, COVID-19 pandemic
15, 104, 128, 140, 151

G

Gallup Poll, US 22, 26
Gates, Bill 144
GDP, as indicator of success 176
gender
gender profile of the top 10% 8,
29–30
inclusivity 152–3
social mobility 57–8
general election, 2019 1, 76, 97, 120,
173
Generation Z 17, 100, 118
gentrification 133–4

Germany 159, 169
Gethin, Stephen 121
Ghosh, J. 132–3
Giddens, A. 64
Gilens, Martin 42–3
gilets jaunes (yellow vest) movement,
    France 115
global financial crisis, 2008 31, 77–9,
    126, 140
global warming *see* climate change
globalisation 39
    offshoring 79, 109, 158
Good Friday Agreement 121
good jobs 55–61
    see also employment
Goodhart, David 96–7
Gove, Michael 84
government debt 140
government employees, as members of
    the top 10% 5
government spending 169–70
    see also public services; welfare state
Graeber, David 46, 66, 75, 129,
    157
Great British Class Survey 2013 39
Green, Duncan 184
Green New Deal 176
Green Party 87, 120, 178
Guinan, J. 82

H
Haldane, Andy 164
hard work 48, 50, 61–73, 162
HC-One 107
healthcare 144, 168
    inequalities 112–14, 138, 139
    NHS 91, 94, 116, 137, 138, 170
    private healthcare 116, 137, 140,
        159, 167–8, 182
Hecht, Katharina 62
higher education 30–1, 58, 136, 147–8,
    183
    elite 17, 26, 28–9, 73, 74, 100
    and employment 57, 61
    inequalities 17, 100, 117–19
    mental health issues 73
    post-1992 28
    and social capital 118
    student debt 37
    US 57, 74
Hills, John 168
HMRC, income survey 5–6
hoarding 135–6, 144
home ownership 33, 52, 110, 111
    see also housing
homelessness 93
    see also housing

House of Commons Committee for
    Business, Energy and Industrial
    Strategy 107
household debt 152
housing 52
    and climate change 114
    house prices 33
    housing costs 110, 111
    inequalities 17, 100, 107–9, 133–4
    insulation grants 176
    mortgages 33, 52, 106, 110
    and state education 137
    see also home ownership; homelessness
human rights 121
Human Rights Act 1998 121

I
immigration, top 10% attitudes towards
    6, 16, 42, 43
income distribution 133, 168
    misconceptions around 1–4
    Palma ratio 22–3
    UK breakdown, 2019/20 7
income from capital 33–4
income tax 178–9, 181
Indian ethnicity, in the top 10% 30
inequalities 53, 77–8, 92–3, 100–23,
    129–30, 153–4, 165–6, 183
    and the COVID-19 pandemic 127
    and education 17, 100–1, 117–19, 136
    and employment 17, 100, 107–9
    global 177
    growth of 14, 32–3
    healthcare 112–14, 138, 139
    higher education 17, 100, 117–19
    housing 17, 100, 107–9, 133–4
    intergenerational 14, 17, 100, 109,
        111–12, 117–18
    labour market 60–1
    and politics 87
    private sector responsibility 69–71
    and the top 10% 8, 17, 101–23
    and the 'undeserving' 148–50
inflation 101, 105
Inflation Reduction Act 2022, US 169
informal work 56–7
inheritance, and housing inequality 111
Institute for Fiscal Studies 26, 105
Institute for Government 104
insulation 125–7, 130, 144
interdependence 175–6
Intergenerational Commission 118
intergenerational inequalities 14, 17,
    100, 109, 111–12, 117–18
International Labour Organization 56
interview panels 40

IPCC (Intergovernmental Panel on
   Climate Change) 114
Ireland 5, 13, 33, 155
isolation 127–31, *131*, 144, 150–1
Ivy League universities, US 57

J
jobs
   see employment
Johnson, Boris 11, 26, 76, 84, 87, 97,
   119, 121
Johnson, Paul 105
Jones, Owen 133, 148

K
Kawachi, I. 116–17
key workers 127, 144, 150, 165
Khan, Shamus 152–3
King's Fund 138
Kwarteng, Kwasi 3, 105

L
labour market 60–1, 79–80
Labour Party/ Labour 1, 2, 44, 76, 80,
   82–3, 84, 85, 89, 120, 122, 180,
   194
   New Labour 9, 78, 85
Lamont, Michèle 44–5
land values 110
Lansley, Stewart 112, 114, 151
Laurison, Daniel 27, 29, 31, 40,
   57
Lawson, Neal 154
Le Pen, Marine 96, 98
left, the
   and Brahmins 41
   social attitudes of the top 10% 16, 4
   2
LGBTQ+ people, top 10% attitudes
   towards 43
Liberal Democrat Party 76, 84, 85, 86,
   102, 120
liberalism
   small-l liberalism 96, 98, 182
life expectancy 79, 115, 138
Lindner, Christian 169
living standards 23–4
   see also cost of living crisis
local government 81–3, 117
local politics 81, 82–3
low-wage work 62, 127
luck 48, 59, 61
luxury consumption, and climate
   change 114–15
Lynch, Mick 178

M
Major, John 60
Make Votes Matter 84
management consultants 47, 59, 70, 86,
   90, 108, 126, 130, 147
Mandler, Peter 148
manners elite 45
market failures 105–7, 141
marketisation 137–9
Markovits, D. 20
Marmot reports, 2010 and 2020
   115–16, 117
Mason, Paul 142
May, Theresa 84, 87
Mazzucato, Mariana 173–4
mean-tested benefits 77, 93–4, 159
media
   control of 120
   as members of the top 10% 5, 26
Members of Parliament (MPs) 5, 76
men
   community involvement 70
   see also gender
mental health
   anxiety 72, 130, 135, 150, 165
   depression 130, 150
   higher education 73
   unequal societies 130
   working hours reduction 171
Merchants 38, 41–2, 43, 45, 46, 47,
   48, 50, 53, 61, 65, 68, 69, 72, 73,
   88–9, 96, 98, 160, 162, 174
meritocracy 6, 11, 18, 19, 20, 39, 47,
   58, 65, 68, 74, 100, 109, 111, 118,
   146–9, 165, 170, 181, 184–5, 186
middle class 33, 39, 40, 133, 136, 148
Mijs, Jonathan 118, 155–6, 156–7
Milanovic, Branco 14, 34
Millennials 17, 100, 117, 118
minority rights, top 10% attitudes
   towards 6, 43
mobility 17–18, 124–5, 144, 148, 167
money, cultural taboos around 3
money elite 45
monopolies 140
   and energy market failure 106–7
morals elite 45
mortgages 33, 52, 106, 110
MPs (Members of Parliament) 5, 76
multinational companies, taxation of
   180
Murdoch, Rupert 120

N
NatCen Social Research 24, 39
National Union of Rail, Maritime and
   Transport Workers 178

Nationality and Borders Bill 2021 120
neoliberalism 142
net zero 174, 176–7
networking 63
    see also social capital
New Labour see Labour Party/Labour
NFTs (non-fungible tokens) 143–4
NHS 91, 94, 116, 137, 138, 170
Nietzsche, F. 46
Nixon, B. 82
Northern Ireland 121

O

Obama, Barack 96
occupation see employment
Occupy movement 181
OECD (Organisation for Economic
    Co-operation and Development)
    data 23, 31
Office for National Statistics (ONS)
    24, 29
offshoring 79, 109, 158
Olson, Dan 144
online shopping, and the COVID-19
    pandemic 134
online working see working from home
ONS (Office for National Statistics)
    24, 29
Organisation for Economic Co-
    operation and Development
    (OECD) data 23, 31
overwork 69, 75
    see also working hours
Oxford Brookes University 29
Oxford University 28–9, 119

P

Pakistani ethnicity, in the top 10% 30
Palma ratio 22–3
Parra, Nicanor 32
Parsons, Tony 3
participation, political 80–5, 172–3
'partygate' scandal 76
Paugam, Serge 49–50
pensions, state 138
performance management 72
Personal Independence Payment 79
PFIs (private finance initiatives) 139
Piketty, Thomas 5, 14, 31, 38, 41, 42,
    113, 180
Polanski, Jack 178
polarisation, political 14, 85–6, 98,
    102, 172
Policing Bill 2021 120
politicians, as members of the top 10%
    5, 26
politics 76–99, 181

centre ground 85–8
contemporary context 77–80
party membership 82–3, 84
political change 184–5
political participation 80–5, 172–3
political polarisation 14, 85–6, 98,
    102, 172
political reform 172–3
and trust 76, 82
populism 11, 14, 16, 76, 77, 98, 102
positionality of authors 8–11
poverty 59, 78, 93, 151, 174, 175
    child poverty 170
    and education 118
    and the 'undeserving' 148–50
precarity, of employment 61, 107–9
presenteeism 64
private education 54, 118–19, 136, 137,
    147–8, 159, 162, 167, 170, 182
    school fees 26, 33, 35, 36, 37
    and social capital 60, 118
    see also education
private finance initiatives (PFIs) 139
private healthcare 116, 137, 140, 159,
    167–8, 182
    see also healthcare
private sector 19–20
    corporate sector 46, 51, 59, 64, 65–6,
        67–8, 71, 88–9, 108, 128, 153
    financial sector 51–2, 88–9
    insecurity in 109
    involvement in public services 139,
        170
    raising expectations of 171
privatisation
    excess profits of privatised companies
        101
    of utility companies 177–8
professionals
    anti-elitist attitudes towards 12, 46, 96
    professionals and managers 24, 25,
        26–8, 39, 55
    see also top 10%
property tax 180–1
protest, right of 120
Protestant work ethic 50
public sector employment 109
public services 159, 173
    cuts in 78–9, 105, 117, 170
    destigmatisation of 170
    and marketisation 137–8
    private sector involvement in 139, 170
    and the top 10% 8, 19, 56, 77, 91–2,
        138–9, 140, 144, 159, 163, 166–8,
        183
    universal 56, 77, 93–5, 144, 159

Putnam, Robert 81, 129, 157, 158

Q

Question Time, BBC 1, 2, 181

R

race and ethnic origin
  and inclusivity 152–3
  and social mobility 58
  of the top 10% 8, 30
Raworth, Kate 135
redistribution 139, 161, 163, 182
  top 10% attitudes towards 6, 42, *42*,
    43, 77
Reed, Howard 151
Reich, Robert 141
relocation *see* mobility
renewable energy 141
  see also climate change; energy costs
Resolution Foundation 2, 34, 112, 163
rich, the *see* top 1%; top 10%
richness 47
right, the 16
  and Brexit 102
  centre right 89, 97
  and control of the media 121
  far right 15, 97–8
  and Merchants 41
  political attitudes of the top 10% 16, 42
rights and responsibilities 158–60
Rivera, Lauren 57, 119
Rosa, Hartmut 129
Rothermere, Lord 120
Russell Group universities 57
Russia-Ukraine war 76, 104, 105–6

S

Saez, E. 31
Salvini, Matteo 98
same-sex marriage, top 10% attitudes
  towards 6, 16, 42
Sandbu, Martin 179
Sandel, Michael 142, 150–1
Sanders, Bernie 96
Savage, Mike 183
savings levels of the top 10% 36
school fees, private education 26, 33,
  35, 36, 37
Schor, Juliet 171
Scotland, devolved government 121
Scottish Greens 121
Scottish National Party 121
self-respect, and employment 55–6
Sherman, Rachel 35, 45–6
Shrubsole, Guy 110
'sink' schools 137
Sinn Féin 121
small-l liberalism 96, 98, 182

'smart' working 64
social capital
  decline in 157–8
  and private education 60, 118
social care 117
  low pay of care workers 103
  market failure in 107
Social Democratic Party of Germany,
  Programme for the Future 159
social media
  'echo chambers' 128
social mobility 19, 28, 36, 57–9
  downward 14, 36, 73, 136, 152,
    162, 182
    children of the top 10% 31–2,
      162
    income and status insecurity
      51–2
  and education 58–60
  meritocracy 6
  and networking 63
  structural barriers to 62
  upward 18, 36, 50, 64, 136
Social Mobility Commission 60
social reproduction 135–7
social security
  top 10% attitudes towards 77
  see also welfare benefits; welfare state
society, attitudes to impact of work on
  65–71, 74–5
sociological imagination 13, 49, 128,
  160
solidarity 94, 127, 142, 157, 158, 159,
  170
'somewheres' 96
Soper, Kate 74
Spain 5, 73, 149, 155, 169
stamp duty 110–11
Starmer, Keir 87
state, the 161
  raising expectations of 173–6
  top 10% attitudes towards 91–5, *92*
state education 36, 60, 119, 136, 137,
  148, 170
status
  and employment 55–7, 68, 74
  status anxiety and insecurity 14,
    51–2, 135, 165
Stevenson, Gary 15
stigma, and unemployment 56
Streib, Jessi 31–2
structure 49
student debt 37
suburbia 40
Summers, A. 179, 180
Sutton Trust 29
Sweden 5, 23, 155

T

tactical voting 172–3
taxation 97, 161, 163, 164, 178–81, 182
  corporation tax 105–6, 113, 180
  council tax 110, 180
  income tax 2, 105–6, 178–9, 181, 185
  property tax 180–1
  stamp duty 110–11
  tax avoidance/evasion 178, 181
  tax cuts 169
  tax fraud 181
  top 10% attitudes towards 8, 42, 43, 77, 88–91, 92
  Truss government tax cuts 105–6
  wealth tax 179
  windfall taxes, energy industry 177
technology
  and acceleration of the pace of life 129
  automation 79, 158, 160
Thatcher, Margaret 105, 180
third sector, as members of the top 10% 5
Thomas, Mark 120
top 1% 2, 4, 13, 14, 15, 32, 41, 52, 64, 65, 93, 126, 128, 162
  and employment 58–9
  enabling of 131–4
  inequality in 155
top 10% 4–7, 8, 11–13, 18, 33
  accumulation and hoarding 135–6, 144
  and austerity policies 1, 11, 13, 16
  barriers to sense of belonging 18, 146–60
  collective denial 139–42
  contradictory isolation of 53–4
  cost of living pressures 14, 15
  and the COVID-19 pandemic 13, 15, 18, 127
    furlough and business support schemes 15, 104, 126–7, 128, 151
  cultural attitudes 42, 84
  demographic profile 8
  economic attitudes 6, 8, 11, 16, 18–19, 42, 42, 77, 92–3, 161–4
  education 28–9, 30–1
  employment 6, 16, 24, 25, 26–8, 55–75
  enabling the wealthy 131–4
  future prospects for 34–7, 95–9, 98, 182-7
  gender profile 8, 29–30
  HMRC income data 5–6
  income and status insecurity 14, 51–2

inequalities 8, 17, 101–23
insulation 125–7, 130, 144
internal diversity of 32
isolation/lack of awareness of others' lives 45–6, 49–50, 127–31, 131, 150–1, 154–7, 164–6
location 8, 29
and marketisation 137–9
and meritocracy 6, 11, 18, 19, 20, 39, 47, 58, 65, 68, 74, 100, 109, 111, 118, 146–9, 165, 170, 181, 184–5, 186
mobility 17–18, 124–5, 144, 148
overview and profile of 13–15, 21–37, 154–5
perceptions of income distribution 38, 47–51
political attitudes 8, 16–17, 42, 76–99
  political participation 80–5
political influence of 5, 11, 76
and public services 8, 19, 56, 77, 91–2, 138–9, 140, 144, 159, 163, 166–8, 183
qualitative analysis of 15–16, 38–54
race and ethnic origin 8, 30
response to social and economic pressures 17–18, 124–45
rights and responsibilities 158–60
and the role of the state 91–5, 92
savings levels 36
social attitudes 6, 8, 16, 18–19, 42, 65–71, 77, 92, 92–3, 161–3, 164–6
social reproduction 135–7
uncertainty and insecurity of 68–9
Törmälehto, Veli-Matti 36–7
Toynbee, P. 89
trade unions 165, 172
  membership 72, 157, 158, 163
Trump, Donald 11, 47, 96, 97, 98
Truss, Liz 105, 141, 186
Trussell Trust 175
trust 130–1
  and politics 76, 82
Trust for London 23–4

U

UBI (Universal Basic Income) 160
UK
  devolved government 121
  Palma ratio 23
UKIP 87
Ukraine-Russia war 76, 104, 105–6
'undeserving,' the 23, 148–50, 163
  see also 'deserving', the

unemployment 56
  welfare benefits 138
Universal Basic Income (UBI) 160
universal welfare benefits 93, 168
  see also welfare benefits
universal public services 56, 77, 93–5,
  144, 159
  see also public services
universities/university education 30–1,
  58, 136, 147–8, 183
  elite 17, 26, 28–9, 73, 74, 100
  and employment 57, 61
  inequalities 17, 100, 117–19
  mental health issues 73
  post-1992 28
  and social capital 118
  student debt 37
  US 57, 74
Unlock Democracy 83
unpaid work 56, 150, 175–6
upper class 38–9, 133
upper-middle class 4, 16, 27, 31–2,
  38–54, 39
  see also top 10%
upward orientation 35, 45–6, 47, 50,
  51
upward social mobility 18, 36, 50, 64,
  136
US
  and the COVID-19 pandemic 141
  downward social mobility 31–2
  elitism in higher education 150–1
  employment and social class 57
  inequalities and social segregation
  156–7
  Inflation Reduction Act 2022 169
  middle class 33
  universities/university education 57,
  74
utility companies, privatisation of
  177–8

V
volunteering 69, 70–1

W
Walker, D. 89
water industry, privatisation of 178
wealth
  distribution of 142
  enabling of the wealthy 131–4
  historical accumulation of 113
  inequalities 112–14
  unequal distribution of 14
wealth tax 179

Weber, Max 50
welfare benefits 138, 159–60, 167–8
  cuts in 78, 79, 169
  increasing of in line with inflation,
  2022 175
  mean-tested 77, 93–4, 159
  universal 93, 168
welfare state 167, 174
  anti-welfare attitudes *42*, 42–3
  top 10% attitudes towards *42*, 93–4
  and the 'undeserving' 149–50
  see also public services
well-off, the
  social attitudes and perceptions of
  21–2
  see also top 1%; top 10%
White ethnicity, in the top 10% 30
Whitmarsh, Lorraine 114
Whyte, William 55–6
Williams, Zoe 134, 178
women
  anti-exclusion policies 43
  community involvement 70
  gender pay gap 30
  life expectancy, decrease in 115
  and online working 64
  top 10% 8, 29–30
  trade union membership 72
  unpaid work 56, 150, 175–6
  working class, and employment 57
  see also gender
Woodward, A. 116–17
work
  hard work 55, 61–73
  see also employment
work-life balance 18, 171
working class 24, 39, 148
  and Brexit 101–2
  and employment 57
working from home 27, 64, 104, 126,
  128, 165
working hours 64
  reduction in 171
World Bank 47
World Inequality Database 13, 32, 54
Wren-Lewis, Simon 78–9, 90

Y
yellow vest (*gilets jaunes*) movement,
  France 115
Young, Michael 184–5
Younge, Gary 181

Z
Zahawi, Nadim 107

"For all its talk of death, *The Collected Regrets of Clover* is never dark or grim. This feel-good story is beautiful, heartwarming, and ultimately hopeful." —*Reader's Digest*

"A warmhearted novel." —*AARP*

"A satisfying experience." —*Library Journal*

"Warm, profound, and expertly told, *The Collected Regrets of Clover* explores how befriending death can help enrich our lives. While infinitely poised in her role as a death doula, Clover's clumsy foray into the world of the living will have you recalling the sweet awkwardness of your first kiss and the thrill of new belonging. This is one of those special books that will leave a handprint on your heart." —Emma Brodie, author of *Songs in Ursa Major*

"I couldn't put this book down. *The Collected Regrets of Clover* is a tender, charming delight, perfect for anyone who loved *The Authenticity Project* or *Eleanor Oliphant Is Completely Fine.*" —KJ Dell'Antonia, *New York Times* bestselling author of *The Chicken Sisters*

"What a beautiful story! I loved the premise, which was skillfully and sensitively executed. The characters are both memorable and relatable, and the subject of death is handled with refreshing honesty and heartbreaking poignancy. This book will be one that I remember for a long time, and it's a story that we can all learn something from." —Ruth Hogan, *Sunday Times* bestselling author of *Madame Burova*

"Clover's story is a heartfelt and delightful deep dive into death. You will turn the last page with a fresh zest for life and absolutely no regrets." —Annabel Monaghan, author of *Nora Goes Off Script*

Praise for *The Collected Regrets of Clover*

"This is a beautiful tale of a vulnerable, compassionate woman who finds that, in order to care for others, she must also let herself be cared for. Even that cliché feels moving, rather than saccharine, in Brammer's capable hands."

—*Kirkus Reviews* (starred review)

"A comforting exploration of grief, love, and human connection that is sure to appeal to fans of books that feel like a warm hug."

—*BookPage*

"Brammer writes with grace and heart about the complicated and complex world of grief. Despite the heavy subject, though, Brammer's debut is never dark or hopeless . . . [and] is ultimately a beautiful story of belonging and connection and, cliché though it may sound, what it really means to live life to its fullest."

—*Shelf Awareness*

"While this heartwarming debut novel deals with death, it never becomes maudlin, instead focusing on what makes a life worth living. Readers who appreciate seeing quirky, isolated characters come into their own, such as in *Eleanor Oliphant Is Completely Fine*, will find much to love in this moving novel."

—*Booklist*

"A tender story of love, life lessons, and letting go. Full of wisdom, it's a novel that handles with profound sensitivity and delicacy important questions that face us all while fostering a joyful sense of hope for the future. Clover is a beguiling character who has so much more to offer the world than she knows, and it's a sheer delight to watch as her horizons expand. *The Collected Regrets of Clover* leaves us contemplating what it means to live our lives to the fullest, without regrets. A beautiful, thought-provoking novel."

—Sarah Haywood, *New York Times* bestselling author of *The Cactus*

Printed in the USA
CPSIA information can be obtained
at www.ICGtesting.com
JSHW021942200524
63489JS00004B/283